KNOW BROTHER
JOSEPH

KNOW BROTHER
JOSEPH

New Perspectives on Joseph Smith's Life and Character

EDITED BY
R. ERIC SMITH
MATTHEW C. GODFREY
MATTHEW J. GROW

DESERET
BOOK

Salt Lake City, Utah

Library of Congress Cataloging-in-Publication Data

Names: Smith, R. Eric, editor. | Godfrey, Matthew C., editor. | Grow, Matthew J., editor.
Title: Know Brother Joseph : new perspectives on Joseph Smith's life and character / R. Eric Smith, Matthew C. Godfrey, Matthew J. Grow.
Description: Salt Lake City, Utah : Deseret Book, 2021. | Includes bibliographical references and in- dex. | Summary: "An anthology of history essays from leading scholars on the life of the Prophet Joseph Smith"—Provided by publisher.
Identifiers: LCCN 2020043856 | ISBN 9781629728742 (hardback)
Subjects: LCSH: Smith, Joseph, Jr., 1805–1844. | Mormon Church—Presidents—Biography. | LCGFT: Biographies.
Classification: LCC BX8695.S6 K56 2021 | DDC 289.3092 [B]—dc23
LC record available at https://lccn.loc.gov/2020043856

Printed in the United States of America
PubLitho, Draper, UT

10   9   8   7   6   5   4   3   2   1

CONTENTS

CONTENTS

PART 2: OHIO AND MISSOURI, 1831–1839

CONTENTS

CONTENTS

PREFACE

When the angel Moroni first visited Joseph Smith in 1823, he said that Joseph's name would be known for good and evil throughout the world. Moroni's statement has never been more true than in the present. Around the globe, millions of members of The Church of Jesus Christ of Latter-day Saints testify that Joseph was a prophet of God who restored Christ's Church. As we write this in April 2020, the Church just completed a general conference that celebrated the Restoration. During this conference, the First Presidency and Quorum of the Twelve Apostles released a "Bicentennial Proclamation to the World" that shared their solemn witness of Joseph's role in the "restoration of the fulness of the gospel of Jesus Christ."

But, if indications on the internet can be believed, Joseph's name evokes instant controversy among others who dismiss him as a fraud. A middle ground also exists: those who are curious and want to understand the phenomenon of a nineteenth-century American prophet. This middle ground also has more adherents than ever before; college classes around the world now include Joseph and the early Latter-day Saints in a variety of contexts.

Major historical figures must be understood anew by each generation, who bring new questions and demand fresh perspectives. These ongoing reassessments are most useful when based upon new information that can lead to enhanced understanding. The study of Joseph Smith at this moment benefits from such an increase in information, thanks largely to the Joseph Smith Papers. For the past decade, the three of us have been privileged to work with many other dedicated and talented historians and editors in compiling and publishing all of Joseph's records.

While most of the documents being published in the Joseph Smith Papers have long been known by historians, publishing them together with the highest professional standards of historical documentary editing has yielded new perspectives on nearly every aspect of Joseph's life. When completed in 2023, the Joseph Smith Papers will contain more than two dozen volumes, perhaps 20,000 published pages. In addition, if measured by the same standard, the Joseph Smith Papers website would add many thousands of pages of material not found in the print edition.

The sheer volume and complexity of the papers makes reading them a daunting prospect even for Latter-day Saints with a deep interest in Joseph. The core of this problem is that the Joseph Smith Papers are intended for scholars. The meticulous presentation of documents, the extensive footnotes, the in-depth introductions, even the size and weight of the volumes—all of these indicate that these are substantial volumes that demand to be taken seriously by anyone researching Joseph. For Latter-day Saints, it can be difficult to wade through the volumes and synthesize the new information. Indeed, it will take a generation (likely more!) of scholars, believers, and detractors to digest and analyze this material.

This book is an attempt to bring insights drawn from the Joseph Smith Papers—and other reputable sources about Joseph and the early Church—to a broader audience. We asked over forty individuals who have studied Joseph to write brief essays. The authors come from a variety of backgrounds—many are historians, while others are editors, writers, and teachers. We envision the result as something like a college course on Joseph and the early Church, with a different professor each day. Most academics are used to writing articles of thirty or forty pages, usually more than 10,000 words. Here, we asked each author to teach about Joseph using only about 1,500 words. Writing concisely, in a format intended for a broader audience, leads hopefully to a focused and accessible approach.

We also asked the authors to consider how studying Joseph's life and papers has influenced their own lives.

We've spent the past decade reading Joseph's mail, scrutinizing his journal, studying his revelations, puzzling over his legal and financial worlds. We have listened to the thoughts of his friends and pondered the words of his enemies. We have followed him seemingly every step from the Palmyra of his youth to Carthage. We are among the small group of individuals who have read every word in the Joseph Smith Papers print edition—most of them many times! For us, it is a great privilege to spend our professional lives with Joseph.

Through our work, we have been able to get to know Joseph as a human being—not as a mythic figure. We have been with him in his triumphs and his failures, his joys and his sorrows. Knowing him as a person has given us even more appreciation for him as a prophet, for how the Lord used him as the instrument to restore the gospel of Jesus Christ. We hope that in these pages, you will also gain new insights into and appreciation for Brother Joseph.

MILLIONS SHALL KNOW BROTHER JOSEPH

By LeGrand R. Curtis Jr.

In April 1830, when The Church of Jesus Christ of Latter-day Saints was organized, William W. Phelps was a 38-year-old editor and publisher of the *Ontario Phoenix* in Ontario, New York. That year, he obtained a copy of the Book of Mormon and received a testimony of its truthfulness. Within less than a year he moved to Kirtland, Ohio, and was baptized and ordained to the Melchizedek Priesthood.[1] In July 1831, he was appointed Church printer.[2] His skill as a writer, editor, and printer was very valuable to the young Church as he moved back and forth between Ohio and Missouri.[3] His accomplishments in the first six years of the Church included helping publish the Book of Commandments, the Doctrine and Covenants, and the Church's first newspaper: *The Evening and the Morning Star.*[4] He helped compile the first hymnbook and wrote several hymn texts, including "The Spirit of God," which was sung at the dedication of the Kirtland Temple and is now sung at every temple dedication.[5]

In 1836 he returned to Missouri, where he continued his duties as a leader of the Church. However, he was excommunicated in March 1838 due to actions he and some other Church leaders had taken. Phelps was reconciled with the Church but soon became estranged again during the persecutions against the Church in Missouri. His bitterness led him to testify against Joseph Smith in 1838, contributing to Joseph's arrest, imprisonment, and suffering. Phelps was excommunicated again in March 1839.[6]

However, in June 1840 a repentant Phelps sought the Prophet's forgiveness and was reconciled with the Church once again. He became, again, a close friend to Joseph and a valiant worker in the cause of the Restoration.[7] As Joseph's clerk, Phelps wrote many important documents in the final years of Joseph's life.[8]

Shortly after Joseph's death, Phelps wrote a poem in honor of his prophet and friend. He titled it "Joseph Smith," and it was first published in the *Times and Seasons.*[9] It became a beloved hymn of the Restoration that we know today as "Praise to the Man." The hymn is a touching tribute to Joseph. Just before the final chorus there is this intriguing sentence: "Millions shall know 'Brother Joseph' again."[10]

It is easy to chalk that line up to sentimental exaggeration by a friend and admirer. After all, at the time of Joseph's death there were only about 26,000 members of The Church of Jesus Christ of Latter-day Saints, and many critics anticipated that the Church would fade into oblivion after Joseph's killing. But the truth is, since Phelps wrote that poem, millions *have* come to know Brother Joseph.

What in Joseph Smith's short life could account for millions eventually knowing him, or at least knowing of him? During Moroni's visits with Joseph on the evening of September 21, 1823, Moroni summarized what was ahead for Joseph by saying that "God had a work for [him] to do."[11] It was what Joseph did in fulfilling that work that has impacted millions and, in a sense, brought them to know him. The following paragraphs describe some of the things that Joseph did as part of the work that God had for him to do.

Joseph translated and published the Book of Mormon.

During Moroni's September 1823 visits, he introduced Joseph to the task of translating and publishing the Book of Mormon. The actual work would not begin until a few years after that, but the effect of that work has been remarkable. The first printing was 5,000 copies. Since that time, over 185 million copies of the Book of Mormon have been printed and distributed in over 90 languages (with selections available in more than 20 additional languages).[12] Thus millions of people have been introduced to Joseph and the restored gospel through the Book of Mormon. Millions have received a testimony of his prophetic call by reading and praying about the Book of Mormon. And, as a side benefit, millions have read portions of Joseph's history in the introduction to the Book of Mormon.

Joseph received the priesthood, including the keys of the priesthood, and organized God's true church.

Another part of the work that God had for Joseph Smith to do was to receive priesthood ordination and then organize the restored Church, through which the blessings of the gospel could be shared with others. In 1829 Joseph Smith, in company with Oliver Cowdery, received the Aaronic Priesthood from John the Baptist, and the Melchizedek Priesthood from Peter, James, and John.[13] In 1830, Joseph organized the Church. In 1836 Joseph and Oliver received the "keys of this dispensation" from Moses, Elias, and Elijah.[14] With the restoration of priesthood authority and keys, and the establishment of the Church, people were able to receive the ordinances that can only be performed through the priesthood. Since the organization of the Church, millions have been blessed by being baptized, confirmed, and receiving other ordinances. Moreover, before and after baptism, these millions have come to know Joseph by learning about his life and teachings.

Joseph began the missionary work that has carried the gospel throughout the world.

From the very beginning of the Church, Joseph Smith called missionaries to proclaim the gospel. In the beginning the missionaries went to various places in the United States and Canada. In 1837 Joseph sent missionaries to Europe, and later he sent them to the South Pacific and other places.[15] The missionary work that he started has expanded onto all continents and is continuing to spread. Each year missionaries tell millions about the Church and its founder, Joseph Smith. Many people also receive tracts from the missionaries recounting Joseph's remarkable story in his own words.

Joseph revealed God's will and His true doctrine.

Joseph Smith was a prophet in every sense of the word. He received revelation for the Church and, in fact, all people in this dispensation. Many of the revelations received by Joseph are in the Doctrine and Covenants. Others are included in the Pearl of Great Price. Yet others can be found in his writings compiled in the Joseph Smith Papers. These papers also include records of speeches given by him, articles he wrote or edited, letters he wrote, and other important writings in which he taught God's true doctrine. Technology and recent historical publications have made it easier than ever for people to know Brother Joseph and the words of God that he taught. A vast trove of information is available in the Joseph Smith Papers volumes and website, josephsmithpapers.org. *Saints, Volume 1* narrates Joseph's life and the Restoration of the gospel like never before. Further materials recently produced by the Church make Joseph even more accessible, including *Revelations in Context,* Church History Topics, short videos, and podcasts.

Church historic sites in Vermont, New York, Pennsylvania, Ohio, Missouri, and Illinois commemorate Joseph's life and ministry, allowing individuals to be in sacred settings where the Lord revealed much to Joseph Smith. These sites have also provided millions of people the opportunity to come to know Joseph through the interpretation of events in his life in their historical context.

Joseph restored ordinances for the dead and led the effort to build temples where ordinances could be performed.

As mentioned earlier, priesthood authority and keys were restored through Joseph Smith, and millions have been blessed by the ordinances that are performed with the priesthood. Those ordinances include temple ordinances. Millions on earth have been blessed by those temple ordinances. But it does not stop there. Because of work for the dead, millions on the other side of the veil have also been blessed. The ordinances for the dead go hand in hand with the preaching to the dead that happens in the spirit world. In Joseph F. Smith's vision of the redemption of the dead (Doctrine and Covenants 138), he saw messengers from various dispensations taking the joyous news of the gospel to those who died without it. Included among the messengers was Joseph Smith himself. Part of the message carried forth in the spirit world is the Restoration of the gospel and that the saving ordinances revealed to Joseph Smith are available to the dead vicariously.

Conclusion

William W. Phelps did not have the priesthood office of prophet. But he was certainly prescient when he looked into the future and penned the line "Millions shall know 'Brother Joseph' again," because millions, on both sides of the veil, have come to know Joseph the Prophet. Joseph did the work that God had for him to do.

Elder LeGrand R. Curtis Jr., a General Authority Seventy, serves as the Church Historian and Recorder.

Notes

1. "Phelps, William Wines" (biographical entry), josephsmithpapers.org; Bruce A. Van Orden, *We'll Sing and We'll Shout: The Life and Times of W. W. Phelps* (Provo, UT: Religious Studies Center, Brigham Young University, 2018), 3, 32–36.

2. "Revelation, 20 July 1831 [D&C 57:11]," josephsmithpapers.org.

3. Phelps and his family moved to Jackson County, Missouri, in 1831. In 1835, he returned to Kirtland for several months, leaving his family in Missouri. (Edward Partridge to Lydia Clisbee Partridge, Aug. 5–7, 1831, Edward Partridge, Letters, 1831–35, CHL; Whitmer, History, 70–71, in *JSP,* H2:79.)

4. "Minutes, 30 April 1832," josephsmithpapers.org; "History, 1838–1856, volume B-1 [1 September 1834–2 November 1838]," p. 592, josephsmithpapers.org; Peter Crawley, *A Descriptive Bibliography of the Mormon Church* (Provo, UT: Religious Studies Center, Brigham Young University, 1997), 1:18.

5. "Minutes, 14 September 1835," josephsmithpapers.org; "Minutes and Prayer of Dedication, 27 March 1836 [D&C 109]," josephsmithpapers.org; Michael Hicks, "What Hymns Early Mormons Sang and How They Sang Them," *BYU Studies* 47, no. 1 (2008): 103.

6. Thomas B. Marsh to Wilford Woodruff, in *Elders' Journal,* July 1838, 36–38; Minute Book 2, 10 Mar. 1838, CHL; Journal, July 8 and 26, 1838, josephsmithpapers.org; William W. Phelps, Testimony, Richmond, MO, Nov. 1838, State of Missouri v. JS et al. for Treason and Other Crimes (Mo. 5th Jud. Cir. 1838), in State of Missouri, "Evidence,"

University of Missouri, Columbia; "Extracts of the Minutes of Conferences," *Times and Seasons,* Nov. 1839, 1:15; Van Orden, *We'll Sing and We'll Shout,* 281, 297.

7. "Letter from William W. Phelps, with Appended Letter from Orson Hyde and John E. Page, 29 June 1840," josephsmithpapers.org; "Letter to William W. Phelps, 22 July 1840," josephsmithpapers.org.

8. See, for example, *General Smith's Views of the Powers and Policy of the Government of the United States* (Nauvoo, IL: John Taylor, 1844).

9. "Joseph Smith," *Times and Seasons,* Aug. 1, 1844, 5:607.

10. *Hymns of The Church of Jesus Christ of Latter-day Saints* (Salt Lake City: The Church of Jesus Christ of Latter-day Saints, 1985), no. 27.

11. "History, 1838–1856, volume A-1 [23 December 1805–30 August 1834]," p. 5, josephsmithpapers.org [Joseph Smith—History 1:33].

12. "Church to Translate Scriptures in 34 More Languages; Will Release Portions Online," https://www.ChurchofJesusChrist.org/church/news/church-to-translate-scriptures-in-34 -more-languages-will-release-portions-online?lang=eng; First Presidency letter, Oct. 9, 2017, https://www.ChurchofJesusChrist.org/bc/content/ldsorg/church/news/2017/11/2-15159 _000_letter.pdf?

13. "History, 1838–1856, volume A-1 [23 December 1805–30 August 1834]," p. 17 ; "Revelation, circa Aug. 1835 [D&C 27:12]," josephsmithpapers.org.

14. "Visions, 3 April 1836 [D&C 110:11–16]," josephsmithpapers.org.

15. "Early Missionaries," Church History Topics, ChurchofJesusChrist.org.

PART 1

VERMONT, NEW YORK, AND PENNSYLVANIA, 1805–1830

THE BIRTH OF A PROPHET: "A SON WHOM WE CALLED JOSEPH"

By Mark L. Staker

The year before Joseph Smith Jr.'s birth, the winds of change blew over his family. On April 16, 1804, the *Evening Post* announced that the ship his father used to send ginseng to China had returned after more than ten months at sea. It was in New York Harbor loaded with teas, porcelain, silk, and rhubarb. His parents must have felt blessed. The imports promised fabulous gains.[1]

Joseph Sr. and Lucy Smith ran a store in East Randolph village, Vermont, on the turnpike three miles down the mountain from their Tunbridge farm. There they were raising six-year-old Alvin, four-year-old Hyrum, and one-year-old Sophronia. But by early May they learned there were problems with their ginseng shipment, and they were broke.[2]

The young couple moved back into the Tunbridge mountains to plan their future. Although Lucy's brothers Stephen and Daniel lived with their families in The Market, the main village in Tunbridge, it was her husband who served as a witness on August 27, 1804, when Lucy's parents, Solomon and Lydia Mack, bought a large farm in neighboring Sharon Township. Her parents turned 72 that September and would need someone to care for them in old age. The elderly couple moved into a small frame home built by early settlers on top of a hill on the west edge of their farm.[3]

By January their local newspaper lamented the "hard winter," although Vermont had a lot of winter still ahead.[4] And Joseph Sr. decided to sell his farm before spring planting began in late May to give buyers a whole growing season. He and Lucy would use the money along with Lucy's savings to pay their debts rather than default on their loan as so many others did. "Although we might be poor," Lucy remembered, "we would have the satisfaction of knowing that we had given no man any cause of complaint; and having a conscience void of offence, [and with] the society of our children and the blessing of health, we still might be indeed happy."[5]

In early spring Lucy walked to a grove of wild cherry trees, probably at the cemetery where her firstborn child was buried, and she knelt to plead for her husband.[6] Then she went home, fell asleep, and dreamed of a beautiful, graceful tree. It rustled in a gentle breeze. "As the wind increased this tree assumed the most lively and animated appearance, and seemed to express in its motions the utmost joy and happiness."[7] Lucy believed that tree represented her husband, who would bend to the wafting of the Holy Spirit. About this time, Lucy was with child. She didn't know it was a son.[8]

Shortly after Lucy's dream, on April 29, 1805, she and Joseph Sr. sold their farm for $600.[9] Lucy remembered, "This was considerable of a trial to us for it deprived us at once not only of the comforts and conveniences of life but also of a home of any description." The family was "free from embarrassment of debt but not from the embarrassment of poverty."[10] That would only get worse.

They moved to nearby Royalton for a few months but were not there long enough to grow a garden or do much work that could pay well. They were there long enough, however, that Lucy began to feel her baby move.

By late summer of 1805, Lucy's parents finished a large, comfortable home in the flatlands by White Brook. They moved from the hill, leaving the small house empty. Joseph Sr. "hired a farm of my father," Lucy recalled, and the Smiths moved to "the Solomon Mack place."[11] By then her pregnancy was far enough along that her husband and children could feel the baby's lively kick.

Ten years earlier, in 1795, Samuel Shepard built the 22-by-24-foot house Joseph and Lucy rented. He hewed heavy timbers, attaching thin, unpainted clapboard, and made his own rough brick for a cooking hearth.[12] He raised the house on the northern crest of a hill next to a flat area big enough for a kitchen garden.[13] Lucy remembered working hard over several years to create "quite comfortable circumstances." It was probably she who planted the roses that grew near the house and brightened it.[14]

Shepard had built their house at an angle to protect against the nor'easters blowing down from Canada. And when he planted the apple orchard, he put it northeast of the home to protect it from those cold gales.[15] The orchard was "quite extensive," even by Vermont's fruitful standards, and was well established by the time Joseph Sr. and Lucy arrived.[16]

Their home was pleasant, but the soil thin, the ground rocky, and the hill too steep for oxen to plow.[17] The large apple orchard helped, but it could not provide a living. Because Joseph Sr. grew up working his mother's dairy, he had other options.[18] And the hill could support pasture and hay. He probably built the large stable for cows that was in the orchard, placed strategically to help block the wind.[19]

By the fall, when the apples began to ripen, Lucy was well along in her pregnancy during the backbreaking work of picking fruit and pressing it into cider. The family of their local midwife usually put up one hundred barrels of cider.[20] Joseph Sr. and Lucy's orchard easily outdid them. Fruit was a crop they could rely on in hard times.[21]

By December, Lucy was uncomfortable. She knew the time for the baby to come was approaching. The cider was aging; the hay was in; the cows may have stopped giving milk. The work slowed down. Joseph Sr. spent his winter teaching school at the local schoolhouse.[22] He made a little more than five shillings six pence a week, enough to buy one bushel of wheat.[23] But he didn't leave town. (East Randolph's newspaper advertised on December 30 he had a letter at the post office that had been there several weeks.)[24]

December was a quiet time. Vermonters, like their Puritan ancestors, didn't celebrate Christmas. There were no decorations, December 25 sermons, or school vacations. There was only work, but less of it. Spinning. Weaving. Mending. Darning. For a brief, exciting few weeks it was wedding time. And the sugar plums went into wedding cakes. Polly Hammon married on December 18, Hulda Mars on December 25, Anna Ladd on December 31. And Emy Bruce's wedding was the last that season on January 7.[25]

Monday, December 23, was a school day. Joseph Sr. taught at a little schoolhouse on the turnpike 1.35 miles south of his home. The midwife lived down the turnpike three miles in the same direction, and a runner would pass the schoolhouse on her way to the midwife, gathering both people at once. There were others who were more important participants in the birth than the father, however. These were the women who helped.[26] Lucy would have initiated the calling of midwife, family, and supporting friends while in labor. Her son Alvin, barely losing his first teeth, would have to make his way through the snow to get help.

Lucy's mother lived just down the hill.[27] It was probably Lydia Mack, after Alvin's visit, who gathered the other women: her son Daniel's wife, Sally Mack, who had moved near Lydia; and her son Stephen's wife, Temperance, who lived six miles further up the turnpike at The Market. Close neighbors may have joined them. A circle of women collected, giving advice, making comments, and arguing opinions that turned the room into a noisy social gathering.[28]

The local midwife, the widow Mary Spalding, neared the end of 50 years of experience delivering more than 3,000 babies with great success and often worked without charge.[29] A midwife saw her prospective mothers "put to bed" but also insured that each "walked her room" regularly to aid progress.[30] Spalding was a woman of few words who filled her time reading and smoking a long, white pipe but could orchestrate the chorus of advice offered by others—as the women worked and labored together to complete this act of creation.[31] The goal of each midwife was to deliver a "living mother of a living son" or "living daughter."[32] Lucy had little to say of the birth, later noting only, "We had a son whom we called Joseph, after the name of his father. He was born December 23d, 1805."[33]

On that day the wind blew northwest, bringing temperate conditions from the south, and "the weather [was] very pleasant—though in the morning it was some snow."[34] A gentle, almost imperceptible breeze also began to blow Christianity into a new direction. Father and Mother Smith started out the previous year thinking God would bless them with wealth. By the time 1805 ended, the winds of change brought them poverty but also a son—Joseph Smith Jr., prophet of the Restoration.

Mark L. Staker is a master curator of Historic Sites for The Church of Jesus Christ of Latter-day Saints.

Notes

1. "Arrivals," *Evening Post,* Apr. 16, 1804, 3.
2. "Lucy Mack Smith, History, 1844–1845," bk. 2, pp. [6]–[8], josephsmithpapers.org.
3. Windsor County Deeds, Book 3:272–73, 485; 5:36, 312, 313, 315; 6:386, 459; 8:456.
4. "The Weather Has Been," *Post Boy,* Jan. 22, 1805, 7.
5. "Lucy Mack Smith, History, 1844–1845," bk. 2, p. [8], spelling and punctuation standardized.
6. Mark L. Staker and Donald L. Enders, *Joseph and Lucy Smith's Tunbridge Farm: An Archaeology and Landscape Study* (Independence: John Whitmer Books, 2020), 56–71.
7. "Lucy Mack Smith, History, 1845," p. 50, josephsmithpapers.org.
8. Staker and Enders, *Joseph and Lucy Smith's Tunbridge Farm*; "Lucy Mack Smith, History, 1844–1845," bk. 2, p. [8].
9. James Adams from Asael Smith, Oct. 11, 1805, Tunbridge Deed Book 3:282.
10. "Lucy Mack Smith, History, 1844–1845," bk. 2, p. [8], spelling and punctuation standardized.
11. "Lucy Mack Smith, History, 1844–1845," bk. 2, p. [8].
12. A photograph of the foundations taken in 1894 shows brick remnants of the original hearth. (See H. L. Bixby, "Vermont Scenes, 1894," PH 6, CHL.)
13. Junius F. Wells, "Report on Joseph Smith's Birthplace, June 1905," 2, CHL.
14. "Lucy Mack Smith, History, 1844–1845," bk. 2, p. [8].
15. T. Michael Smith, Kirk B. Henrichsen, and Donald L. Enders, "The Birthplace Home of Joseph Smith Jr.," *Mormon Historical Studies* 6, no. 2 (Fall 2005): 31–32, 40–41; Susan L. Fales, "'The Spirit of the Place': The Clifford Family and the Joseph Smith Farm," *Journal of Mormon History* 33, no. 3 (Fall 2007): 152–86.
16. Wells, "Joseph Smith's Birthplace," 19; Evelyn M. Wood Lovejoy, *History of Royalton, Vermont: With Family Genealogies, 1769–1911* (Burlington: Free Press Printing, 1911), 417.

17. Smith, Henrichsen, and Enders, "Birthplace Home," 37–38; Lovejoy, *History of Royalton*, 747; Zadock Thompson, *History of Vermont, Natural, Civil and Statistical, in Three Parts* (Burlington: Chauncey Goodrich, 1842), 160.

18. Mary Smith's dairy is discussed in Staker and Enders, *Joseph and Lucy Smith's Tunbridge Farm*, 10, 14–18.

19. Wells, "Joseph Smith's Birthplace"; "Lucy Mack Smith, History, 1845," p. 51.

20. Phineas Spalding, *Spalding Memorial and Personal Reminiscences; and Caroline A. Spalding, Life and Selected Poems* (Haverhill, NH: Cohos Steam Press, 1887), 31.

21. "Lucy Mack Smith, History, 1844–1845," bk. 3, p. [3].

22. "Lucy Mack Smith, History, 1844–1845," bk. 2, p. [8].

23. Two schoolhouses have been suggested as the place where Joseph Sr. taught (Larry E. Dahl, "Vermont," in *Sacred Places*, vol. 1, *New England and Eastern Canada: A Comprehensive Guide to Early LDS Historical Sites,* ed. LaMar C. Berrett [Salt Lake City: Bookcraft, 1999], 98–99). One was on the Turnpike Road near the Smith house. The other was three-eighths of a mile west of the Smith home in Royalton Township, but it cannot be the correct school because it had a female teacher (see Lovejoy, *History of Royalton*, 196–97, 199, 288).

24. "List of Letters Remaining in the Post-Office Randolph," *Weekly Wanderer,* Dec. 30, 1805, 3.

25. See Sharon Township Records, 1768–1820, 1:115.

26. Laurel Thatcher Ulrich, "'The Living Mother of a Living Child': Midwifery and Mortality in Post-Revolutionary New England," *William and Mary Quarterly* 46, no. 1 (Jan. 1989): 35.

27. "Testimony of Harvey Smith," in Wells, "Joseph Smith's Birthplace."

28. Laurel Thatcher Ulrich, *A Midwife's Tale: The Life of Martha Ballard, Based on Her Diary, 1785–1812* (New York: Knopf, 1990), 66.

29. Spalding, *Spalding Memorial,* 8, 15–16; Joel Munsell's Sons, *American Ancestry: Giving the Name and Descent, in the Male Line, of Americans Whose Ancestors Settled in the United States Previous to the Declaration of Independence, A.D. 1776* (Albany, NY: Joel Munsell's Sons, 1899), XII:95; Lovejoy, *History of Royalton,* 895, 900.

30. Ulrich, *Midwife's Tale,* 196.

31. See Spalding, *Spalding Memorial,* 8.

32. See Ulrich, "Midwifery and Mortality," 30–31, especially footnote 9.

33. "Lucy Mack Smith, History, 1845," p. 51.

34. Hiram Harwood, "Harwood Diaries, March 22, 1805–December 20, 1806," Bennington Museum Research Libraries, Bennington, Vermont, spelling standardized.

UNITED AND DEDICATED: JOSEPH SMITH'S FAMILY

By Kyle R. Walker

In 1842, as Joseph Smith was reflecting on those who had been most loyal to him and the Church he helped establish, he included some lines in his journal about his parents. Joseph summarized, "Words and language, are inadequate to express the gratitude I owe to God for having given me so honorable a parentage."[1] The influence of his entire family profoundly shaped Joseph's developing personality and his future prophetic role.

Joseph was reared in a religious home, where biblical teachings were discussed and practiced. Joseph Sr. and Lucy Mack Smith established a pattern of regular religious habits from the time the children were very young, including prayers both morning and night. William Smith, the second-to-youngest brother in the family, recalled that "we always had family prayer since I can remember. I well remember father used to carry his spectacles in his vest pocke[t] . . . and when us boys saw him feel for his specks, we knew that was A signal to get ready for prayer, and if we did not notice it mother would say, 'William,' or whoever was the negligent one, 'get ready for prayer.'"[2] Family prayer appears to have been a joint effort by the Smith parents in which Joseph Sr. and Lucy took turns being voice. The Smith children recounted that during family prayer their parents, both father and mother, "pourd out their Souls to God the doner of all blessings, to keep and gard their children . . . from sin and from all evil works."[3]

After evening prayer, the Smith family typically sang a hymn. Recalling this daily routine, some of the children said that the family typically only sang one or two selections of hymns. This practice of hymn-singing in the home was a pattern typical of some Protestant families and imbued the Smith children with fondness for spiritual hymns throughout their lives.[4]

Joseph portrayed his father and mother as "goodly parents who spared no pains to instructing me in the christian religion."[5] Palmyra neighbors remembered that Mother Lucy utilized the Bible as the family's "first primer."[6] When Lucy later spoke at a gathering of Saints in Nauvoo, she recounted how she had instilled religious values into the minds and hearts of her children. One of the ways she had accomplished this was by teaching them stories from the Bible at a very young age—"about Joseph in Egypt and such things, and when they are four years old they will love to read their Bible."[7]

Lucy had a profound influence on the desire of Joseph and her other children to attend regular church meetings, as well as revival camp meetings. "My mother, who was a very pious woman and much interested in the welfare of her children," recalled William, "made use of every means which her parental love could suggest, to get us engaged in seeking for our souls' salvation, or . . . 'in getting religion.'" Through spiritual instruction in the home, as well as attending worship services, Lucy helped all of her children become individuals who sought truth.[8] Lucy was instrumental in fanning the fires of faith that eventually led Joseph into the Sacred Grove.

Joseph Smith took comfort in the fact that his father was the first person to believe his account of his earliest visions.[9] Perhaps that was because his father also believed in heavenly manifestations. He had experienced his own series of seven spiritual dreams during the years 1811–19. One dream was very similar to Lehi's dream, as recorded in the Book of Mormon; Joseph Sr. saw "a tree" bearing fruit that could make one happy. In the last of this series of dreams, a heavenly messenger revealed that this was the final time he would visit, and Joseph Sr. was left somewhat puzzled regarding his eternal welfare: "there is but one thing which you lack, in order to secure salvation," the messenger told him. As Joseph Sr. sprang forward to get pen and paper to write down the message, he awoke before he could record what he had heard. This final dream occurred in 1819, foreshadowing what would occur the following year when Joseph Jr. experienced his First Vision. The events and teachings Joseph Sr. learned from these dreams put the entire family in a mindset where they were prepared to accept visions, angelic visitors, and miracles.[10]

When Moroni visited Joseph on September 21–22, 1823, he instructed Joseph to share what he had learned with his father. With Moroni's encouragement, Joseph shared the events with his entire family. Thus, the Smith family's involvement with the coming forth of the Book of Mormon came directly from the angel's instruction. Moroni also issued a warning that once Joseph had obtained the plates, the Smith family name "would be cast out as evil by all people." Based on this instruction and forewarning, Lucy recounted her view that it wasn't just Joseph's mission to bring forth a sacred book of scripture, but that of her entire family.[11]

In the ensuing years, Joseph went to his family in great confidence. Mother Lucy recollected with fondness the time when the family was preparing to receive the plates, during 1823–27. Joseph had learned from Moroni details about Book of Mormon culture, warfare, and patterns of religious worship, which he also shared with his family. "I presume our family presented an aspect as singular as any that ever lived upon the face of the earth," wrote Lucy in her history, "all seated in a circle, father, mother, sons, and daughters, and giving the most profound attention to a boy, eighteen years of age, who had never read through the Bible in his life."[12]

As the light of the Restoration began to settle during the decade of the 1820s, Joseph Sr., Lucy, and their children became their son's and brother's greatest support. "We all had the most implicit confidence in what he [Joseph] said," remembered William about his brother's character.[13] The Smiths diligently helped safeguard the sacred record once Joseph had the plates in his possession, and throughout the process of translation. The family experienced much persecution and made great sacrifices to assist in the publication of the Book of Mormon.

Three of the Eight Witnesses of the Book of Mormon were Smiths. Joseph's parents were baptized on the day of the Church's organization, April 6, 1830, and the rest of the family all soon joined the faith, including spouses of the married Smith children.[14] Alvin, the eldest brother, who passed away just two months after Moroni's initial visits, manifested his support of Joseph's mission. On his dying bed, Alvin's last charge to Joseph was for him to "do everything that lies in your power to obtain the Record."[15] The surviving Smith family followed Joseph Smith to Ohio, Missouri, and Illinois. Joseph Sr. served as Church patriarch, and the Prophet Joseph valued his father's counsel and considered him a trusted adviser.[16] Lucy led a branch of the Church in their migration from New York to Ohio, and by the Nauvoo period of Church history was revered among the Saints as "'Mother' of [all] the 'mothers in Israel.'"[17] His brothers served in prominent leadership positions in the early Church—Hyrum as a member of the First Presidency, and William as an Apostle. Samuel fulfilled many missions and served as a bishop in Nauvoo.[18] Don Carlos was appointed president of the high priests quorum in Kirtland at the age of 19, and he helped edit and publish several Church newspapers.[19] The three Smith sisters, Sophronia, Katharine, and Lucy, contributed heavily to the completion of the Kirtland Temple, and Lucy participated with her mother in the Female Relief Society at Nauvoo.[20]

Nowhere is the support of the Smith family more evident than in the relationship of Joseph and his brother Hyrum. According to a history of the Church, just a day before they were murdered, Joseph said, "Could my brother Hyrum but be liberated it would not matter so much about me." However, Hyrum was determined not to leave his side.[21] Ultimately, the two brothers gave their lives for the cause they had espoused. The same might be said of the entire Smith family, as they unitedly joined their labors and dedicated their lives to the restored gospel of Jesus Christ. The Smiths' collective efforts were indispensable to the foundation and expansion of the early Church.

Kyle R. Walker is a faculty member at BYU–Idaho and has published extensively on the Joseph Smith Sr. and Lucy Mack Smith family.

Notes

1. Journal, Aug. 23, 1842, in *JSP,* J2:115–16.
2. John W. Peterson, "Wm. B. Smith's Last Statement," *Zion's Ensign,* Jan. 13, 1894, 6.
3. William Smith, "Notes Written on 'Chambers' Life of Joseph Smith,'" ca. 1875, 29, CHL.
4. Smith, "Notes Written," 29; Michael Hicks, *Mormonism and Music: A History* (Urbana: University of Illinois Press, 1989), 4.
5. History, ca. Summer 1832, in *JSP,* H1:11.
6. John Stafford, interview, as cited in William H. Kelley, "The Hill Cumorah, and the Book of Mormon," *Saints' Herald,* June 1, 1881, 167.
7. Jennifer Reeder and Kate Holbrook, eds., *At the Pulpit: 185 Years of Discourses by Latter-day Saint Women* (Salt Lake City: Church Historian's Press, 2017), 23.
8. William Smith, *William Smith on Mormonism* (Lamoni, IA: Herald Steam Book and Job Office, 1883), 6.
9. "History, 1838–1856, volume C-1 [2 November 1838–31 July 1842]," p. 20 [addenda], josephsmithpapers.org.
10. Lucy Mack Smith, *Biographical Sketches of Joseph Smith the Prophet, and His Progenitors for Many Generations* (Liverpool: S. W. Richards, 1853), 73–74.
11. Smith, *Biographical Sketches,* 82–84.
12. Smith, *Biographical Sketches,* 84.
13. Peterson, "Wm. B. Smith's Last Statement," 6.
14. History, ca. June–Oct. 1839 ("Draft 1"), 9, 11, in *JSP,* H1:366, 372; Smith, *Biographical Sketches,* 151.
15. Smith, *Biographical Sketches,* 88.
16. "History, 1838–1856, volume C-1 [2 November 1838–31 July 1842]," p. 21 [addenda], josephsmithpapers.org; History, 1834–36 (Oct. 11, 1835), in *JSP,* H1:101.
17. Smith, *Biographical Sketches,* 172–83; Juanita Brooks, ed., *On the Mormon Frontier: The Diary of Hosea Stout, 1844–1861* (Salt Lake City: University of Utah Press, 1964), 22–23, as cited in Reeder and Holbrook, *At the Pulpit,* 22.
18. Dean L. Jarman and Kyle R. Walker, "Samuel Harrison Smith," in *United by Faith: The Joseph Sr. and Lucy Mack Smith Family,* ed. Kyle R. Walker (American Fork, UT: Covenant Communications; Provo, UT: BYU Studies, 2006), 205–36.
19. Kyle R. Walker, "'As Fire Shut Up in My Bones': Ebenezer Robinson, Don Carlos Smith, and the 1840 Edition of the Book of Mormon," *Journal of Mormon History* 36, no. 1 (Winter 2010): 1–33.
20. Mary Salisbury Hancock, "The Three Sisters of the Prophet Joseph Smith, Part II," *Saints' Herald,* Jan. 18, 1954, 10; Jill Mulvay Derr et al., eds., *The First Fifty Years of Relief Society: Key Documents in Latter-day Saint Women's History* (Salt Lake City: Church Historian's Press, 2016), 38, 45, 49.
21. "History, 1838–1856, volume F-1 [1 May 1844–8 August 1844]," p. 168, josephsmith papers.org.

RECEIVING GRACE FOR GRACE: JOSEPH SMITH'S CONVERSION PROCESS

By Rachel Cope

In the early nineteenth century, a period of revivalism, later known as the Second Great Awakening, fostered an interest in powerful manifestations of the Holy Spirit and ignited a desire within the hearts and minds of countless Christians to seek the gift of salvation. Hoping to feel the power of religion, spiritual seekers attended revival meetings, engaged in devotional activities, participated in prayer meetings, pondered upon scriptural passages, and prayed intently within private settings, such as groves of trees or personal chambers.[1] As many conversion narratives from the time attest, the desire to experience divine redemption stood at the heart of this emerging evangelical world—a world in which individuals such as Joseph Smith actively participated. Joseph's conversion story highlights the lengthy process through which earnest Christians of the time sought, found, and received the gift of grace—a reminder that seeking religious guidance and feeling the presence of God require patience and time.

The prevalence of revival meetings in antebellum America cultivated sincere religious curiosity within many hearts and minds. To seekers of salvation, revivalism denoted "times of spiritual awakening in which the church is quickened, wanderers reclaimed, and sinners saved."[2] Revivals also marked periods of spiritual "refreshing."[3] They served as a call to ponder and contemplate, to revitalize or initiate faith, to experience conversion, and to attain a forgiveness of sins.[4] Those seeking "to get Religion too" and "to feel & shout like the Rest," as Joseph described it, typically attended revivals.[5] Immersed in this context, they became increasingly aware of their need for redemption. As revival participant Emilie Royce Bradley concluded, "The Lord did not need me, but I needed him."[6]

Although a few people experienced justification—or the "remission of sin and absolution from guilt and punishment"—immediately upon attending a revival, the vast majority of seekers spent days, weeks, months, and even years before God's spirit, voice, or presence assured them that they had been cleansed through the blood of their Redeemer.[7] Forgiveness, justification, and conversion typically involved deep internal struggles within both the heart and the mind. Hearing, feeling, knowing, seeing, experiencing, and understanding the voice and presence of the divine took time.[8]

The patience and perseverance required of a religious seeker is powerfully manifest throughout the story of Joseph Smith. His narrative, while unique in many ways, is also strikingly similar to much religious memoir of the time.[9] It reminds us that even those who are considered the most spiritual of individuals—such as prophets, preachers, and missionaries—struggle to feel and hear the voice of God. Experiencing conversion, recognizing spiritual promptings, feeling a sense of deep forgiveness, drawing closer to the divine, and reaching a sanctified or holy state are lifelong processes for all of God's children.[10] No one is exempt from the difficult journey of mortality. Even the Savior "received not of the fulness at the first but received grace for grace and he received not of the fulness but continued from grace to grace until he received a fulness." And with His help, Joseph's story reminds us, we too can "receive grace for grace."[11]

Joseph's conversion story does not begin in a grove of trees, nor does it emerge within the context of a revival meeting. His spiritual sensibilities had been ignited during childhood. Raised in a spiritually reflective and deeply devotional family, Joseph grew up believing it was possible to receive guidance from the divine.[12] Feelings, impressions, dreams, and visions—all of which took time to unfold—were a reality within the Smith household.[13] As Joseph approached his teenage years, revival meetings were held near his home. "Indeed the whole district of Country seemed affected by it," he recalled. While attending these gatherings, he witnessed conversion experiences, including those of family members.[14] But Joseph, like other earnest seekers, remained uncertain about his own spiritual welfare. He struggled to feel what he perceived everyone else to be feeling.

As a result of his uncertainty, indeed, confused by the abundance of religious options he encountered, Joseph became "seriously imprest with regard to the all important concerns for the wellfare of [his] immortal Soul." He too wanted to experience the peace others described as they received divine assurance of forgiveness. He wanted to "feel" religion. But as he continued to attend revival meetings, Joseph found himself developing more questions than answers. Drawn to deep spiritual contemplation, he began to search in and ponder upon the scriptures.[15] For approximately three years, he reflected upon salvation and became increasingly concerned about the state of his soul. Like so many of his contemporaries, he was "distressed" by his sins.[16] He wondered, much like Emilie Royce Bradley, why "light did not break in upon [him] suddenly."[17] Joseph longed for justification; he wanted to know that he had been washed clean through the blood of his Redeemer.

Determined to hear and know God in a more profound way, and resolved to feel divine influence in his life, Joseph eventually decided to act upon a scripture that encouraged him to "ask of God." He later recalled that he "reflected on it again and again, knowing that if any person needed wisdom from God, I did, for how to act I did not know and unless I could get more wisdom than I then had [I] would never know." For the first time in his life, Joseph decided to pray vocally—to speak privately—to God.[18]

Joseph eventually entered the woods near his home to commune with the divine. Upon finding a secluded spot, he knelt to pray. Like other seekers of mercy, he struggled to articulate his thoughts and feelings. Speaking to God so directly and personally—asking to be forgiven of his sins, pleading for mercy, light, and truth—must have felt overwhelming and intimidating to a teenage boy. Like other seekers of salvation, he must have wondered if God would really listen to him. He had attempted to feel God's presence and power before, but his attempts had failed. Could this time be different?

Consumed by feelings of unworthiness, Joseph sensed a state of darkness surrounding him that seemed to bind his tongue. In that empty moment, he felt entirely overcome by evil—his soul seemed "doomed to sudden destruction."[19] Symbolically speaking, Joseph saw and felt the full effects of sinfulness, the condition of the human soul in its unregenerate state. All seemed lost, hopeless, bleak. His unworthiness loomed before him. His sinfulness seemed all-consuming.

While enveloped in this state of utter despair, Joseph remembered his purpose for entering the woods. He had come seeking his Savior; he had come to plead for redemption. "I cried unto the Lord for mercy for there was none else to whom I could go and obtain mercy," he recalled.[20] As Joseph made this humble plea, darkness dissipated. His intense feelings of despair and fear dissolved. Former burdens became light and feelings of guilt disappeared. Joseph then witnessed a "piller of light above the brightness of the sun at noon day." It came "down from above and rested upon me," he explained. "I was filled with the spirit of god and the Lord opened the heavens upon me and I saw the Lord."[21] In that glorious moment, the Savior of humankind assured a teenage boy that his sins had been forgiven. He had received the gift of justification; he was clean and pure. The peace that had once eluded Joseph now filled his soul.

Although accounts of Joseph's First Vision often focus on the origins of the Church, it is also a story about a personal conversion process—a story of a young man seeking and experiencing the power of redemption. Joseph's spiritual journey began long before he entered the grove of trees, and it continued throughout his life. For years, he had attended revival meetings where he witnessed and listened to professions of faith. But in those contexts, he did not immediately encounter a sense of peace; salvific assurance seemed out of reach. In such moments, God felt distant to him.

As Joseph continued to pray, search, seek, and ponder—as he engaged his heart and mind in an ongoing spiritual quest that lasted for years— he slowly came to recognize that he had always been receiving direction from the divine. He had just mistakenly expected redemption to come in the form of an event rather than a process. Before his desire to feel God's grace could be met, he had to develop spiritual maturity that enabled him to see that God spoke "line upon line, precept upon precept." He revealed "here a little and there a little."[22]

Joseph's conversion thus extended well beyond his experience in the Sacred Grove: The appearance of Moroni, the translation of the Book of Mormon, the loss of translated text, the restoration of priesthood power, the organization of the Church, the slow but steady receipt and under- standing of revelation, the struggle to comprehend and live the law of consecration, the dedication of the Kirtland Temple, the difficulties and seeming failures of Zion's Camp, the loneliness and despair in Liberty jail, the rise of the city of Nauvoo, the emergence of the Relief Society, and the recognition that relationships are eternal all contributed to Joseph's growth in grace, to his journey from justification to sanctification. Indeed, his spir- itual pilgrimage was complex and nuanced—stretching from periods of humble teenage seeking to periods of growing prophetic insightfulness. Joseph evolved from skeptic, to hopeful convert, to faithful believer, and he had to make a continuous effort to keep Christ at the center of his life.[23]

Joseph's conversion narrative—a story of ongoing spiritual growth— accurately represents religious experiences of the time. The answers he sought, the changes he anticipated, and the forgiveness he longed to attain came slowly. His story illustrates that religious life is a pilgrimage, an on- going journey, a process that unfolds over time. Hearing, understanding, receiving, and applying the gift of redemption was and is a continuing process that requires patience, hope, perseverance, and tenacity.

Rachel Cope is an associate professor of Church history and doctrine at Brigham Young University.

Notes

1. See Brett M. Grainger, *Church in the Wild: Evangelicals in Antebellum America* (Cambridge, MA: Harvard University Press, 2019).
2. L. D. Davis, *The History of the Methodist Episcopal Church in Cortland* (Syracuse, NY: William T. Hamilton, 1855), 122–23.
3. *Presbyterian Magazine,* Jan. 1821, 1:21.
4. See Davis, *History of the Methodist Episcopal Church,* 122–23.
5. "Alexander Neibaur, Journal, 24 May 1844, extract," p. [23], josephsmithpapers.org.
6. Papers of Emilie Royce Bradley, Diary, June 26, 1831, Dan Beach Bradley Family Papers, Oberlin College Archives, Oberlin College Library, Oberlin College, Oberlin, Ohio. Emilie Royce (1811–45) of Clinton, New York, served as a Christian missionary in Thailand until her death from tuberculosis in 1845.
7. Noah Webster's 1828 dictionary states that justification was "an act of free grace by which God pardons the sinner and accepts him as righteous, on account of the atonement of Christ." (*American Dictionary of the English Language,* s.v. "justification," http://websters dictionary1828.com/Dictionary/justification.)
8. See Rachel Cope, "'In Some Places a Few Drops and Other Places a Plentiful Shower': The Religious Impact of Revivalism on Nineteenth-Century New York Women" (PhD diss., Syracuse University, New York, 2009).
9. See Bruce Hindmarsh, *The Evangelical Conversion Narrative: Spiritual Autobiographies in Early Modern England* (Oxford: Oxford University Press, 2005); and Christopher Jones, "The Power and Form of Godliness: Methodist Conversion Narratives and Joseph Smith's First Vision," *Journal of Mormon History* 37, no. 2 (2011).
10. Noah Webster's 1828 dictionary defines sanctification as follows: "In an evangelical sense, the act of God's grace by which the affections of men are purified or alienated from sin and the world, and exalted to a supreme love to God." (*American Dictionary,* s.v. "sanctification," http://webstersdictionary1828.com/Dictionary/sanctification).
11. "Revelation, 6 May 1833 [D&C 93:12–13]," josephsmithpapers.org.
12. "Lucy Mack Smith, History, 1844–1845," bk. 2, pp. [3]–[4], josephsmithpapers.org.
13. "History, circa June 1839–circa 1841 [Draft 2]," pp. 2–3, josephsmithpapers.org; "Lucy Mack Smith, History, 1845," josephsmithpapers.org.
14. "History, circa June 1839–circa 1841 [Draft 2]," 1–2.
15. "History, circa Summer 1832," pp. [1]–[3], josephsmithpapers.org; "Lucy Mack Smith, History, 1844–1845," book 3, p. [10].
16. "History, circa Summer 1832," p. [2].
17. Emilie Royce Bradley, Diary, June 26, 1831.
18. James 1:5–6; "History, circa June 1839–circa 1841 [Draft 2]," 2–3.
19. "History, circa June 1839–circa 1841 [Draft 2]," 3; "Lucy Mack Smith, History, 1845," p. [75]. For experiences similar to Joseph's, see Emilie Royce Bradley Papers; Catherine Livingston Garrettson Papers, Garrettson Family Papers, United Methodist Archives and History Center, Drew University, Madison, New Jersey; and Charles G. Finney, *Memoirs of Rev. Charles G. Finney* (New York: A.S. Barnes, 1876).
20. "History, circa Summer 1832," p. [3].
21. "History, circa Summer 1832," p. [3].
22. 2 Nephi 28:30; Isaiah 28:10.
23. Richard L. Bushman, "Joseph Smith and Modernism," *BYU Studies Quarterly* 59, no. 2 (2020): 121–34.

HEARING HIM:
THE DILEMMA BETWEEN HEAD
AND HEART THAT LED TO
JOSEPH SMITH'S FIRST VISION

By Steven C. Harper

I remember the day I recognized Joseph Smith's dilemma. It was lunchtime. I was sitting outside reviewing copies of his First Vision accounts again. I was hoping to hear something I had been deaf to before—and I was rewarded. As I focused on how frequently Joseph used the word *mind,* I eventually picked up on a distinction he was making—a struggle between his head and heart. Then I heard him clearly: before the First Vision, his heart and his mind were at odds, and in no small way.

His dilemma was acute. He chose potent words to describe it. "My mind become seriously imprest," he said, "with regard to the all important concerns for the wellfare of my immortal Soul." He said his "mind bec[a]me excedingly distressed for I bec[a]me convicted of my sins."[1] He said he was "wrought up in my mind." The stakes were high. It was "of the first importance that [he] should be right, in matters that involve eternal consequences," but he was "perplexed in mind."[2] His "mind was called up to serious reflection and great uneasiness."[3]

The core dilemma in Joseph Smith's First Vision accounts is hidden in plain sight. It is easy to overlook. A chapter in *Americanist Approaches to The Book of Mormon* illustrates how easy. This chapter compares Joseph's experience to some early American conversion narratives and concludes that Joseph's accounts lack angst and typical "transformations of the heart." The author notes, "Nowhere in Smith's first vision is there a description of the agonies and ecstasies of conversion." Joseph "presents himself not as one whose heart needs changing but one whose mind needs persuading." That either-or is overstated. The author depicts Joseph's accounts as trying to resolve "cognitive dissonance" or intellectual incongruity *rather than* ravishing a sinful heart with infinite love."[4] Those phrases present a false dilemma.

Joseph's vision accounts present his actual dilemma. He had a choice between an undesirable theology that made intellectual sense or a theology that *promised* to ravish his sinful heart with God's love but *never did.* Joseph's salvation depended on knowing how to act relative to this choice, and how to act he did not know. He worked hard on the problem. He wanted to feel God's love and forgiveness, but he checked his emotions. He felt *and* he thought. He attended various churches as often as possible.[5]

At Methodist meetings Joseph watched penitent sinners receive a gift of God's grace that would enable them to choose Christ.[6] Joseph said that "he wanted to get Religion too wanted to feel & shout like the Rest but could feel nothing."[7] Methodism taught him to expect that desirable experience. Did failure to get it mean that Presbyterianism was correct? He hoped not. Methodism appealed to Joseph's heart, but Presbyterianism fit the observable facts. It made sense, terrible sense. Christ had only atoned for a few, and he was not one of them. Joseph's head inclined him to one conclusion; his heart, the other. How could he know which was right? His immortal soul was at stake. No matter how much thought he put into it, he did not know if his conclusions were right. No matter how much he followed his heart, he did not know if it was leading him right.

That is the context for Joseph's vivid description of the "confusion and strife amongst the different denominations." He said, "It was impossible for a person young as I was and so unacquainted with men and things to come to any certain conclusion who was right and who was wrong." He could not discern which nuance of which theology was right. Every professor of every option wielded the Bible skillfully.[8] Joseph described what occurred in his mind "in the midst of this war of words, and tumult of opinions." He thought often: "Who of all these parties are right? Or are they all wrong together? And if any one of them be right which is it? And how shall I know it?"[9]

While he was "laboring under the extreme difficulties caused by the contests of these parties of religionists," Joseph learned from James 1:5 that he could ask God directly.[10] He went to the woods to do so. He returned from the grove forgiven and full of God's love. He also felt settled for the first time regarding the churches. In his *mind,* he had often thought they could all be wrong. His *heart* rejected that possibility, however, since it seemed to leave him no good options.[11] Now his heart could be at peace with what his head recognized.

Some eight decades later, in 1902, B. H. Roberts was named an assistant church historian and tasked with turning Joseph Smith's history into books (eventually becoming the multivolume *History of the Church*).[12] Roberts had gathered Joseph's history from back issues of the *Millennial Star* and bound it into three volumes, which he annotated. Joseph's history says that he "often said to myself, what is to be done? Who of all these parties are right? Or are they all wrong together?" Later, Joseph asked two glorious personages who stood above him in the air "which of all the sects was right, (for at this time it had never entered into my *heart* that all were wrong)."[13]

Which was it, Roberts wondered? Had Joseph considered the option that all of the churches were wrong or not?[14] Roberts knew that in 1842 Joseph said that at about age 14 he began to notice "a great clash" between churches and considered "that all could not be right, and that God could not be the author of so much confusion."[15] So Roberts decided to delete the presumed contradiction. He simply omitted the line *for at this time it had never entered into my heart that all were wrong* when he edited the *History of the Church.*[16]

That made it even more difficult to hear Joseph's dilemma. Once in a while it happens, however. Once in a while, after spending lots of time with Joseph's attempts to describe what defied description, it is possible to hear him. He had an awful dilemma. One choice said that Jesus Christ atoned for a limited few, and Joseph was not one of them. The other choice said that Joseph could access God's grace and choose salvation through Jesus Christ. The second choice was desirable but Joseph could not get the conversion experience it promised. That seemed to leave Joseph only one terrible option, until James directed him to ask of God, who introduced him to His Only Begotten Son.

Though it is hard to hear Joseph's dilemma, there is an extremely good reason to do whatever it takes to hear him: He testified that he saw and heard the Father say, "This is my beloved Son, Hear him."[17]

Steven C. Harper is a professor of Church history and doctrine at Brigham Young University and is editor in chief of *BYU Studies Quarterly*.

Notes

1. "History, circa Summer 1832," pp. 1–2, josephsmithpapers.org.
2. "Journal, 1835–1836," p. 23, josephsmithpapers.org.
3. "History, circa June 1839–circa 1841 [Draft 2]," p. 2, josephsmithpapers.org.
4. Grant Shreve, "Nephite Secularization; or, Picking and Choosing in the Book of Mormon," *Americanist Approaches to The Book of Mormon*, ed. Elizabeth Fenton and Jared Hickman (New York: Oxford University Press, 2019), 207–29. Quoted passages are from page 208, emphasis added.
5. "History, circa June 1839–circa 1841 [Draft 2]," pp. 2–3.
6. John H. Wigger, *Taking Heaven by Storm: Methodism and the Rise of Popular Christianity in America* (Urbana: University of Illinois Press, 1998), 16–20; Roger E. Olson, *Arminian Theology: Myths and Realities* (Downers Grove, IL: InterVarsity Press, 2006), 158–78.
7. "Alexander Neibaur, Journal, 24 May 1844, extract," p. [23], josephsmithpapers.org.
8. Overviews of the theological environment include E. Brooks Holifield, *Theology in America* (New Haven: Yale University Press, 2003), and Mark A. Noll, *The Rise of Evangelicalism* (Downers Grove, IL: InterVarsity Press, 2003).
9. "History, circa June 1839–circa 1841 [Draft 2]," p. 2.
10. "History, circa June 1839–circa 1841 [Draft 2]," p. 2.
11. "Journal, 1835–1836," p. 24.
12. Truman G. Madsen, *Defender of the Faith: The B. H. Roberts Story* (Salt Lake City: Bookcraft, 1980), 162–64, 289–90.
13. "History, circa June 1839–circa 1841 [Draft 2]," pp. 2–3, emphasis added. Compare to "History of Joseph Smith," *Times and Seasons,* Apr. 1, 1842, 3:748.
14. On page 3 of his "History of Joseph Smith from the Millennial Star," Roberts wrote the following in pencil: "contradiction with statement in Wentworth letter [one illegible word] see preceding." (History of Joseph Smith, 3 vols., in B. H. Roberts Collection, 1883–1933, CHL.)
15. "'Church History,' 1 March 1842," p. 706, josephsmithpapers.org.
16. B. H. Roberts, ed., *History of The Church of Jesus Christ of Latter-day Saints,* vol. 1 (Salt Lake City: Deseret News, 1902), 6.
17. "History, circa June 1839–circa 1841 [Draft 2]," p. 3.

"WE FOUND HIM TO BE A BOY OF TRUTH": THE FRIENDS OF YOUNG JOSEPH SMITH

By Larry E. Morris

Lucy Mack Smith's history notes that in the autumn of 1825, "a man, by the name of Josiah Stoal [Stowell], came from Chenango county, New York, with a view of getting Joseph [Jr.] to assist him in digging for a silver mine."[1]

Joseph added in his later history that Stowell "had heard something of a silver mine having been opened by the Spaniards in Harmony, Susquahanah [Susquehanna] County, State of Pennsylvania, and had previous to my hiring with him been digging in order if possible to discover the mine."[2]

Born in 1770, Stowell was a respected farmer and sawmill owner in Bainbridge, New York, about 130 miles southeast of the Smith farm in Manchester, New York.[3] It is somehow fitting that Stowell was the first person, other than members of the Smith family and scriptural figures, mentioned by name in Joseph's history. Stowell's visit to the Smith farm triggered a series of events that reveal much about young Joseph's ability to make lasting friendships, even in the midst of controversy.

"Things Invisible to the Natural Eye"

Adding a crucial detail not mentioned by Joseph, Lucy's history mentions that Stowell "came for Joseph on account of having heard that he

30

possessed certain keys, by which he could discern things invisible to the natural eye"[4]—a reference to young Joseph's use of a seer stone to search for lost articles or buried treasure. As historians with the Joseph Smith Papers note, "Several of [Joseph Jr.'s] neighbors recounted his participation in treasure-seeking activities between 1823 and 1826 in locations ranging from the Palmyra-Manchester area to Harmony."[5]

Regarding such activities, Ronald W. Walker has written, "There were hundreds and probably thousands of these 'money diggers,' all seeking troves of fabled coins, mines, jewels, and other valued prizes."[6] Indeed, there were village seers throughout western New York, and in the greater Palmyra area, others possessed and used seer stones. For many rural people at this time, including the Smiths, folk magic blended easily with their Christian beliefs.[7]

Stowell's hired hands, including Joseph and his father, searched for almost a month without success, boarding for a time at the Isaac Hale home in Harmony, where Joseph first met his future wife, Emma Hale. Stowell gave up the venture but was clearly impressed with Joseph Jr. because he hired him as a laborer. Through the winter, Joseph, who turned 20 in December 1825, worked on the farm and attended school.

It must have been quite a shock to Joseph, when, in March 1826, in connection with his using a seer stone to help search for the mine, he was arrested and tried as a disorderly person. The charge was brought not by Stowell but by Peter Bridgeman, a nephew of Stowell's wife, Miriam. Bridgeman apparently wanted to protect Josiah from being defrauded by Joseph.

In 1877, William Purple, who attended the hearing and took notes, said that Joseph testified and told how he had discovered his seer stone, even exhibiting it at the judge's request.

The key witness was Stowell himself, who made it clear that he needed no protection from Joseph and reportedly "swore that the prisoner possessed all the power he claimed, and declared he could see things 50 feet below the surface of the earth, as plain as the witnesses could see what was on the Justice's table, and described many circumstances to confirm his words." Since Stowell's testimony could not be impeached, concluded Purple, "the prisoner was discharged, and in a few weeks left the town."[8]

An 1886 account of the hearing, however, claims that Joseph was found guilty. Given the contradiction between the two accounts and the lack of an 1826 document clearly reporting the verdict, the outcome of the case remains in question.[9]

"The Best Hand He Ever Hired"

Late in 1826, after Moroni's annual visit at the hill in western New York where the gold plates were buried, Joseph was back in southern New York, again seeking work. Stowell, unable to hire Joseph at that time, apparently sent him to a friend by the name of Joseph Knight, a prosperous landowner who lived a few miles south of Stowell, on the opposite side of the Susquehanna River. Knight operated a gristmill and owned 140 acres of fields, with "two dwelling houses, a good barn, and a fine orchard."[10]

"My father . . . hired many hands," wrote Joseph Knight Jr. "In 1827 [1826] he hired Joseph Smith. Joseph and I worked together. . . . My father said Joseph was the best hand he ever hired. We found him [to be] a boy of truth." Joseph told the junior Knight and his father that a personage had appeared to him and told him of a gold book. "My father and I believed what he told us, I think we were the first after his father's family."[11]

Newel, another son in the Knight family, expressed similar sentiments. "To him [Joseph] I was particularly attached," wrote Newel. "His noble deportment, his faithfulness, his kind address could not fail to gain the esteem of those who had the pleasure of his acquaintance. . . . In all his boyish sports or amusements, I never knew any one to gain advantage over him and yet he was always kind and kept the good will of his playmates."[12]

"The Virtues and Good Qualifications of the Faithful Few"

After Joseph and Emma married in South Bainbridge in January 1827, none other than Stowell moved them to Manchester. That September, Stowell and Joseph Knight Sr. were both present at the Smith farm when Joseph arrived there after obtaining the plates from Moroni.

"After Brackfirst [breakfast] Joseph Cald me into the other Room," Knight wrote of that memorable day, "and he set his foot on the Bed and leaned his head on his hand and says, 'Well I am Dissopinted.' 'Well,' says I, 'I am sorry.' 'Well,' says he, 'I am greatly Dissopinted; it is ten times Better then I expected.'" Joseph next described the height, width, and thickness of the plates and said they appeared to be gold. But he seemed most impressed with the "glasses or the urim and thummem" and said, "I can see anything; they are Marvelus."[13]

In his history, Joseph told how Knight assisted him and Oliver Cowdery as they translated in Harmony, noting that the elderly gentleman "several times brought us supplies (a distance of at least thirty miles) which enabled us to continue the work when otherwise we must have relinquished it for a season."[14]

Josiah Stowell was baptized into the Church of Christ (the original name of the Church) but did not migrate west with the Saints, remaining in New York. In February 1843, Stowell, then a 73-year-old widower, dictated a statement that showed that his affection for Joseph and his testimony of the Restoration had never wavered: "He [Stowell] has been acquainted with him [Joseph Smith] 6 years & he never knew anything of him but that was right als[o] know him to be a Seeer & a Phrophet & Believe the Book of mormon to be true."[15]

Ten months later, Stowell asked fellow Church member Martha Campbell to write a letter for him. "Brother Smith by the request of Brother Stowell," opened the letter, "I now set down to write you he is quite unwell & is sometimes fearfull that he cannot stand it through the winter & wishes me to say to you that he wants your prayers, & the prayrs of all the saints for the recovery of his health to inable him to gather among the Saints."[16]

Campbell concluded the letter by reiterating Stowell's hope to "meet with the saints" and "hear the word of the Lord," but those hopes were not realized: Josiah died on May 12, 1844. Less than seven weeks later, Joseph and his brother Hyrum were killed by a mob at Carthage jail.

"News of the murders stunned the Knights," writes their biographer William G. Hartley, "whose friendship with Joseph Smith spanned more than fifteen years, and Hyrum had been their friend nearly as long."[17]

Newel Knight expressed the feelings of the entire family when he said that "two of the best men that ever lived, lost their lives for the truth's sake. . . . I have shared in the blessings of the Gospel which they have enjoyed, and been a partaker of the sorrows and troubles and fierce persecutions which they have endured."[18]

Joseph Knight Sr. had lived a life of stalwart faithfulness, moving with the Colesville branch first to Ohio and then to Missouri. Driven from Missouri with his family, he had settled in Nauvoo. He was on his way west when he died at age 74 at Mount Pisgah, Iowa, on February 2, 1847.

Less than two years before his own death, the Prophet Joseph had offered a moving tribute to his loyal friend:

> While I contemplate the virtues and the good qualifications and characterestics of the faithful few, which I am now recording in the Book of the Law of the Lord, of such as have stood by me in every hour of peril, for these fifteen long years past; say for instance; my aged and beloved brother Joseph Knights [Knight] Senr, who was among the number of the first to administer to my necessities, while I was laboring, in the commencement of the bringing forth of the work of the Lord, and of laying the foundation of the Church of Jesus Christ of Latter Day Saints: for fifteen years has he been faithful and true, and even handed, and exemplary and virtuous, and kind; never deviating to the right hand nor to the left. Behold he is a righteous man."[19]

Larry E. Morris is an independent writer and historian and a former editor with the Joseph Smith Papers Project.

Notes

1. Lucy Mack Smith, *Biographical Sketches of Joseph Smith the Prophet, and His Progenitors for Many Generations* (Liverpool: S. W. Richards, 1853), 91.
2. Joseph Smith, History, 1838–1856, vol. A-1, 8, in *JSP,* H1:234 [Joseph Smith—History 1:56].

3. See "Stowell, Josiah, Sr." (biographical entry), josephsmithpapers.org.

4. Smith, *Biographical Sketches,* 91–92.

5. *JSP,* H1:237, note 65.

6. Ronald W. Walker, "The Persisting Idea of American Treasure Hunting," *BYU Studies* 24, no. 4 (1984): 430.

7. Richard Lyman Bushman, *Joseph Smith: Rough Stone Rolling* (New York: Knopf, 2005), 48–52.

8. "Appendix: Reminiscence of William D. Purple, 28 April 1877 [*People v. JS*]," p. [3], josephsmithpapers.org; see also Dan Vogel, *Early Mormon Documents* (Salt Lake City: Signature Books, 2002), 4:127–37.

9. "Appendix: Docket Entry, 20 March 1826 [*People v. JS*]," p. [1], josephsmithpapers.org; see also Vogel, *Early Mormon Documents,* 4:239–56.

10. *Broome County Republican,* May 5, 1831, cited in William G. Hartley, *Stand by My Servant Joseph: The Story of the Joseph Knight Family and the Restoration* (Provo, UT: Joseph Fielding Institute for LDS Church History; Salt Lake City: Deseret Book, 2003), 5; see also "Knight, Joseph, Sr." (biographical entry), josephsmithpapers.org.

11. Joseph Knight Jr., "Incidents of History from 1827 to 1844," 1, cited in Hartley, *Stand by My Servant Joseph,* 11. For the original, see Joseph Knight, Autobiographical Sketch, 1862, p. 1, CHL.

12. Cited in Hartley, *Stand by My Servant Joseph,* 12. For the original, see Newel Knight, Autobiography and Journal, ca. 1846, pp. 1–2, CHL.

13. Cited in Larry E. Morris, *A Documentary History of the Book of Mormon* (New York: Oxford University Press, 2019), 78. For the original, see Joseph Knight, Reminiscences, undated, image [3], CHL.

14. Joseph Smith, History, 1838–1856, vol. A-1, 20, in *JSP,* H1:304.

15. Cited in Mark Ashurst-McGee, "The Josiah Stowell Jr.—John S. Fullmer Correspondence," *BYU Studies* 38, no. 3 (1999): 114. For the original, see John S. Fullmer Correspondence with Josiah Stowell Jr., Feb. 1843, CHL.

16. "Letter from Martha Campbell, 19 December 1843," p. [1], josephsmithpapers.org.

17. Hartley, *Stand by My Servant Joseph,* 348.

18. Cited in Hartley, *Stand by My Servant Joseph,* 349.

19. "Reflections and Blessings, 16 and 23 August 1842," josephsmithpapers.org.

"A MARVEL AND A WONDER": A WRITER'S VIEW ON JOSEPH SMITH AND THE BOOK OF MORMON

By Angela Hallstrom

Let's start this essay with a confession: although I am a professional writer and have spent most of my adult life training myself, and others, to put thoughts down on paper, I have delayed writing this piece until the last possible moment. I've hemmed, I've hawed, and I've avoided the blinking cursor on my computer screen for one simple reason.

Writing is hard.

This is not a controversial opinion. Most people don't relish the thought of composing a cover letter or writing a research paper. Yet some are surprised to learn that those of us who write for a living can still find the process daunting. I assure you, though, that most of my writer friends would find the following words, penned by Joseph Smith in a letter to William W. Phelps in 1832, strikingly apt. "Oh Lord God deliver us in thy due time from the little narrow prison," Joseph wrote, metaphorically describing the limitations of the written word, "almost as it were totel darkness of paper pen and ink and a crooked broken scattered and imperfect language."[1]

Joseph Smith was many things—an agile thinker, a dynamic teacher, and a powerful religious leader—but he was not a well-trained or particularly skilled writer. When the Book of Mormon was published in 1830,

24-year-old Joseph had received little formal education. His wife, Emma, was asked later in her life by her son whether Joseph would have been capable of writing the Book of Mormon himself. She did not mince words in her response.

"Joseph Smith . . . could neither write nor dictate a coherent and well-worded letter; let alone dictating a book like the Book of Mormon," Emma said. She went on to explain that even though she was an active participant in the translation of the plates, she could describe the coming forth of the Book of Mormon only by using the language of miracles. "It is marvelous to me," she said, "'a marvel and a wonder,' as much so as to anyone else."[2]

My personal testimony of the gospel, as found in The Church of Jesus Christ of Latter-day Saints, is multifaceted. Experiences ranging from private spiritual witnesses to reminders of the practical benefits of Church membership have helped me "stay in the boat," as President M. Russell Ballard has urged us, even when I grapple with difficult questions or trials of my faith.[3] But one vital, foundational aspect of my testimony is the Book of Mormon itself. Not only do I find deep meaning in the spiritual message of the book, but, like Emma, I find the very fact of its existence a "marvel and a wonder" I cannot ignore.

The manuscript that Joseph Smith delivered to publisher Egbert B. Grandin for printing in the summer of 1829 tells an epic story, spanning a thousand years, of the rise and fall of a great civilization. It features hundreds of named characters and geographical locations; a complicated narrative style that includes digressions, flash-forwards, and multiple narrators; and a sophisticated exploration of religious ideas. Joseph dictated that manuscript, which soon became a 588-page book, in three months' time.[4]

It would be astonishing for any 24-year-old farm boy with a haphazard education to produce the Book of Mormon in the way that I, and other writers, typically produce our manuscripts: we research, take notes, think, pace, create an outline, write the first five chapters before hitting a wall, lay awake at night full of existential dread, muster the energy to gird one's loins and begin again, write, write, cut, cut, rewrite, rewrite, send it to a trusted reader or editor, rewrite again, and so on until it is published. For a book the length and complexity of the Book of Mormon, this process almost always takes years.

Not only did Joseph produce the Book of Mormon in three months— he *dictated* it. Let's return again to Emma's description of Joseph's translation method: "Your father would dictate to me hour after hour; and when returning after meals, or after interruptions, he would at once begin where he had left off, without either seeing the manuscript or having any portion of it read to him. . . . It would have been improbable for a learned man to do this; and, for one so ignorant and unlearned as he was, it was simply impossible."[5]

Joseph himself did not talk much about how he translated the Book of Mormon, other than to say it was done by the "gift and power of God."[6] But several eyewitnesses, including scribes like Martin Harris and Oliver Cowdery, described the process in much the same way as Emma did. They said that Joseph dictated the text as it came to him, with the aid of a seer stone or the Nephite interpreters that he found buried with the plates, later known as the Urim and Thummim. The manuscript that resulted does not appear to have been edited or revised beyond corrections, like fixing spelling errors, that Joseph's scribes made during a dictation session. By all available accounts, the completed text was delivered to the printer just as it was dictated: a massive stream of words that went on, page after page, without any punctuation. The typesetter would later add the commas, apostrophes, and periods that made the prose readable.[7]

During my master's program in creative writing, I shared the classroom with many people in their mid-20s, just like Joseph was in 1829, who had aspirations to write their own epic novels, some of them taking place in imagined locations with a complex cast of characters spanning multiple generations. Again and again, my classmates and I found the first drafts of these novels to be convoluted, confusing, or at least in need of a good deal of work. I was more interested in writing short stories than epic novels, but my first drafts, too, had plot holes, point of view problems, and scores of other issues. My classmates and I did not worry too much about these initial, messy attempts, however. First drafts are called "rough drafts" for a reason—getting our words down on paper was just the first step of many steps in the writing process.

As a student, writer, editor, and teacher, I have read thousands of initial attempts at fiction writing. But the Book of Mormon, the ultimate "first draft," does not fall prey to the problems that so many of these manuscripts contain. Yes, sometimes the prose of the Book of Mormon is a little clunky, but inelegant sentence structure is usually one of the last things a writer is concerned about when she is trying to wrestle an unwieldy novel into submission. The biggest problems in a first draft are usually structural: the point of view is not stable (is the narrator writing the story at the time it happens or 20 years in the future?); the writer has lost track of time and place (wasn't the main character supposed to be in London last Christmas?); important plot points are introduced that are never resolved (what happened to the gun Patricia hid in her nightstand?). Many writers even have a hard time staying in a stable verb tense, as the story shifts from past tense to present tense and back again.

Then we have the Book of Mormon. If, as Joseph Smith maintained, it is a record of an ancient people that he translated by the gift and power of God, its style, structure, and means of production make sense, albeit a kind of sense that requires a person to believe in miracles. But if, as some of Joseph's critics have alleged, the book is a product of Joseph's imagination—a fictional "novel" that he dictated, line after line, and did not revise—its lack of major structural issues is so astounding that its existence borders on the miraculous as well.

Take, for example, the book of Mosiah. The book begins in 124 BC with the reign of King Benjamin in Zarahemla, but after a few chapters it flashes back to around 200 BC to tell the story of Zeniff, who left Zarahemla to reclaim the land of Lehi-Nephi. A "story-within-a-story" like this is hard enough for a writer to pull off smoothly in a first draft, but Zeniff's narrative is just one of several in the book of Mosiah. There are so many characters, places, and zigs and zags through time that I am probably not the only one to Google "book of Mosiah timeline chart" in order to feel prepared to teach a Sunday School class of 14-year-olds. Yet somehow, Joseph kept all these characters, places, and overlapping narratives straight. According to Emma's account, Joseph did not have a book or manuscript to read from as he dictated,[8] let alone a color-coded timeline cheat sheet.

Among other examples, I am also impressed by the fact that this book features three major narrators—Nephi, Mormon, and Moroni—each with a particular voice, style, and purpose in writing. The ability to create a distinctive narrative voice that is maintained throughout a long piece is one of the hallmarks of a talented, experienced fiction writer. Whether Joseph was a talented writer can be debated, but he was certainly inexperienced. To me, the reason Nephi's, Mormon's, and Moroni's narrative voices are so consistent is because their portions of the book were in fact written by three separate people.[9]

Joseph Smith would probably not use the word "writer" to describe himself, but he had no trouble calling himself "prophet." Those who participated in the translation of the Book of Mormon were also convinced they had witnessed God working through man.

"My belief is that the Book of Mormon is of divine authenticity—I have not the slightest doubt about it," Emma said.[10]

As I work to conclude this essay—going back to my notes, typing then deleting, reading my words aloud to hear what I should change and what I should keep—I find that I have to agree.

Angela Hallstrom works for the Church History Department as a writer and literary editor on the *Saints* project.

Notes

1. "Letter to William W. Phelps, 27 November 1832," josephsmithpapers.org.
2. Joseph Smith III, "Last Testimony of Sister Emma," *Saints' Herald,* Oct. 1, 1879, 289–90.
3. M. Russell Ballard, "Stay in the Boat and Hold On!" *Ensign,* Nov. 2014, 89.
4. For a detailed timeline of the translation of the Book of Mormon, see John W. Welch, "The Miraculous Timing of Translation of the Book of Mormon," in *Opening the Heavens: Accounts of Divine Manifestations, 1820–1844,* ed. John W. Welch (Provo, UT: Brigham Young University Press; Salt Lake City: Deseret Book, 2005).
5. Joseph Smith III, "Last Testimony of Sister Emma," *Saints' Herald,* Oct. 1, 1879, 290.
6. Preface to the Book of Mormon, 1830 edition.
7. See "Book of Mormon Translation," Gospel Topics, ChurchofJesusChrist.org; and

Historical Introduction to "Printer's Manuscript of the Book of Mormon, circa August 1829–circa January 1830," josephsmithpapers.org.

8. Joseph Smith III, "Last Testimony of Sister Emma," *Saints' Herald,* Oct. 1, 1879, 289.
9. See Grant Hardy, *Understanding the Book of Mormon: A Reader's Guide* (New York: Oxford University Press, 2010).
10. Joseph Smith III, "Last Testimony of Sister Emma," *Saints' Herald,* Oct. 1, 1879, 290.

PLAIN, PRECIOUS, AND EXPANSIVE: WHAT JOSEPH TAUGHT ABOUT JESUS AND HIS GOSPEL

By Keith A. Erekson

In a letter to a recent convert in September 1839, Joseph Smith made two connected observations. First, he noted that "time and experience will teach us more and more, how easily falsehood gains credence in general, rather than truth." Second, he pointed out that this tendency toward error occurred most "especially in taking into consideration the plan of salvation; the plain simple order of the gospel of Jesus Christ."[1] Living in a theological environment swarming with errors and falsehoods, Joseph repeatedly emphasized the plain truths of the plan of salvation and gospel of Jesus Christ. Indeed, there is much that we know about the Savior *because* of Joseph. Two hundred years later, as falsehoods continue to enjoy credence, even among practicing Latter-day Saints, we would do well to understand the expansiveness of Joseph's plain and precious teachings about Jesus Christ.

The early pages of the Book of Mormon linked the success of falsehood with the absence of plain truth and tied both to Joseph Smith's work. Pleading for an explanation of his father's allegorical vision, Nephi sees the future of world history in which "there are many plain and precious things taken away from the book, which is the book of the Lamb of God." As a result, "an exceedingly great many do stumble, yea, insomuch that Satan hath great power over them." But, mercifully, God would not "suffer that the Gentiles shall forever remain in that awful state of blindness" caused "because of the plain and precious parts of the gospel of the Lamb which have been kept back." No, the ultimate antidote to blindness and stumbling would come when Jesus would "bring forth unto them, in mine own power, much of my gospel, which shall be plain and precious."[2] As the Book of Mormon came off the press in the spring of 1830, Joseph and his earliest followers were already acknowledging it as containing "the fullness of the gospel of Jesus Christ to the Gentiles and also to the Jews." In time, this perception of Joseph's restorative work would grow to include all of his translations and revelations.[3]

Sometimes, we look too narrowly at the way plain and precious truths about the gospel of the Lamb have been restored. Speakers and teachers may point to the Joseph Smith Translation footnotes in the Bible that add additional words or passages, or compare biblical passages reproduced in the Book of Mormon. For example, a passage from Isaiah 48 is copied into 1 Nephi 20, with an additional seven-word phrase. Whereas the version preserved in the Bible describes the house of Israel as having "come forth out of the waters of Judah," the Book of Mormon appends this clarification, "or out of the waters of baptism."[4] There it is! The essential ordinance of baptism restored to the text.

Joseph held a far more expansive view of the word of God, one that did not turn on the simplicity of a few extra words, the presence of a comma, or the nuances among prepositions. In an epistle to the Saints, Joseph teased out the meaning of an Old Testament passage by saying, "I might have rendered a plainer translation to this, but it is sufficiently plain to suit my purpose."[5] Joseph expressed the revelations he received in words, acknowledging that our "crooked broken scattered and imperfect language" became a "little narrow prison almost."[6] The message of the Lamb of God was larger than the words used to convey it.

How did Joseph reveal a richer view of the plain and precious gospel of Jesus Christ? One contribution came through translating Nephi's scriptural analysis. After quoting 13 chapters from Isaiah, Nephi states that his "soul delighteth in plainness," so he offers six chapters of his own, plainer commentary. Isaiah wrote "many things which were hard for many . . . people to understand"—complex prophecies, rich with historical connections and multiple meanings. For Nephi, speaking plainly did not mean oversimplifying but rather communicating with clarity and completeness, resulting in a straightforward pronouncement on "the doctrine of Christ," given "according to the plainness of my prophesying."[7] Nephi thus links the lost plain and precious truths with the gospel of Jesus Christ.

At an even broader level, Joseph's revelations restored plain teachings not just about the gospel of the Lamb but also about the character of the Lamb Himself. Readers of the Old Testament encounter a Jehovah who often appears in its pages as vengeful, angry, petty, and willing to enact genocide on a whim. Plagues, lightning, and famine are the visible signs of this god's presence. Behind the scenes he seems quite willing to strike deals with the devil over the temptation of Job. He looks unmoved by selfishness and brutality, greed and ambition, sadness and tragedy. He eliminates the entire population of the earth save eight.

How different a view of Jehovah appears in the revelations to Joseph Smith! In the Book of Mormon, when the brother of Jared approaches Jehovah for assistance, he is startled to see the hand of God before seeing all of Jehovah, a being who is eager to reveal Himself and minister personally. In the book of Moses, when Enoch sees the future sufferings of the world in vision, he is startled also to see Jehovah's tears: "How is it that thou canst weep," he asks, "seeing thou art holy, and from all eternity to all eternity?" The Lord responds that the people of the earth "are the workmanship of mine own hands, and I gave unto them their knowledge, in the day I created them; and in the Garden of Eden, gave I unto man his agency," and yet they chose to become "without affection, and they hate their own blood."[8] The weeping of Jehovah and His revelation of its cause prompts Enoch to weep with Him. "That single, riveting scene," declared Elder Jeffrey R. Holland, "does more to teach the true nature of God than any theological treatise could ever convey."[9] When we see no respite to our personal pains or to larger structural injustices such as racism or discrimination, there is immense comfort in knowing that He weeps with us.

The New Testament narrates the life of Jesus of Nazareth from His birth to Mary, through His baptism and ministry, to His Crucifixion and Resurrection. But it is the Book of Mormon testimony of Alma that adds the precious, personal details that "he shall go forth, suffering pains and afflictions and temptations of every kind" so "that he may know according to the flesh how to succor his people according to their infirmities."[10]

In the New Testament, Jesus speaks of His atoning sacrifice metaphorically as a "cup" that cannot pass from Him.[11] In the revelations to Joseph Smith He speaks plainly, without metaphor. "I am Jesus Christ the son of God," he declares, "who was crusified for the sins of the World" so "that they may become the [children] of God." Through Joseph we learn of the personalized, pleading dialogue that Jesus, our Advocate, will have with His Father: "Father behold the sufferings & death of him who did no sin in whom thou wast well pleased Behold the Blood of thy son which was shed the blood of him whom thou gavest that thyself might be glorified wherefore Father spare these my Brethren that Believe on my name that they may come unto me And have everlasting life."[12]

From Joseph Smith we learn that it is a modern error to assume that "Christ-centered" messages come only from the Bible or ancient scripture. To Joseph, the Jehovah of the Old Testament and the Messiah of the New was also a Living Christ, both visible and describable. "His eyes were as a flame of fire; the hair of his head was white like the pure snow, his countenance shone above the brightness of the sun," records Joseph's journal of the Lamb's 1836 visit to the Kirtland Temple. And "his voice was as the sound of the rushing of great waters, even the Voice of Jehovah, saying, I am the first and the last. I am he who liveth. I am he who was slain. I am your Advocate with the Father."[13]

For Joseph, the seeker, the modern prophet who drew truth from gold plates and Egyptian scrolls as well as from encounters with Protestant preachers and social movements, the plain and precious message of deity could be found everywhere. It was "a voice of mercy from heaven" as well as "a voice of truth out of the earth." There were "glad tidings for the dead" as well as "a voice of gladness for the living and dead." The plain and precious truths about the plan of salvation and the gospel of the Lamb were so expansive as to be a cause of courage and rejoicing. The earth would "break forth into singing" while the dead would "speak forth anthems of eternal praise," and every heart would "rejoice, and be exceedingly glad."[14]

Keith A. Erekson is an author, speaker, and public historian who serves as the director of the Church History Library.

Notes

1. Joseph Smith to Isaac Galland, Sept. 11, 1839, in *JSP,* D7:9.
2. 1 Nephi 13:28, 29, 32, 34.
3. Articles and Covenants, ca. Apr. 1830, in *JSP,* D1:121 [D&C 20:9]; see also Vision, Feb. 16, 1832, in *JSP,* D2:184 [D&C 76:14].
4. Joseph added the phrase parenthetically to what is now 1 Nephi 20:1 in the 1840 edition of the Book of Mormon. (See "Book of Mormon, 1840," p. 53, josephsmithpapers.org.)
5. "Letter to the Church, 7 September 1842 [D&C 128]," p. 6, josephsmithpapers.org [D&C 128:18].
6. Joseph Smith to William W. Phelps, Nov. 27, 1832, in *JSP,* D2:320. The quoted words are in Joseph Smith's handwriting.
7. 2 Nephi 25:4, 1; 31:2; see also 3 Nephi 11:31–39; 27:13–21.
8. Moses 7:29, 32–33; Ether 3.
9. Jeffrey R. Holland, "The Grandeur of God," *Ensign,* Nov. 2003, 72.
10. Alma 7:11, 12.
11. See John 18:11; Matt. 26:39, 42; Mark 14:36; Luke 22:42.
12. Revelation, Dec. 7, 1830, in *JSP,* D1:220 [D&C 35:2]; Revelation, ca. Mar. 7, 1831, in JSP, D1:275 [D&C 45:4–5]; see also Revelation, June 8, 1831, in *JSP,* D1:333 [D&C 53:2].
13. Visions, Apr. 3, 1836, in *JSP,* D5:226–28 [D&C 110:3–4].
14. "Letter to the Church, 7 September 1842 [D&C 128]," pp. 6–8, josephsmithpapers.org [D&C 128:19, 22].

THE PROPHET, THE BOOK, AND THE SAINTS

By Janiece Johnson

On a Monday morning in 1834, a fledgling group of Saints attending a Church conference heard Joseph Smith declare, "Take away the book of Mormon, and the revelations, and where is our religion? We have none."[1] For centuries, the Protestant world had been bound by the idea of "sola scriptura"—meaning God's words and authority were found solely in the Bible. Joseph's translation of the Book of Mormon boldly breached that boundary, and his continuing revelations ensured that more of God's word would cascade to those who would receive it. Though Joseph would do much in his 38 years, his translation of the Book of Mormon stands as one of his most significant and enduring offerings to the Saints.

It is unlikely that any of those early Saints were shocked by Joseph's assertion; many had converted to the Book before they even considered becoming followers of Joseph Smith or members of the Church he organized. Years before the label *Latter-day Saints* became commonplace, this people's first nicknames would be based in the Book of Mormon: it was the Book that initially distinguished them from other Christian congregations.[2] For some a testimony came easily; in fact, some felt the truth of the Book before they ever read a page. William W. Phelps dated his conversion to June 9, 1830, the date he purchased a Book of Mormon. Though he wouldn't meet Joseph or be baptized for another year, already his "heart was there."[3] Mary Ann Angell would often tell of the first time she held the Book and how "the Spirit bore witness to her . . . of the truth of its origin, so strongly that she could never afterwards doubt it." She shared it with friends for two years before she was baptized.[4] Methodist lay minister Phineas Young preached the Book of Mormon and Methodism for a year until he decided he could not reconcile the two. He had to choose. His relationship with the new Book had grown so much that he felt he must leave Methodism and "cleave" to the Book.[5]

One of the ways that the book functioned was as a signal—a sign that pointed to Joseph as a prophet and attested to the opening of the heavens and the restoration of charismatic gifts.[6] But it was much more than a symbol. Joseph consistently preached the value of the Book's contents—elevating it alongside the Bible. In the fall of 1830, Joseph received a revelation that taught, "The Book of Mormon & the Bible are given of me for thine instructio[n]."[7] In February 1831, another revelation to Joseph commanded "the Elders Priests & Teachers of this Church" to "teach the scriptures which are in the Bible and the Book of mormon."[8] In a letter written in 1834, Joseph taught of "the pure principles of godliness as contained in the Scriptures of the old and new Testaments, the Book of Mormon and the revelations and commandments of Jesus Christ, which have been given to his Church in these last days."[9]

The Book of Mormon was a central spring for the organization and evolution of the Church. Scholars have demonstrated that the Book of Mormon shaped early Latter-day Saint ecclesiastical structure, liturgical form, and missionary efforts.[10] However, just as significant is the mark the Book left on the Saints themselves. In 1841, Wilford Woodruff recorded Joseph declaring that "the Book of Mormon was the most correct of any Book on earth and the keystone of our religion and a man would get nearer to God by abiding by its precepts than any other book."[11] This is a claim about practice—about how individuals read and applied the Book to their lives. The existence of the Book alone is not sufficient to change the lives of individuals. We must learn the Book's content and "abide by its precepts" if it is to bring us to God.

The stories, language, and lexicon of the Book created a new world for the early Saints. The new world did not eradicate their old world—they were still a people of the Bible—but the Book of Mormon expanded the world of the Bible they already inhabited. The Saints were used to reading and finding personal application in Bible stories; now, the Book of Mormon prophet Nephi pleaded with his readers to "liken" the scriptural narrative to themselves.[12] Six hundred pages offered a multitude of narrative possibilities for likening. The new Book offered them prophecies they eagerly waited to fulfill and patterns to live out their own holy narratives. Different elements of the narrative reached out to different individuals; examples drawn from the text varied as much as the individuals applying the text.

As early converts to the Book of Mormon began to develop a relationship with it, the text transformed their lives. Some saw themselves in the Book's narrative—they saw the stories parallel their own lives. After years of caring for her paralyzed husband and family, Drusilla Hendricks related how she often felt "like the old Nephite women while they were traveling in the wilderness, for they became strong like unto the men." As Drusilla read the First Book of Nephi she saw that God intervened in her life by nourishing her and strengthening her in her own wilderness just as He had done for the women in Nephi's narrative.[13]

Similarly, as a missionary in 1840, Brigham Young wrote his wife, Mary Ann Angell Young, "I never have witnessed the hand of the Lord so visible in all my life as I have since I left home this time. My heart is like the charit[y] of Aminadab."[14] Reading the book of Helaman, Brigham felt a kinship with Aminadab—a repentant Nephite who enabled his Lamanite brethren to break through the darkness that surrounded them and see Nephi and Lehi conversing with angels while in a jail.[15] Aminadab's witness opened the way for the repentance of these Lamanites so that they could receive an outpouring of the Spirit. This story affected Brigham to such a degree that he alluded to the same incident multiple times in sermons in the following years.[16] Though it was an obscure reference, Brigham seemed confident that Mary Ann would recognize it— he didn't explain it. Mary Ann had been reading and studying the Book even longer than he had. The reference reminded Brigham of a significant spiritual moment for him and unified him and Mary Ann in their shared witness of scripture.

Unique Book of Mormon echoes and allusions began to lightly pepper some Saints' writings about their lives. Others used more pepper, and the Book began to transform their whole manner of self-expression. Many would begin their own personal histories as Nephi did: "having been born of goodly parents."[17] Joseph Smith was one of those who reproduced Nephi's language as he first wrote his history in the summer of 1832. "I was born in the town of Charon in the State of Vermont North America on the twenty third day of December AD 1805 of goodly Parents," Joseph declared. The Book of Mormon offered the Saints a pattern to emulate as they wrote and lived out their own sacred narratives.

One of Joseph's goodly parents, Lucy Mack Smith, was one of the Book of Mormon's earliest converts. In an 1831 letter, she told her brother and sister-in-law of the Book of Mormon. Though the Book had been published just nine months earlier, it had already changed how Lucy expressed herself; more than half of this letter contains unique Book of Mormon language.[18] Early the next year, as she led a group of New York Saints to Kirtland, Ohio, she saw a parallel with the travels of Lehi and his family. As the group encountered difficulty, she "called them all round" and preached to them. They had "set out just as Father Lehi did to travel by the commandment of the Lord to a land that the Lord will show unto us if we are faithful," she declared. "I want you all to be solemn and lift your hearts to God in prayer continually that we may be prospered."[19] Like Lehi and his family, Lucy and the Saints would be successful if they were faithful. The Book of Mormon would continue to shape her understanding of her life and the role of her family as well as her verbal expression. In 1844, as she began dictating her history of her son, she channeled Book of Mormon prophets as she quoted, paraphrased, and alluded to the Book. Lucy even structured her history after the pattern of the small and large plates.[20]

These were not the only ways that the Book of Mormon shaped the lives of its early converts. Some replicated the stories of the Book, hoping for miraculous results. Others used the heroic and faithful examples from the Book as a pattern for their lives. Many illuminated their relationship with the Book through handmade indices, marginalia, dedications, and underlining in their own books. As the early Saints expanded their notion of scripture, the Book's narrative reached into their lives and opened a new world that they could choose to inhabit. If we, like them, value the Book and its revelatory contributions, it will change our lives and bring us, too, "nearer to God."

Janiece Johnson is a Laura F. Willes Research Fellow at the Neal A. Maxwell Institute for Religious Scholarship at Brigham Young University, working on early Book of Mormon reception.

Notes

1. Minutes and Discourse, Apr. 21, 1834, in *JSP*, D4:15.
2. Elements of this essay were previously published in Janiece Johnson, "Becoming a People of the Books: Toward an Understanding of Early Mormon Converts and the New Word of the Lord," *Journal of Book of Mormon Studies* 27 (2018): 1–43.
3. William W. Phelps, "Letter No. 6," Feb. 24, 1835, *Latter Day Saints' Messenger and Advocate,* Apr. 1835, 1:97; "Annual Conference," *Deseret News,* Apr. 11, 1860, 45, 48.
4. Emmeline B. Wells, "Heroines of the Church: Biography of Mary Ann Angell Young," *Juvenile Instructor,* Jan. 1, 1891, 26:17.
5. Phineas Howe Young, "Life of Phineas Young—Written by Himself," Autobiography, 1838, L. Tom Perry Special Collections, Harold B. Lee Library, Brigham Young University, Provo, UT (hereafter Perry Special Collections).
6. Grant Underwood, "Book of Mormon Usage in Early LDS Theology," *Dialogue* 17, no. 3 (1984): 35–74; Jan Shipps and John W. Welch, eds., *The Journals of William E. McLellin, 1831–1836* (Provo, UT: BYU Studies, 1994), 6–7; Terryl Givens, *By the Hand of Mormon* (New York: Oxford University Press, 2002), 82–88.
7. "Revelation, October 1830–B [D&C 33:16]," p. 45, josephsmithpapers.org.
8. "Revelation, 9 Feb. 1831 [D&C 42:12]," in "Revelation Book 1," p. 63, josephsmith papers.org.
9. "Letter to J. G. Fosdick, 3 February 1834," p. 23, josephsmithpapers.org.
10. See Mark Ashurst-McGee, "Zion Rising: Joseph Smith's Early Social and Political Thought" (PhD diss., Arizona State University, 2008); Scott Faulring, "Book of Mormon: A Blueprint for Organizing the Church," *Journal of Book of Mormon Studies* 7, no. 1 (1998): 60–71; Appendix 3: "Articles of the Church of Christ," June 1829, in *JSP,* D1:368–70; Michael Hubbard MacKay and Gerrit Dirkmaat, *From Darkness unto Light: Joseph Smith's Translation and Publication of the Book of Mormon* (Provo, UT: Religious Studies Center, Brigham Young University; Salt Lake City: Deseret Book, 2015), 147; Ryan G. Tobler, "The Only Way to Be Saved: Early Mormonism and the Sacrament of Baptism," *Journal of Mormon History,* forthcoming; Gerald E. Smith, *Schooling the Prophet:*

How the Book of Mormon Influenced Joseph Smith and the Early Restoration (Provo, UT: Neal A. Maxwell Institute Press, 2015).

11. Wilford Woodruff, Journal, Nov. 28, 1841, CHL.

12. First Book of Nephi, chap. 6, Book of Mormon, 1830 ed.; now 1 Nephi 19:23.

13. Chapter 5 in the first edition, and 1 Nephi 17 in every Book of Mormon edition post-1879. Quoted in Kenneth W. Godfrey, Audrey M. Godfrey, and Jill Mulvay Derr, eds., *Women's Voices: An Untold History of the Latter-day Saints, 1830–1900* (Salt Lake City: Deseret Book, 1982), 88.

14. Ronald O. Barney, "Missionary Letters of Brigham Young to His Wife," *BYU Studies,* vol. 38, no. 2 (1999): 183.

15. Helaman 2 in the 1830 edition, and Helaman 5 in every Book of Mormon edition post-1879.

16. Richard S. Van Wagoner, ed., *The Complete Discourses of Brigham Young* (Salt Lake City: Smith-Pettit Foundation, 2009), 1:360, 444, 445.

17. 1 Nephi 1:1; see also Erastus Snow, Autobiography, 1818–37, CHL; Archibald Gardner, Autobiography, 1857, 3, Perry Special Collections; Solomon Chamberlain, Autobiography of Solomon Chamberlain, 1, Perry Special Collections.

18. Lucy Mack Smith to Solomon Mack, Jan. 6, 1831, CHL.

19. Lucy Mack Smith, History, 1844–45, 18 books, bk. 11, [2–3], [8–10], CHL; Lavina Fielding Anderson, ed., *Lucy's Book: A Critical Edition of Lucy Mack Smith's Family Memoir* (Salt Lake City: Signature Books, 2001), 511, note 3.

20. Anderson, *Lucy's Book,* 281.

EMMA, JOSEPH, AND THE REVELATION "UNTO ALL"

By Jennifer Reeder

In February 1879, in the Riverside Mansion in Nauvoo, Illinois, Joseph Smith III and Alexander Smith interviewed their mother, Emma Hale Smith Bidamon, concerning her belief in the spiritual claims of their father—her first husband. They wanted to know before she died how she viewed the remarkable events of the Restoration. She answered affirmatively, "[I] believe the Church to have been established by divine direction. I have complete faith in that."[1]

Emma Smith experienced her own divine direction through a revelation known today as Doctrine and Covenants section 25. Like her husband's accounts of the First Vision, this revelation powerfully manifested the connection of earth and heaven and that the Lord cared deeply for her. Joseph received the revelation for Emma in early July 1830.[2] The recorded words reveal the Lord's specific direction to Emma; at the same time, they are his "voice unto all."[3] In the October 2019 women's session of general conference, President Russell M. Nelson invited all to prayerfully study the section.[4] Emma's revelation contains valuable doctrine echoing, in a way, Joseph's First Vision and providing a pattern for all people who seek God.

Joseph went into the grove in the early spring of 1820 seeking truth regarding the spiritual state of his soul and direction on which church to join. Immediately upon kneeling in the woods to pray, he was disrupted by doubt and fear.[5] At the darkest moment, he saw a burning light coming down from heaven, and in the light he saw God the Father and His Son, Jesus Christ. Years later, after Joseph had found reassurance from personal experience in his pursuit of revelation and authority, he was able to help others obtain that same divine comfort.

Similarly, Emma sought comfort and assurance following the disturbing events surrounding her baptism in late June 1830. She had traveled with Joseph to Colesville, New York, to help establish the Church there among Joseph Knight's family and other believers. Angry neighbors destroyed a dam erected on the farm for baptism, but early in the morning of June 28, the dam was repaired, and Oliver Cowdery baptized Emma and others. Joseph planned to confirm the new members soon afterward. Instead, he was arrested for disorderly conduct and taken to court and jail.[6] Worried, Emma immediately gathered a group of women to pray for Joseph.[7] After his release, Joseph found his wife "awaiting with much anxiety" at the home of her sister Elizabeth Hale Wasson.[8] The Smiths returned home to Harmony, Pennsylvania, where Emma received a divine manifestation—not a visitation of heavenly beings, but through the words of her prophet-husband, who had become intimately acquainted with the divine.

The darkness and fear Joseph initially experienced in the Sacred Grove was immediately overcome with light. The Father called Joseph by name, commanding him to listen to His Son, Jesus Christ.[9] Then Christ spoke, also calling Joseph by name: "Joseph my son thy sins are forgiven thee."[10] Nearly the same wording was given to Emma from the Lord.

"Hearken unto the voice of the Lord your God, while I speak unto you, Emma Smith, my daughter. . . . Thy sins are forgiven thee."[11] She, too, was known of God, her sins were forgiven, and she found comfort. God spoke directly to her, as He had spoken to Joseph.

Joseph had been inspired to seek God by reading from the Bible: "If any of you lack wisdom, let him ask of God."[12] As a recipient of divine revelation, he then invited others to seek God for themselves. The Lord encouraged and empowered Emma to obtain her own personal revelation. She was instructed to act "as it shall be given thee by my spirit." Emma would "receive the Holy Ghost" by the laying on of hands; Joseph confirmed her a month later, in August 1830.[13] These words revealed the Lord's love for and trust in her. His promise of divine assistance and direction would expand her well beyond her own abilities and partner her with Christ.

Emma's revelation followed patterns in the revelations previously bestowed upon Joseph Smith Sr., Hyrum Smith, Samuel Smith, Martin Harris, Oliver Cowdery, Joseph Knight, and David Whitmer. One of those patterns was a delineation of distinct responsibilities. For example, Joseph Sr., Hyrum Smith, and Knight were assigned to help build up God's kingdom on earth.[14] Emma was commissioned to a similar work: "thou shalt be ordained under [Joseph's] hand to expound Scriptures & exhort the Church according as it shall be given thee by my spirit." The Lord instructed her to do that by, first, making "a selection of Sacred Hymns . . . to be had in my Church" and, second, fulfilling her role as "an Elect Lady whom I have called."[15]

These were unusual tasks—expounding, exhorting, and hymn selecting—for a woman of Emma's time. In expounding, she was by definition tasked to "explain, to lay open the meaning, to clear of obscurity, to interpret," while in exhorting, she was to "encourage, to embolden, to cheer, to advise, to excite or to give strength, spirit or courage."[16] The Lord also instructed Emma that her "time shall be Given to writing & to Learning."[17] While living in Kirtland, Ohio, she sent hymns to William W. Phelps in Independence, Missouri, who printed them in *The Evening and the Morning Star*, a newspaper distributed somewhat widely among the Saints. *A Collection of Sacred Hymns, for the Church of the Latter Day Saints* was published in Kirtland in time for the dedication of the Kirtland Temple in early 1836.[18] Though she did not write the hymns, Emma's selection certainly preached doctrine and cheered and encouraged the Saints, both collectively and individually, through worship. The Lord told Emma in 1830, "My Soul delighteth in the song of the heart yea the song of the righteous is a prayer unto me & it shall be answered with a blessing upon their heads."[19] When Joseph dedicated the temple, Emma's hymns united the Saints in worship and great spiritual manifestations.

A second way in which Emma expounded scripture and exhorted the Church was through the Relief Society. On March 17, 1842, twenty women gathered on the second floor of the red brick store in Nauvoo and were organized by the Prophet Joseph "after the pattern, or order, of the priesthood," or "according to the ancient Priesthood."[20] The women elected Emma as president, and Joseph read from 2 John to teach that Emma was an "Elect lady, . . . elected to preside." He explained that she had been ordained in July 1830, at the time of her revelation, "to expound the scriptures to all; and to teach the female part of community."[21] Sarah Kimball, present at the first Relief Society meeting, recalled that Joseph taught the women, "I have desired to organise the Sisters in the order of the Priesthood. . . . The organization of the Church of Christ was never perfect until the women were organised."[22] Emma led the women in providing relief to the poor and saving souls, as instructed by Joseph.[23]

Another pattern in revelation includes counsel accompanied by warnings or promises. This demonstrates one way the Lord speaks to His children. The Lord told Emma in section 25, "If thou art faithful and walk in the paths of virtue before me, I will preserve thy life, and thou shalt receive an inheritance in Zion." He also directed her to "keep my commandments continually & a crown of righteousness thou shalt receive."[24] Notice the grammatical structure, suggesting blessings attached to specific instruction.

From the perspective of the twenty-first century, we can see examples of how this divine charge to be faithful worked out in Emma's life, years after the revelation was given. As gossip about plural marriage and slander of Joseph's moral integrity swirled around Nauvoo in 1842 and 1843, Emma taught the Relief Society, as recorded in the minutes: "Our way was straight— said we wanted none in this society but those who *could* and *would* walk straight and were determined to do good."[25] She extended the invitation to all female members to walk in paths of virtue.

Emma's life was, in fact, preserved: she died at the age of 75 in April 1879.[26] Shortly before her passing, her nurse reported a dream in which Joseph brought Emma to a beautiful mansion, where she found a baby in the nursery—Don Carlos, who had died at the age of 14 months in Nauvoo. Emma excitedly picked up her son and asked her husband about the other children. He said, "Emma, be patient, and you shall have all your children." She then turned and saw the glorified Jesus Christ. A few days later, Emma called for Joseph at her death.[27] She too, like her prophet-husband, had seen the Savior, and she too received that "crown of righteousness" and "an inheritance in Zion" promised to her decades earlier. These are principles promised "unto all."[28]

Jennifer Reeder is the nineteenth-century women's history specialist at the Church History Department and the project lead of the Discourses of Eliza R. Snow.

Notes

1. Joseph Smith III, "Last Testimony of Sister Emma," *Saints' Herald,* Oct. 1, 1879, 289.
2. For more detail on the dating of this revelation, see Historical Introduction to "Revelation, July 1830–C [D&C 25]," josephsmithpapers.org.
3. "Revelation, July 1830–C [D&C 25:16]," p. 35.
4. Russell M. Nelson, "Spiritual Treasures," *Ensign,* Nov. 2019, 77.
5. "Journal, 1835–1836," pp. 23–24, josephsmithpapers.org.
6. "History, 1838–1856, volume A-1 [23 December 1805–30 August 1834]," pp. 42–45, josephsmithpapers.org.
7. John S. Reed, "Some of the Remarks of John S. Reed, Esq., as Delivered before the State Convention," *Times and Seasons,* June 1, 1844, 5:551.
8. "History, 1838–1856, volume A-1 [23 December 1805–30 August 1834]," p. 47.
9. "History, circa June 1839–circa 1841 [Draft 2]," p. 3, josephsmithpapers.org.
10. "History, circa Summer 1832," p. 3, josephsmithpapers.org.
11. "Revelation, July 1830–C," in Doctrine and Covenants, 1835 ed., p. 178, sec. 48, v. 1 [D&C 25:1, 3], josephsmithpapers.org. The original manuscript of the revelation to Emma Smith is not extant. The earliest known version is the circa March 1831 hand-written copy in Revelation Book 1. The revelation was first published, with some wording changes, in the Book of Commandments in 1833. Additional wording changes were made when the revelation was published in the first (1835) edition of the Doctrine and Covenants. The language in our current scriptures closely tracks that of the 1835 edition. For general information about the process by which Joseph Smith and others revised and edited the revelations for publication, see "Joseph Smith–Era Publications of Revelations," josephsmithpapers.org.

12. James 1:5–6.
13. "Revelation, July 1830–C [D&C 25:7–8]," p. 34; "History, 1838–1856, volume A-1 [23 December 1805–30 August 1834]," pp. 51–52.
14. "Revelation, February 1829 [D&C 4]," josephsmithpapers.org; "Revelation, May 1829–A [D&C 11]," josephsmithpapers.org; "Revelation, May 1829–B [D&C 12]," josephsmith papers.org.
15. "Revelation, July 1830–C [D&C 25:7, 11, 3]," pp. 34–35.
16. *An American Dictionary of the English Language,* ed. Noah Webster (New York: S. Converse, 1828), s.vv. "exhort," "expound."
17. "Revelation, July 1830–C [D&C 25:8]," pp. 34–35.
18. While the copyright year is 1835, most likely the book was typeset for the press that year and then actually printed in 1836. (See Michael Hicks, *Mormonism and Music: A History* [Urbana: University of Illinois Press, 2003], 20.)
19. "Revelation, July 1830–C [D&C 25:12]," p. 35.
20. "First Organisation," n.d., ca. July 1880, Relief Society Record, 1880–92, p. 5, CHL; "Nauvoo Relief Society Minute Book," Mar. 31, 1842, p. 22, josephsmithpapers.org.
21. "Nauvoo Relief Society Minute Book," Mar. 17, 1842, pp. 8–9.
22. Sarah M. Kimball, Reminiscence, Mar. 17, 1882, The First Fifty Years of Relief Society (website), churchhistorianspress.org.
23. "Nauvoo Relief Society Minute Book," June 9, 1842, p. 63.
24. "Revelation, July 1830–C," in Doctrine and Covenants, 1835 ed., p. 178, sec. 48, v. 1 [D&C 25:2]; "Revelation, July 1830–C [D&C 25:15]," p. 35.
25. "Nauvoo Relief Society Minute Book," Mar. 31, 1842, p. 23.
26. See "Smith, Emma Hale" (biographical entry), josephsmithpapers.org.
27. Alexander Hale Smith, "Sermon at Bottineau, N.D.," July 1, 1903, *Zion's Ensign,* Dec. 31, 1903, 7.
28. "Revelation, July 1830–C [D&C 25:16]," p. 35.

PART 2

OHIO AND MISSOURI, 1831–1839

"GOD IS MY FRIEND": JOSEPH SMITH AND ADVERSITY

By R. Eric Smith

Joseph Smith was born to poor tenant farmers in Vermont. At age 38, he was shot by a mob, in a jail, in a small town in Illinois. In between, he faced so much adversity that his story is almost the stuff of myth. Around age 7, Joseph endured a painful leg surgery that required him to use crutches for several years. At 14, he was rejected and ridiculed when he reported on his First Vision to a minister. When Joseph was 17, his older brother Alvin died—one of four brothers who predeceased him. At 20, Joseph was criminally prosecuted for using a seer stone—the first of many times the law was used to harass him. When he was 22, his and Emma's firstborn child died—the first of six children that they buried. At 25, he undertook the first of three migrations that forced him to start again with little. At 26, he was attacked and beaten. At 32, he was sentenced to death. Though he survived that peril, he languished in jail while his family and thousands of followers were driven out of their homes and exiled. At 36, he declared bankruptcy because he had taken on so much personal debt to build up the Church. In his final two years he rebuffed waves of legal and personal attacks, some from former friends, and started looking for places outside of the United States for his people to settle.[1] Notwithstanding all this and more, he never turned against God, never denied his testimony that God and Christ had spoken to him, and never stopped preaching the gospel, building temples, and guiding the Saints.

An entire book could be written about the adversity Joseph faced and his response to it. In fact, responding to adversity with faith and fortitude may be the overarching theme of Joseph's life. As with Paul, his New Testament hero, tribulation became second nature to Joseph, and he rejoiced in it because he knew that trials are necessary to prepare us for the glories to come.[2] This essay explores only one aspect of Joseph's experience with adversity: his willingness to obey God regardless of the circumstances.

Somehow, Joseph made up his mind early in his prophetic career that he would do whatever God asked him to do. This was perhaps partly in response to the rebuke he received from the Lord after he let Martin Harris borrow the first pages of the Book of Mormon translation. The Lord told Joseph his failing in that episode was fearing man more than God; had Joseph been faithful, God would have "extended his arm" and been with Joseph "in evry time of trouble."[3] Joseph appears to have decided that he would never disappoint the Lord again. We may be inclined to think Joseph had an easier time obeying because of the visions he had seen. But many others who shared some of those marvelous experiences did not remain true. Joseph's steadfastness must be found, rather, in his character.

Joseph's obedience was not half-hearted, not of the *All right, I guess I'll do it* variety. No, he responded to the Lord's commands with alacrity, as historian Richard Bushman put it. Bushman was talking specifically about how, in the fall of 1832, Joseph and Newel K. Whitney set off from Ohio to New York City shortly after Whitney was commanded to travel there, even though Emma Smith was in the late stages of pregnancy and Whitney was still recovering from a leg injury earlier that year.[4] Family and personal considerations seemed to hardly enter Joseph's calculus after God told him to do something. (I am mindful that for nearly every challenge Joseph faced, Emma endured an accompanying trial—sometimes of a different sort, but no less sore. As you read the accounts in this essay about how Joseph met adversity, reflect on what they also reveal about Emma's sacrifice, support, strength, and faith.)

Two other examples from the same period further demonstrate how remarkably prompt Joseph was to act on instruction from the Lord. In late 1830, Joseph and a group of Saints were living in New York, where most of them had homes, extended families, and work opportunities. On December 30, a revelation told Joseph to "go to the Ohio," meaning to move with the Saints roughly 300 miles to eastern Ohio, where another small group of believers was living.[5] If the Lord suddenly told me to up-root my family and move to a different state, how long would it take me to get there? Surely He would be all right with me taking time to get a good price on my home, tie up business, and say goodbye. But Joseph responded swiftly. He arrived in Kirtland, Ohio, in the middle of winter, on February 4, 1831. Emma bore twins three months later.[6]

An episode the following year showing Joseph's alacrity has elements of both the heartbreaking and the incredible. The twins Emma bore in April 1831 both died at birth, and Joseph and Emma then adopted new-born twins, named Joseph and Julia, from a Church member whose wife had died.[7] On March 1, 1832, as these twins approached their first birth-day, Joseph was commanded to travel to Missouri, 900 miles away. Joseph had been there the prior summer to designate Independence as a gather-ing place for the Church. Now the Lord wanted him to return to coun-sel with the Saints.[8] (Fortunately, in our own day, long trips away from spouses and children to carry out Church assignments are not generally required.)

On March 20, Joseph received by revelation answers to two ques-tions he had asked the Lord about the Missouri trip. In answer to the first question, Joseph was told to buy paper and take it to Missouri for the printing of the Book of Commandments. In answer to the other, he was instructed to set aside the New Testament translation for the time being and to proceed to Missouri with "no delays."[9] Four days later, Joseph and Sidney Rigdon were tarred and feathered by a mob outside their homes in Hiram, Ohio—a brutal attack intended to humiliate and warn. We have heard this story before, so perhaps it no longer seems remarkable to us that Joseph preached a Sabbath sermon the next day, with some of his assailants in the crowd.[10] How many of us would have taken that day off?

And now comes the part that to me is almost hard to believe, in showing both the amount of affliction Joseph was asked to suffer and how obedient he was. On March 29, five days after the tarring and feathering, the infant Joseph died a month shy of one year. He had been sick when his father was dragged outdoors by the mob, and exposure to the cold night air might have contributed to his death.[11]

Now, surely, the Prophet would take some time to grieve the loss and to recover from his beating? No. On April 1, presumably after the burial of his son, Joseph left Ohio for the long trip to Missouri.[12] His responsiveness to the commandment of the Lord seems superhuman, but Joseph was only an ordinary person who had made up his mind to obey.

On the return trip from Missouri, Joseph's traveling companion Newel Whitney broke his leg in a stagecoach accident. Though Joseph was anxious to return to Emma and their one surviving child, he delayed his return home for several weeks to help his friend recover.[13] A letter Joseph wrote Emma during this time gives clues into the source of his uncommon fortitude. "I will endeavor to be Contented the Lord asisting me," he wrote, after mentioning how unpleasant his situation was. "I will try to be contented with my lot knowing that God is my friend in him I shall find comfort I have given my life into his hands." For Joseph, God was a friend who would assist and comfort him in any situation. And Joseph had also given his entire life over to God—not only pushing his own desires, fears, and welfare aside but letting them be completely swallowed up in whatever God asked. "I Count not my life dear to me," Joseph told Emma.[14] He meant it, as his martyrdom proved.

That Joseph was faithful to God even to the point of giving the last full measure of devotion encourages me to press forward and stay true even in times of extreme difficulty. In recent years I have dealt with a diagnosis of stage IV cancer, probably the greatest trial of my life. It can be hard to push anxiety and despair from my mind, to continue to perform my labors in family, Church, and occupation with optimism and determination. Serendipitously, my work as an editor for the Joseph Smith

Papers means that Joseph's example has been continually before my eyes. Thinking of his faith, his physical courage, and his steely resolve fortify me against what I must endure. Above all, Joseph points me directly to God, the only true source of comfort. I have felt that comfort!

When we do what God asks, when we search for Him, when we cry out for help, He provides the peace, strength, and guidance we need to make it through any adversity. I add my voice to that of Brother Joseph: God is our friend and is with us in times of trouble.

R. Eric Smith is the editorial manager and a general editor of the Joseph Smith Papers Project.

Notes

1. "Events," josephsmithpapers.org; Richard Lyman Bushman, *Joseph Smith: Rough Stone Rolling* (New York: Knopf, 2005).
2. "Letter to 'All the Saints in Nauvoo,' 1 September 1842 [D&C 127:2]," p. [1], josephsmithpapers.org; see also, for example, Letter to Church Leaders in Jackson County, Missouri, Aug. 18, 1833, in *JSP*, D3:264; Letter to Edward Partridge, Dec. 5, 1833, in *JSP*, D3:371; and Letter to the Church and Edward Partridge, Mar. 20, 1839, in *JSP*, D6:367.
3. Revelation, July 1828, in *JSP*, D1:8 [D&C 3:7–8].
4. Bushman, *Rough Stone Rolling*, 188; Revelation, Sept. 22–23, in *JSP*, D2:303 [D&C 84:114].
5. Revelation, Dec. 30, 1830, in *JSP*, D1:227 [D&C 37:1].
6. "Mormonism," *Painesville Telegraph*, Feb. 15, 1831, [1]; "History, 1838–1856, volume A-1 [23 December 1805–30 August 1834]," p. 92, josephsmithpapers.org; "Joseph Smith Pedigree Chart," josephsmithpapers.org.
7. "Joseph Smith Pedigree Chart."
8. Revelation, Mar. 1, 1832, in *JSP*, D2:199 [D&C 78:9].
9. Revelation, Mar. 20, 1832, in *JSP*, D2:217–18.
10. "Part 4: Missouri, Indiana, and Ohio, Spring and Summer 1832," in *JSP*, D2:195; "History, 1838–1856, volume A-1 [23 December 1805–30 August 1834]," pp. 205–8.
11. "History, 1838–1856, volume A-1 [23 December 1805–30 August 1834]," p. 209; "Joseph Smith Pedigree Chart."
12. "Part 4: Missouri, Indiana, and Ohio, Spring and Summer 1832," in *JSP*, D2:196.
13. Historical Introduction to Letter to Emma Smith, June 6, 1832, in *JSP*, D2:247.
14. Letter to Emma Smith, June 6, 1832, in *JSP*, D2:249, 251.

RECORDING THE FIRST VISION: JOSEPH SMITH'S DECISION TO SHARE HIS VISIONARY EXPERIENCES

By Robin Scott Jensen

In recent years, *Saints: Volume 1,* the Joseph Smith Papers, *Teachings of Presidents of the Church: Joseph Smith,* and other Church publications have made extraordinary amounts of information about Joseph Smith's history and teachings easily accessible. The response by Latter-day Saints has been impressive. Millions of members have used these resources to be inspired and informed. Appropriately, our interest is usually in what Joseph Smith said or did—that is, we focus on the *content* of the historical records.

Investigating the *context* of historical records—that is, when, why, how, and by whom they were created—can often help us understand the content better. For example, if you are reading a statement from Joseph Smith, it can make a significant difference whether he wrote the document himself, spoke to the Saints with a clerk capturing his words, or asked a scribe to compose a letter. Looking at context also helps us appreciate the time, effort, and expense that went into creating these documents. The records from which we learn Joseph's history did not simply spring into existence. Someone had to decide that something was worth documenting, and—in a time when paper, ink, and pens were not as affordable as they are now—had to buy the materials and write down the words; and other people had to value, preserve, and pass down those records. Given these factors and Joseph's poverty, culture, and education level, it is remarkable how many records were created.

Consider the story of the First Vision. For members of the Church, the details of what happened when God and Jesus Christ appeared to Joseph on that spring day in 1820 are familiar. Such detail comes to us because Joseph relayed the experience both verbally and in writing. Yet he didn't record an account of the vision on paper until 1832, twelve years after the event.[1] Why?

Joseph seemed to be averse at first to even speaking of the First Vision and his other heavenly manifestations. This may have been because soon after he experienced the vision, he shared it with a minister who rejected it.[2] Because of this rejection, at least according to one scholar, Joseph did not even tell his immediate family about the First Vision.[3] Likewise, George A. Smith, Joseph's cousin, recalled a letter his family received from the young prophet while he was translating the Book of Mormon. According to George A.'s recollection, Joseph called his cousin's family to repentance and denounced the religions of the day but said nothing of his heavenly visions.[4]

Joseph was reluctant to share the First Vision and the visitations of the angel Moroni with the larger public as well. The preface to the first edition of the Book of Mormon—a perfect forum for Joseph to explain the divine context surrounding the discovery and translation of the book— makes no mention of Moroni's visits.[5] Perhaps taking cues from their son, Joseph's parents mirrored his reticence. When Oliver Cowdery boarded with Joseph Smith Sr. and Lucy Mack Smith in late 1828 (at a time when Joseph and Emma were living in Pennsylvania), he showed an interest in the stories then circulating about Joseph and the golden plates. Lucy and her husband refused to tell Cowdery anything "for a long time" until he finally gained their trust.[6]

Joseph's reluctance to share his heavenly visitations with others seems to be a major reason why he did not give an account in writing for so long. The reason did not have to do with literacy; the Smiths were a literate—though not literary—family. As farmers, they made business records, such as statements indicating their debts and what money was owed to them.[7] They also kept in touch with extended family through correspondence.[8] As his network of believers grew, Joseph also wrote letters to offer words of encouragement, oversee logistics of printing the Book of Mormon, and convey his belief in the restored gospel.[9] But he evidently did not produce any records capturing his innermost thoughts, such as a journal.

Perhaps Joseph did not produce such personal records in the 1820s simply because he felt no inclination to express himself on paper; perhaps agricultural life was work enough. We don't have, after all, a flood of diaries from agrarian workers in nineteenth-century New York. Joseph also may have felt that language was an imperfect medium—comparing it to a "little narrow prison"—in which to share or understand sacred events.[10]

Yet as Joseph progressed in his calling as a prophet, he learned about the importance of written records. As he began translating the Book of Mormon in 1827 and 1828, he must have recognized the role records played in transmitting God's word to His children. Indeed, that record depicted a civilization that had lost its belief in God because it did not have written scripture.[11] Martin Harris's loss of the pages of the initial translation taught Joseph the necessity of better preserving records. As he recommenced translating the Book of Mormon in 1829, Joseph captured the sacred revelations he received from God more systematically (he had only written down one revelation in 1828). Committing those commandments to paper, rather than just expressing them verbally, likely helped him recognize the greater permanence of the written record.

The recorded commandments quickly became essential to early believers. As Joseph recorded—on paper—broad doctrinal revelations or divine answers to questions from his friends and family, he captured God's words so that readers could remember and follow the directives. As early believers in the Book of Mormon read from these revelations, as well as from the Book of Mormon, they became increasingly comfortable with the idea of seeing principles of their growing faith in writing. For Joseph, the importance of recording God's instructions was reiterated in April 1830, when the Lord commanded him to keep a record on the same day the Church was established.[12]

Although Joseph was learning the importance of recording the words of God, he still did not produce writings conveying his own experiences or feelings. The Prophet's earliest documents show a man committed to capturing the newly revealed gospel in writing but not as enthusiastic about transmitting his own thoughts on paper. Nowhere do we have Joseph's early comments on the revelations or other latter-day scripture. The prophet and translator set God's words to paper before his own.

In 1832 Joseph began to document the Church and his own life in a different way. That year Joseph started five record-keeping projects: a revelation book, a history, a journal, a letterbook, and a minute book.[13] Ironically, he left no written statements of why he began keeping more extensive records—we only know of the change because of the records themselves. Each of these records filled a distinct need for the growing Church. Joseph would need a revelation book, letterbook, and minute book to document the Church's activities and provide a central repository for official communications. Keeping a journal would allow him to document and reflect on his activities. A history permitted Joseph to interpret the meaning of his visionary experiences.

This 1832 history came more than 12 years after the First Vision occurred, but that vision was one of the first things he recorded during this explosion of administrative and personal records. The history, probably written in the summer of 1832, noted Joseph's birth and family circumstances and then "quickly moved to the events that marked the beginning of his career as a prophet," including his First Vision and the beginnings of the translation of the Book of Mormon.[14] It bears Joseph's handwriting and that of his clerk Frederick G. Williams. The autobiographical content, however, makes clear that Joseph was the sole author.

Even though the history is only six pages, it offered a significant addition to the extant writings of Joseph. By the time he ceased work on the history, he had *doubled* the amount of surviving personal records produced up to that point. In other words, the entire known documentary record of Joseph Smith before summer 1832—excluding the Book of Mormon, his revelations, and other sacred translations—is only a few hundred words longer than the essay you are currently reading.[15]

After years of documenting God's words to him, Joseph now recorded his own words about the vision in his 1832 history. As Joseph came to rely more and more upon the written record for God's word, he slowly recognized that his own voice mattered to himself and his followers. The First Vision quickly became a foundational event for Joseph in his retelling of his early history. As he increasingly expressed himself in writing, he gained more experience in writing about his visionary experience. The 1832 history paved the way for additional histories he created in subsequent years to document his amazing life. The prophet and seer did not just *experience* marvelous events—he *recorded* them on paper so they could be shared, kept, and treasured. His words have become part of our sacred history.

Robin Scott Jensen is an associate managing historian of the Joseph Smith Papers Project.

Notes

1. See Doctrine and Covenants 20:5 for a brief mention of the First Vision without any detail attached to the event. (Articles and Covenants, ca. Apr. 1830, in *JSP,* D1:121 [D&C 20:5].)
2. Joseph Smith, History, 1838–56, vol. A-1 ("Draft 2"), 3, in *JSP,* H1:216.
3. Steven C. Harper, *First Vision: Memory and Mormon Origins* (New York: Oxford University Press, 2019), 11. When Moroni appeared to Joseph in 1823, he commanded Joseph to tell his father about the angel's appearance. This may suggest that Joseph had been reluctant to share his religious experiences with his family. (Joseph Smith, History, 1838–56, vol. A-1 ["Draft 2"], 7, in *JSP,* H1:232.)
4. History of George A. Smith, ca. 1857–75, p. 2, CHL.
5. Preface to Book of Mormon, ca. Aug. 1829, in *JSP,* D1:92–94.
6. "Lucy Mack Smith, History, 1844–1845," bk. 7, p. [12], josephsmithpapers.org.
7. See, for example, "List of Services, between circa 12 January and 6 February 1819," josephsmithpapers.org.
8. See Lucy Mack Smith to Solomon Mack, Jan. 6, 1831, CHL; and History of George A. Smith, ca. 1857–75, p. 2, CHL.
9. See, for example, Letter to Oliver Cowdery, Oct. 22, 1829, in *JSP,* D1:94–97; and Letter to Newel Knight and the Church in Colesville, Aug. 28, 1830, in *JSP,* D1:172–77.
10. Joseph Smith to William W. Phelps, Nov. 27, 1832, in *JSP,* D2:320.
11. See Omni 1:17.
12. Revelation, Apr. 6, 1830, in *JSP,* D1:129 [D&C 21:1].
13. Journal, 1832–34, in *JSP,* J1:3–51; "Letterbook 1," josephsmithpapers.org; Revelation Book 2, in *JSP,* MRB:407–665; "Minute Book 1," josephsmithpapers.org; History, ca. Summer 1832, in *JSP,* H1:3–22. Joseph had already started a book in which his revelations were recorded around spring 1831, but this book was carried to Missouri in late

1831 so that the revelations could be published. Thus, he needed a second manuscript book in Ohio for his revelations. (See Source Note and Historical Introduction for Revelation Book 1, in *JSP,* MRB:3–7.)

14. Historical Introduction to History, ca. Summer 1832, in *JSP,* H1:4–5.

15. This quantification, derived from online transcriptions available at josephsmithpapers.org, is based on the word count of the following documents: Preface to Book of Mormon, circa August 1829; a letter to Oliver Cowdery, October 22, 1829; a letter to Martin Harris, February 22, 1831; a letter to Hyrum Smith, March 3–4, 1831 (excluding a letter from Oliver Cowdery that Joseph copied into this letter to Hyrum); a note Joseph wrote in a record book on March 8, 1832; and a letter he wrote to Emma Smith, June 6, 1832. It does not include the letters Joseph cowrote with John Whitmer in the latter half of 1830. The total word count (including canceled words) of these documents is approximately 2,050. The word count of the 1832 history is approximately 2,060.

READING THE FIRST VISION IN LIGHT OF JOSEPH SMITH'S OTHER EARLY VISIONS

By Kathleen Flake

In the summer of 1832, Joseph Smith took up his pen and started to write a history of the Church, possibly in response to the command "there Shall a Record be kept among you," which had been given two years earlier on the date of the Church's organization.[1] While others would later be called to obey that commandment and keep a record of the continuing progress of the Church, Joseph alone experienced the first events that called it into being. He never finished this version of what he called "A History of the life of Joseph Smith Jr. an account of his marvilous experience and of all the mighty acts which he doeth in the name of Jesus Ch[r]ist the son of the living God of whom he beareth record and also an account of the rise of the church of Christ in the eve of time according as the Lord brought forth and established by his hand."[2] In his introduction, however, Joseph outlined the events that constituted that history, all of which are well known to us today: Joseph's First Vision and the appearances of Moroni; John the Baptist; and Peter, James, and John.

When the Prophet took up the task again six years later, he followed this same outline. An excerpt of this 1838 history became what we know today by the much simpler title "Joseph Smith—History" and is published in the Pearl of Great Price. Focusing on the decade leading up to the organization of the Church, the "History" is composed of four events in the young prophet's life. These events are usually spoken of individually and taught in isolation from one another. In this essay, I invite you to think about them as having a specific shared purpose that gives not only coherence but additional meaning to the History. Such a reading of these stories enables us to see them anew and deepen our understanding of each as a related step in, as Joseph put it, "the rise of the church of Christ in the eve [or evening, the latter days] of time." Finally, attending to their relatedness reveals that these "marvelous experiences" are not merely autobiographical. They portray "the rise" also of a prophet, the decade-long education and spiritual maturation of a young man to found and lead the kind of church he initially sought—one that could save him and, as the History testifies, us.

We are helped in this experiment with seeing the familiar anew by the descriptive references to each event in Joseph's 1832 manuscript. They differ markedly from how we refer to them today and help us see what mattered to Joseph about these "marvelous" events. What we call the "First Vision," he described as "receiving the testamony from on high." He did not link the label *testimony* to a particular part of his experience in the grove, and, of course, there were many elements of that vision that could be considered a testimony. But, in this 1832 version of the First Vision, the text narrows the field of possibilities to a particularly powerful and personal moment for Joseph: his being forgiven of his sins.

While it can rightly be said that Joseph Smith began his religious life wanting to know which church was true, the 1832 history shows it is more accurate to say he wanted to know which church could truly save him. "My mind [had] become," he wrote, "excedingly distressed for I become convicted of my sins and by searching the scriptures I found that . . . there was no society or denomination that built upon the gospel of Jesus Christ . . . and I felt to mourn for my own sins and for the sins of the world." Thus, in the 1832 account of the First Vision, the first declaration or "testimony" of the Lord was the assurance "Joseph my son thy sins are forgiven thee." This was followed by a simple exhortation to "go thy way walk in my statutes" and by a relatively long and universal indictment of the world: all to the effect that "none doeth good no not one." With this, the Lord's instruction ended, and Joseph is portrayed as satisfied, even joyful: "My soul was filled with love and for many days I could rejoice with great Joy."[3] He had obtained the forgiveness he sought, and his quest for salvation was complete.

In contrast, the 1838 account is more institutionally oriented, both in its definition of Joseph's quest and in the words he heard. "My object," he wrote, "in going to enquire of the Lord was to know which of all the sects . . . to join."[4] Though this version does not contradict the 1832 account, it marks a shift in narrative focus, from relief of one's personal sin to institutional authority to offer such relief. Joseph noted that God twice forbade him to join any church. Moreover, not the world, but religious institutions were faulted. What the 1832 account implied, the 1838 makes explicit. Contemporary churches did not have the power to save him; they did not even seek the power. "They teach for doctrines the commandments of men," he was told, "having a form of Godliness but they deny the power thereof."[5] Writing in 1838, not long after the dedication of the Kirtland Temple, Joseph brings a mature prophet's understanding to his First Vision and its significance that is no longer merely personal. Rather, the necessity of a church being endowed with "power from on high" or "the power of Godliness" was the most significant "testimony" of his first spiritual experience.[6]

The centrality of this theme—the need for a church with divine power—is further evidenced by the three events that form the greater part of Joseph's pre-history of the Church and that solve the problem identified in the First Vision: where is the power of salvation to be found on earth? The second evidence that power was to be restored was demonstrated by the "marvelous" production of the Book of Mormon and his years of tutoring by Moroni and others before and during its translation. Joseph labels this event "seccondly the ministering of Angels," emphasizing the multiplicity of heavenly messengers associated with this aspect of his calling.[7] One imagines these years as Joseph's personal School of the Prophets, taught by the prophets.

Next came John the Baptist, who ordained Joseph to the lesser priesthood. Here is how he described it in his 1832 blueprint: "thirdly the reception of the holy Priesthood by the ministring of Aangels to administer the letter of the Gospel—the Law and commandments as they were given unto him—and the ordinencs."[8] The emphasis on "Law" in this description may show the influence of Joseph's later experiences on his retrospective understanding of his early years. For example, the 1832 history was written a year after Joseph received the commandment to "go to the Ohio," with the promise that "there I will give unto you my law."[9] As Joseph grew through experience with the priesthood, his understanding of the significance of John the Baptist's appearance would have likewise grown. He would have realized it was about more than answering his and Oliver's prayer to be baptized.

Less is known about the circumstances that catalyzed the fourth "marvelous experience" in Joseph's pre-history: the ordination to the higher priesthood by Peter, James, and John.[10] Most scholars assume that this ordination was prompted by the many references to priesthood in the Book of Mormon. In the 1832 account Joseph defines the event as a bestowal of "the Kees [keys] of the Kingdom . . . the continuation of the blessings of God."[11] Also, in 1832, shortly after or possibly while continuing to think about this unfinished history, Joseph received a revelation that made explicit the connection between the first and fourth events of Joseph's pre-history—that is, that explained how a church with the "power of Godliness" came into being. "This greater Priesthood . . . holdeth the key . . . of the knowledge of God therefore in the ordinences thereof the power of Godliness is manifest."[12]

In each of the three events that followed the First Vision, or first "testimony," divine power was conveyed and made executable. In this manner and over a decade, the problem identified in the First Vision was solved: the "power of Godliness" was restored and made institutionally available to humanity.[13] Many years later and referring to "the keys of the Kingdom," Joseph observed, "Now the great and grand secret of the whole matter and the sum and bonnum [summum bonum, or greatest good] of the whole subject that is lying before us consists in obtaining the powers of the Holy priesthood. For him, to whom these Keys are given there is no difficulty in obtaining a knowledge of facts in relation to the salvation of the children of men, both as well for the dead as for the living."[14] With each passing year, the Prophet both learned and taught the extent of the "testimony" of salvation through Jesus Christ. Today, in the Pearl of Great Price, we have not only Joseph's story and an account of the "rise of the church of Christ in the eve of time," but also his testimony of it.

Kathleen Flake is the Richard Lyman Bushman Professor of Mormon Studies at the University of Virginia.

Notes

1. Revelation, Apr. 6, 1830, in *JSP,* D1:129 [D&C 21:1].
2. History, ca. Summer 1832, in *JSP,* H1:10.
3. History, ca. Summer 1832, in *JSP,* H1:10–13.
4. History, ca. June 1839–ca. 1841 (Draft 2), in *JSP,* H1:214 [Joseph Smith—History 1:18].
5. History, ca. June 1839–ca. 1841 (Draft 2), in *JSP,* H1:214 [Joseph Smith—History 1:19]; see Isaiah 29:13; Matthew 15:8; and 2 Timothy 3:5.
6. See Revelation, Jan. 2, 1831, in *JSP,* D1:232 [D&C 38:32]; and Revelation, Sept. 22–23, 1832, in *JSP,* D2:295 [D&C 84:20].
7. History, ca. Summer 1832, in *JSP,* H1:10. Regarding multiple angelic visitations, see Alexander L. Baugh, "Parting the Veil: The Visions of Joseph Smith," *BYU Studies* 38, no. 1 (1999): 27–28.
8. History, ca. Summer 1832, in *JSP,* H1:10.
9. Revelation, Jan. 2, 1831, in *JSP,* D1:232 [D&C 38:32].
10. For such details as are presently known, see John W. Welch, ed., *Opening the Heavens: Accounts of Divine Manifestations, 1820–1844* (Provo, UT: Brigham Young University Press; Salt Lake City: Deseret Book, 2005), 218–26.
11. History, ca. Summer 1832, in *JSP,* H1:10.
12. Revelation, Sept. 22–23, 1832, in *JSP,* D2:295 [D&C 84:19–20].
13. See History, ca. June 1839–ca. 1841 (Draft 2), in *JSP,* H1:214.
14. "Letter to the Church, 7 September 1842 [D&C 128:11]," p. 4, josephsmithpapers.org.

"KNOWLEDGE SAVES A MAN": JOSEPH SMITH'S DEVOTION TO LEARNING

By Petra Javadi-Evans

In studying the life of Joseph Smith, we find a man who strove to prepare himself and the Saints "in all things" through learning.[1] He spent his life learning, teaching, and encouraging others to do the same. Joseph believed that all learning—all knowledge—would enhance spiritual understanding, edify the mind, increase abilities, and develop faith so that a person could be a better influence for good in the world and help build the kingdom of God physically upon the earth and in the hearts of God's children.

The events leading to the First Vision are evidence that from his youth, Joseph was an intelligent, inquisitive, and self-motivated learner. In his desire to secure personal salvation, he investigated different churches, listened to various preachers, studied the scriptures, and took his questions to God. It's true that Joseph's formal education was scant and incomplete; he had been "deprived of the benefit of an education," and the minimal instruction in "reading, writing, and the ground rules of arithmetic . . . constituted [his] whole literary acquirements."[2] However, what he lacked in formal education, he made up for by seizing and creating opportunities to learn throughout his life, using the knowledge he acquired to further the work of building the kingdom of God and encouraging others to do the same.

Joseph understood that building the kingdom of God required divine and secular knowledge, and he considered the two types of information to be both vital and fully compatible. For Joseph, all knowledge was worth obtaining: "The Glory of God is intelligence, or, in other words, light and truth."[3] He taught the Saints that learning was part of their eternal salvation: "If a person gains more knowledge and intelligence in this life through his diligence and obedience than another, he will have so much the advantage in the world to come."[4]

Divine knowledge was of the greatest importance to Joseph. He understood that life eternal was to know "the only true God, and Jesus Christ."[5] Joseph spent his life trying to understand the mysteries of God and to teach them to the Saints. He studied the Bible throughout his life, examining not only its teachings but also the ancient languages in which it was recorded. Joseph wove biblical teachings throughout the letters he wrote and the sermons he gave. Letters to family, friends, associates, and strangers are full of biblical allusions.[6] And though he apparently never wrote down his sermons beforehand, the ease with which he incorporated scriptures into them suggests not only an extraordinary ability to recall scriptures but also a deep understanding of them.[7]

Joseph loved languages, and he studied other languages as a catalyst to expand his understanding of the scriptures. Beginning in the mid-1830s and for the remainder of his life, he studied Egyptian, Hebrew, Greek, and German.[8] While his skill with these languages was sometimes rudimentary, his exposure to each of them acted as steppingstones to additional scripture and distinct teachings about the nature of God, humanity, and the plan of salvation.[9]

Joseph and other Saints believed that some of the most important divine knowledge could be gained in the temple. A December 1832 revelation commanded the Saints to build a temple in Kirtland. It would function as a "house of prayer, a house of fasting, a house of faith, a house of learning, a house of glory, a house of order, a house of God."[10] The temple was a place where the Saints could receive spiritual instruction and be "endowed with power from on high."[11] The Saints believed that they would receive an outpouring of spiritual power which would enable them to use their talents, gifts, and knowledge with greater ability and to greater effect in their efforts to become like God and build His kingdom on the earth.

Joseph knew that becoming like God and building His kingdom meant that the mind "must stretch as high as the utmost heavens, and search into and contemplate the lowest considerations of the darkest abyss, and expand upon the broad considerations of eternal expanse— [thou] must commune with God."[12] For Joseph the broad expanse of eternity encompassed secular learning as well. In 1832 he received a revelation that the Saints should gain an understanding of earthly things, including "things which have been, things which are, things which must shortly come to pass; things which are at home, things which are abroad; the wars and the perplexities of the nations, and the judgments which are on the land; and a knowledge also of countries and of kingdoms."[13]

Later, in 1844, Joseph told members of the Council of Fifty that he wanted "every man to get knowledge, search the laws of nations, and get all the information they can." He didn't want them to "decide in favor of anything until" they knew it. "Every man ought to study geography, governments, and languages, so that he may be able to go forth to any nation and before any multitude with eloquence," he said.[14] Learning was necessary so that the Saints would be "prepared in all things," and enabled to magnify their callings and complete the missions entrusted to them.[15]

Joseph went to great efforts to inspire learning among the Saints by creating opportunities for them to gather and study the divine and secular side by side. An early member wrote of the excitement the Saints felt: "They had been previously commanded to seek learning and study the best books . . . which inspired them with an extravagant thirst after knowledge."[16]

Beginning in Kirtland, Joseph and other elders attended the School of the Prophets and its successor, the School for the Elders. They received "instruction in doctrine and principle," grammar, and other subjects in order to help them "go forth and declare the true doctrines of the kingdom according to the mind and will of God."[17] Later in Nauvoo, Joseph organized the women into a charitable and educational association called the Female Relief Society of Nauvoo. He taught the sisters that they were to get "instruction through the order which God has established" and that "knowledge and intelligence" would begin to flow down. It was the "beginning of better days," he said.[18]

These organizations were a part of Joseph's design for the kingdom of God on earth, a physical Zion—a gathering place for the Saints.[19] Joseph envisioned that Zion would have not only a temple and churches to teach gospel truths but also a university for teaching the arts and sciences; physical Zion would require men and women who understood both God's law and the laws of men.[20] Joseph knew of this necessity firsthand since he served not only as prophet and president of the Church but also as mayor and a justice of the peace of Nauvoo. Court records and city council records indicate that he dedicated much of his time to the study of law, governance, and politics.[21] His sermons near the end of his life indicate that his spiritual knowledge likewise continued to expand and that he continued to impress upon the Saints the importance of perpetual learning.[22]

On April 7, 1844, two and a half months before he was martyred, Joseph explained: "Here, then, is eternal life—to know the only wise and true God; and you have got to learn how to be gods yourselves, . . . by going from one small degree to another, and from a small capacity to a great one."[23] Joseph's life was a testimony to the idea that divine truths and secular truths could coexist, that indeed they must if one wants to build the kingdom of God and receive exaltation. The Church of Jesus Christ of Latter-day Saints continues to emphasize both gospel study and secular education. And it all began with the founder of the Restoration, who was a question-asker and an answer-finder. Joseph declared, "Knowledge saves a man."[24]

Petra Javadi-Evans is an editor with the Joseph Smith Papers Project and the Church Historian's Press.

Notes

1. Revelation, Dec. 27–28, 1832, in *JSP,* D2:341 [D&C 88:80].
2. History, ca. Summer 1832, 1–2, in *JSP,* H1:11, spelling and punctuation standardized.

3. Revelation, May 6, 1833, in *JSP,* D3:89 [D&C 93:36], spelling and punctuation standardized.

4. Journal, Apr. 2, 1843, and Clayton, Journal, Apr. 2, 1843, in *JSP,* J2:325, 404 [D&C 130:19].

5. "Discourse, 7 April 1844, as Reported by Thomas Bullock," josephsmithpapers.org, spelling and punctuation standardized; John 17:3.

6. See Letter to Newel Knight and the Church in Colesville, Aug. 28, 1830, in *JSP,* D1:174–76; Letter to Emma Smith, Aug. 16, 1842, in *JSP,* D10:401–6; and "Letter to James Arlington Bennet, 17 March 1843," josephsmithpapers.org.

7. See Discourse, Mar. 20, 1842, in *JSP,* D9:291–94; "Discourse, 22 January 1843, as Reported by Wilford Woodruff," josephsmithpapers.org; and "Discourse, 21 January 1844, as Reported by Wilford Woodruff," josephsmithpapers.org.

8. See Journal, Oct. 1. 1835; Nov. 17, 19–21, 23, and 26–27, 1835; Dec. 4–8, 14, 23, 26, and 30, 1835; Jan. 4–Mar. 29, 1836, in *JSP,* J1:67, 105, 107, 109–11, 115–17, 122, 135, 137, 140–211; Journal, Dec. 22, 1842; Feb. 3, 5, 8, 13–14, 20, and 22–23, 1843; Mar. 1 and 6, 1843, in *JSP,* J2:191, 254–56, 263–64, 267, 276, 279, 297; and Journal, May 7, 1843; Mar. 18 and 22, 1844; May 23, 1844; June 3, 1844, in *JSP,* J3:13, 205, 207, 257, 270.

9. See "Discourse, 8 April 1843, as Reported by William Clayton–A," josephsmithpapers .org; Joseph Smith, Letter to the Editor, *Times and Seasons,* May 15, 1843, 4:194; and "Discourse, 7 April 1844, as Reported by Thomas Bullock," josephsmithpapers.org.

10. Revelation, Dec. 27–28, 1832, in *JSP,* D2:345 [D&C 88:119], spelling and punctuation standardized.

11. Revelation, Jan. 2, 1831, in *JSP,* D1:232 [D&C 38:32].

12. Letter to the Church and Edward Partridge, Mar. 20, 1839, in *JSP,* D6:368, spelling and punctuation standardized.

13. Revelation, Dec. 27–28, 1832, in *JSP,* D2:341–42 [D&C 88:77–80], spelling and punctuation standardized.

14. Council of Fifty, "Record," Apr. 11, 1844, in *JSP,* CFM:93, spelling and punctuation standardized.

15. Revelation, Dec. 27–28, 1832, in *JSP,* D2:341–42 [D&C 88:80].

16. John Corrill, *Brief History,* 12, in *JSP,* H2:154, punctuation standardized.

17. Letter and Revelation to Harvey Whitlock, Nov. 16, 1835, in *JSP,* D5:62, spelling and punctuation standardized.

18. Discourse, Apr. 28, 1842, in *JSP,* D9:406.

19. Revelation, Aug. 2, 1833–B, in *JSP,* D3:205–6 [D&C 94:1–2]; Plat of the City of Zion, ca. Early June–June 25, 1833, in *JSP,* D3:125; Letter to Church Leaders in Jackson Co., MO, June 25, 1833, in *JSP,* D3:151; Council of Fifty, "Record," Apr. 18, 1844, in *JSP,* CFM:128.

20. Act to Incorporate the City of Nauvoo, Dec. 16, 1844, in *JSP,* D7:483.

21. See "Introduction to Nauvoo City Council Records," josephsmithpapers.org; and "Decision," *Wasp* (Nauvoo, IL), Mar. 22, 1843, [2]–[3].

22. See "Discourse, 13 August 1843–A, as Reported by Willard Richards," josephsmithpapers .org; and "Discourse, 10 March 1844, as Reported by Wilford Woodruff," josephsmith papers.org.

23. "Discourse, 7 April 1844, as Reported by Thomas Bullock," josephsmithpapers.org, spelling and punctuation standardized.

24. "Conference Minutes," *Times and Seasons,* Aug. 15, 1844, 5:616.

"BE STILL AND KNOW THAT I AM GOD": JOSEPH SMITH AND THE EXPULSION OF THE SAINTS FROM JACKSON COUNTY, MISSOURI

By Matthew C. Godfrey

When many members of The Church of Jesus Christ of Latter-day Saints contemplate Joseph Smith, they think about the prophet of the Restoration, one who was receiving constant revelation from the Lord, including grand visions and marvelous visitations from heavenly beings. Certainly, Joseph Smith experienced such remarkable spiritual manifestations. Yet he also had times in his life when he could not get answers to prayers, when God felt more distant—something that most Latter-day Saints experience at some point in their lives. At these times, Joseph— like us—had to patiently wait on the Lord's timetable, trusting He would eventually provide answers and comfort.

From the time the Church was organized in 1830, one of the key doctrines preached by Joseph was the establishment of the City of Zion on the American continent. The Book of Mormon prophesied of this occurrence. When Christ appeared to the Nephites after His Resurrection, He told them that in the last days, a New Jerusalem would be built on the land of the Nephites' inheritance, that all of the Lord's people would be gathered there, and that He would come down from heaven and be in their midst.[1]

Early in 1831, revelations given to Joseph Smith discussed the New Jerusalem, or City of Zion, that would be established.[2] The Saints were told that they needed to purchase land for "an inheritance which shall hereafter be appointed" and which would be called the New Jerusalem. That city, the revelation stated, would be "a land of peace a City of refuge a place of safety for the saints of The most high God."[3]

Because of these prophesies, the Saints were understandably anxious to learn where the New Jerusalem would be built. In June 1831, a revelation told Joseph Smith and Sidney Rigdon that if they would travel to Missouri—where Oliver Cowdery and others sent to preach to American Indians were staying—the Lord would reveal to them "the land of [their] inheritance."[4] Accordingly, Joseph, Sidney, and about two dozen elders traveled from Ohio to Missouri in summer 1831.[5]

After Joseph reached Missouri, he and the others went to Independence in Jackson County—the state's westernmost county.[6] In Independence, Joseph contemplated the prophecies of the City of Zion being built on the American continent and asked the Lord where the temple in the New Jerusalem would be located.[7] Joseph then received a revelation declaring that "the land of Missorie" was the place where the City of Zion would be built, and Independence would be the "centre place."[8]

Although Joseph returned to Ohio, other Saints began moving to Jackson County to establish the New Jerusalem. By 1833, approximately 1,200 Church members lived in the area.[9] Unfortunately, the Saints ran afoul of other Missouri citizens because of cultural differences and other misunderstandings. These tensions erupted into violence in July 1833, resulting in the destruction of the Church's printing shop, the tarring and feathering of Bishop Edward Partridge, and a forced agreement from Church leaders to evacuate the county by April 1834.[10]

After hearing about the violence against the Saints in July 1833, Joseph pleaded with the Lord to deliver them from their enemies. "O Lord what more dost thou require at their hands before thou wilt come and save them?" Joseph asked. But answers were not forthcoming. "I verily know that he [the Lord] will spedily deliver Zion for I have his immutible covenant that this shall be the case," Joseph wrote to the Saints in Missouri in August. "But god is pleased to keep it hid from mine eyes the means how exactly the thing will be done."[11]

With no further direction other than to hold on to their Jackson County land, the Saints began looking into legal options to stay in the county. When those opposed to the Church heard about this, another round of violence broke out. This time, mobs drove the Saints from their homes and forced them from the county in November 1833.[12] The City of Zion seemed dead.

Seeking both comfort and direction, Edward Partridge wrote to Joseph Smith. Stunned by what had occurred, Edward wondered what the Saints in Missouri should do. "Some of our br[ether]n. have their fears that we shall be driven from city to city & from sinagouge to sinagouge," he declared, "& few be left to receive an inheritance in the land."[13] With Church members suffering, impoverished, and sick, Edward—and the Church as a whole—needed direction.

In such an instance, one might expect the Lord to pour out revelation to His prophet. Instead, the Lord's August silence continued even though the situation of the Saints had worsened. Zion seemed abandoned, not delivered—and the Lord was still withholding answers.

Without much to offer in the way of direction, Joseph replied to Edward on December 10, 1833. He told Edward that there were two questions he had posed to the Lord: "why God hath suffered so great calamity to come upon Zion" and "by what means he will return her back to her inheritance" (the same question he had posed in August). But Joseph could not get answers. "The Lord has kept [them] hid from my eyes," Joseph told Edward. "They are not plainly shewn unto me." Yet God gave Joseph a reassuring prompting: "Be still and know that I am God."[14] At a moment when the Saints were in great trouble and had a pressing need for direction, the Lord was silent—except to tell Joseph to trust Him.

This is an instructive experience for all Latter-day Saints. Many will face moments—even periods of great distress—when it feels like God is not answering their prayers. These may be times when we are struggling or times when those we love are struggling and we are pleading to God on their behalf. Even Joseph was not immune to this. He too had to trust in God and wait on the Lord for answers, he too had to watch those he loved suffer, and he too had moments of feeling powerless to do anything for them.

Yet for Joseph, the answers and God's help finally came. On the evening of December 16, 1833, Joseph received a revelation (now section 101 of the Doctrine and Covenants). The first part of that revelation explains why the Lord allowed the Saints to be expelled from Jackson County—the first question Joseph said he had asked God. The second part of the revelation is a parable about a nobleman who loses his land to his enemies and asks his servant to gather the strength of his house to take back the land.[15] That was the answer to Joseph's second question.

Although Joseph did not receive an immediate answer to his prayer, God did not leave him comfortless—and eventually, He gave Joseph the instruction he needed. Joseph's ability to trust in the Lord's timetable throughout the summer and fall of 1833 and maintain his faith in God can serve as a lesson to those struggling to get answers from the Lord or struggling to feel His presence or support. In those cases, the admonition to "be still, and know that I am God" still applies.

Matthew C. Godfrey is the managing historian and a general editor of the Joseph Smith Papers Project.

Notes

1. 3 Nephi 21:22–24; see also Ether 13:2–8.
2. See, for example, Revelation, Feb. 9, 1831, in *JSP*, D1:250 [D&C 42:6–9].
3. Revelation, ca. Mar. 7, 1831, in *JSP*, D1:280 [D&C 45:64–67].
4. Revelation, June 6, 1831, in *JSP*, D1:328 [D&C 52:3–5].
5. William W. Phelps, "Extract of a Letter from the Late Editor," *Ontario Phoenix* (Canandaigua, NY), Sept. 7, 1831, [2]; Joseph Smith manuscript history, vol. A-1, 126, CHL.
6. Letter from Oliver Cowdery, Apr. 8, 1831, in *JSP*, D1:292; Joseph Knight Sr., Reminiscences, 9, MS 3490, CHL; Peter Whitmer Jr., Journal, Dec. 1831, [1], MS 5873, CHL.
7. Joseph Smith Manuscript History, vol. A-1, 127.
8. Revelation, July 20, 1831, in *JSP*, D2:7–8 [D&C 57:1–3].
9. "The Elders Stationed in Zion to the Churches Abroad, in Love, Greeting," *The Evening and the Morning Star* 2 (July 1833): 6.
10. "A History, of the Persecution, of the Church of Jesus Christ of Latter Day Saints in Missouri," December 1839–October 1840, in *JSP*, H2:207–11.
11. Letter to Church Leaders in Jackson County, Missouri, Aug. 18, 1833, in *JSP*, D3:263–64.
12. "A History, of the Persecution," in *JSP*, H2:213–222.
13. Letter from Edward Partridge, between Nov. 14 and 19, 1833, in *JSP*, D3:348.
14. Letter to Edward Partridge and Others, Dec. 10, 1833, in *JSP*, D3:377; see also Psalm 46:10.
15. Revelation, Dec. 16–17, 1833, in *JSP*, D3:389–97 [D&C 101].

TERRIBLE REBUKE AND UNBOUNDED BENEVOLENCE

By Matt Lund

In describing the Prophet Joseph Smith, Parley P. Pratt coupled two characteristics that seem paradoxical. Joseph's rebuke was "terrible as the lion," Parley wrote, and yet his benevolence was "unbounded as the ocean."[1] Similarly, Eliza R. Snow, who had "ample opportunity" to judge the Prophet's daily walk and conversation, observed his affectionate and forgiving nature but also his "severe and cutting rebukes."[2] The pairing of these qualities may appear incompatible, particularly for a prophet of God. Yet, it was often Joseph's loving concern for others that led him to reprove sharply. Additionally, he believed in showing increased love afterward toward those he rebuked. For Joseph, compassion and mercy went hand in hand with reproof.

The Lord's interaction with Joseph provided a pattern. Distressed over his own sins in his youth, Joseph cried "unto the Lord for mercy," and the Lord spoke to him in a vision, saying, "Joseph, my son, thy sins are forgiven thee." Joseph testified that his soul was filled with love and for many days he rejoiced.[3] In this earliest account of the First Vision, Joseph emphasized God's benevolence. Through the many revelations that followed, the Prophet personally witnessed and experienced the Lord's compassion, mercy, loving counsel, encouragement, praise, and desire to protect and bless.[4]

Joseph also experienced divine reproof. The Lord severely chastised the Prophet after the loss of 116 pages of the original Book of Mormon manuscript. "How oft you have transgressed the commandments and the laws of God," the Lord declared, "and have gone on in the persuasions of men." Joseph should have been more faithful, not fearing man more than God. Yet, the Lord softened His words of reproof with encouragement to repent and reminded Joseph of God's mercy.[5]

The Lord often reproved the Saints both individually and collectively, sometimes mildly and at other times severely.[6] Yet, the Lord taught that His chastening is an expression of His love. "Whom I love I also chasten that their sins may be forgiven," the Lord declared.[7] As with Joseph in the episode with the lost manuscript pages, the Lord reproved the Saints but then provided encouragement and reminders of His mercy. As Joseph came to learn of God's love, he showed the same uncompromising expectation that people can do better. The Lord's revelations taught him the need for both compassion and reproof in helping the Saints become the people the Lord intended.

Joseph's compassion is shown in a letter he wrote to Harvey Whitlock, a member who had become estranged from the Church. In 1835, Harvey wrote in despair to Joseph that he had sunk himself in "crimes of the deepest dye." He asked Joseph if he was still within the Lord's reach of mercy and pleaded with the Prophet to inquire of the Lord on his behalf.[8] Joseph replied that upon reading Harvey's letter, "the floodgates of my heart were broken up: I could not refrain from weeping, I thank God, that it has entered into your heart, to try to return to the Lord and to his people." In his reply, Joseph included a revelation in which the Lord admonished Harvey to return to Him, forsake his sins, and live a more virtuous life. If he did so, his sins would be "blotted out from under heaven." Joseph also conveyed God's love. "He has heard your prayers," Joseph wrote, "and holds forth the hand of paternal affection for your return." He assured Harvey that the Saints were willing to receive him again into full fellowship.[9]

Just as Joseph acted as the messenger of divine mercy, he also acted as voice for divine reproof. "Verily thus Saith the Lord," a November 1835 revelation began, "mine anger is kindle[d] against my servant Reynolds Cahoon because of his covetous and dishonest principles in himself and family." If Reynolds did not repent and set his house in order, chastisement awaited him. The Lord commanded Joseph to "go and declare unto him these words." Joseph immediately delivered this message. Reynolds humbly "acknowledged that it was verily so."[10]

One week later, the Prophet "took up a labour" with several Church members, including his uncle John Smith, his counselor Sidney Rigdon, and John Corrill. Joseph corrected each of them: his uncle for remarks made to a congregation regarding the case of an excommunicated Church member; Rigdon for publicly disputing John Smith's remarks, which Joseph felt undermined his uncle's influence in the Church; and Corrill for not partaking of the sacrament. Each showed contrition.[11]

Joseph once remarked to the Saints that his frequent admonitions were part of his prophetic duties. Whether serving as voice for the Lord or acting according to his own judgment, Joseph labored to correct errors he perceived in Church members. He recognized that taking "such a course of conduct was not calculated to gain the good will of all." He did not reprove them to "incur their displeasure or mar their happiness" but rather because he loved them. Reproof became necessary for their temporal and spiritual welfare.[12] Yet, Joseph acknowledged that he sometimes reproved too harshly. "I have sometimes spoken to[o] harsh from the impulse of the moment," he told members of the Quorum of the Twelve, "and inasmuch as I have wounded your feelings brethren I ask your forgiveness, for I love you."[13]

Joseph's example during the expedition of the Camp of Israel, later known as Zion's Camp, reveals how his loving concern for others converged with his willingness to reprove. During the long journey to Missouri, Joseph walked alongside his men, ate the same food, slept in the same tents, and experienced the same hardship. The Prophet denied himself any special privileges. On one occasion, he discovered that some men had been served sour bread, "while he had received good sweet bread from the same cook." The Prophet reproved the cook for his partiality, saying he "wanted his brethren to fare as well as he did, and preferred to eat his portion of sour bread with them."[14]

The hardships of the journey produced grumbling and strife among some in the company. Sylvester Smith, a member of the Kirtland high council, was one who frequently complained and quarreled with others. On one occasion, Joseph sharply reproved Sylvester for refusing to share his bread with Parley Pratt. Apparently, Sylvester had more than he needed, yet he turned Parley away telling him to look elsewhere. It may have been because Parley was not of his company. After Joseph learned of the incident, he told Sylvester he had done wrong. The Prophet did not want anyone to retire to bed hungry because others refused to share their food. When Sylvester justified his actions, Joseph said he had acted "contrary to the principles of Christ" and that his "mind was darkened in consequence of this covetous spirit."[15]

On another occasion, Sylvester and his company entered camp one evening marching to the tune of a fife. This may have excited Joseph's watchdog, which barked and snapped at Sylvester, who in turn threatened the dog and "used much abusive language to Joseph."[16] The next morning, Joseph reproved several men for their contentious spirit. To help them see what he meant, the Prophet imitated their attitude and language by saying, "If a dog bites me I will kill him—if any man insults me, I will kill him—if any man injures me, I will injure him." Sylvester responded, "If that dog bites me I'll kill him." Joseph rejoined, "If you kill that dog, I'll whip you." The Prophet then asked the men if they were not ashamed by this sort of behavior. Joseph said that he was. Such conduct was unbecoming a follower of Christ.[17] The Prophet desired to help camp members live so as to merit the guidance and blessings of the Lord.

After returning to Kirtland, Sylvester criticized the Prophet's leadership, saying he had behaved improperly during the expedition. Before the Kirtland high council Sylvester charged Joseph with "criminal conduct," claiming he had been slandered by the Prophet's public rebukes. The council exonerated Joseph.[18] Sylvester eventually published an apology.[19] Though Sylvester was released from the high council, a few months later the Prophet called him as one of the initial members of the Seventy.[20]

Indicative of his forgiving nature, Joseph evinced no hard feelings toward Sylvester.

Years later, Joseph articulated the duty of priesthood bearers to lead through kindness, long-suffering, and love unfeigned. They also had a duty to reprove "betimes with sharpness, when moved upon by the Holy Ghost" and then show an "increase of love" afterward toward the person.[21] This mix of love and sharp reproof characterized the personality and leadership of Joseph Smith. Like the Lord, he loved others enough to reprove them. Though at times he acted hastily and even harshly, Joseph considered his fellow Latter-day Saints worth the time and trouble to correct. In this way, he strove to help them live up to the Lord's expectations and qualify for His rich blessings.

Matt Lund is an instructor and curriculum writer for Seminaries and Institutes of Religion.

Notes

1. Parley P. Pratt, *Autobiography of Parley P. Pratt* (Salt Lake City: Deseret Book, 1985), 32.
2. Edward Tullidge, *The Women of Mormondom* (New York: Tullidge and Crandall, 1877), 65–66.
3. History, ca. Summer 1832, in *JSP*, H1:11–12.
4. For examples, see Revelation, June 1829, in *JSP*, D1:71 [D&C 18:10–15]; Revelation, Sept. 1830, in *JSP*, D1:178–79 [D&C 29:1–3]; Revelation, Aug. 12, 1831, in *JSP*, D2:39–40 [D&C 61:2]; Revelation, Aug. 2, 1833, in *JSP*, D3:200–201 [D&C 97:1–5]; Revelation, Oct. 12, 1833, in *JSP*, D3:324 [100:1–8]; and Letter to the Church and Edward Partridge, ca. Mar. 20, 1839, in *JSP*, D6:362, 365–66 [D&C 121:1–9].
5. Revelation, July 1828, in *JSP*, D1:8 [D&C 3:6–7].
6. For examples, see Revelation, Sept. 1830, in *JSP*, D1:185 [D&C 28:5–6]; Revelation, Sept. 1830, in *JSP*, D1:187–88 [D&C 30:1–2]; Revelation, May 9, 1831, in *JSP*, D1:306–7 [D&C 50:6–8]; Revelation, May 6, 1833, in *JSP*, D3:90 [D&C 93:41–50]; Revelation, Dec. 16–17, 1833, in *JSP*, D3:389–90 [D&C 101:1–9]; and Revelation, June 22, 1834, in *JSP*, D4:73–74 [D&C 105:2–6].
7. Revelation, June 1, 1833, in *JSP*, D3:106 [D&C 95:1].
8. Letter from Harvey Whitlock, Sept. 28, 1835, in *JSP*, D4:443–46.
9. Letter and Revelation to Harvey Whitlock, Nov. 16, 1835, in *JSP*, D5:60–62.
10. Journal, Nov. 1, 1835, in *JSP*, J1:81; see also Revelation, Nov. 1, 1835, in *JSP*, D5:29–30.
11. Journal, Nov. 8, 1835, in *JSP*, J1:86.
12. Discourse, Apr. 6, 1837, in *JSP*, D5:356.
13. Minutes, Jan. 16, 1836, in *JSP*, D5:152.
14. George A. Smith, Memoirs, 26, 39, CHL.

15. Minutes, Aug. 28–29, 1834, in *JSP*, D4:126, 131–32.

16. George A. Smith, Memoirs, 34–35.

17. Minutes, Aug. 28–29, 1834, in *JSP*, D4:129–30; George A. Smith, Memoirs, 35.

18. Minutes, Aug. 11, 1834, in *JSP*, D4:97–101; Minutes, Aug. 23, 1834, in *JSP*, D4:108–9; Resolutions, ca. Aug. 23, 1834, in *JSP*, D4:110–14; Minutes, Aug. 28–29, 1834, in *JSP*, D4:120–35.

19. Sylvester Smith to Oliver Cowdery, Oct. 28, 1834, in *Latter Day Saints' Messenger and Advocate*, Oct. 1834, 1:10–11.

20. Minutes, Sept. 24, 1834, in *JSP*, D4:173–74; Minutes, Discourse, and Blessings, Mar. 1, 1835, in *JSP*, D4:272.

21. Letter to Edward Partridge and the Church, ca. Mar. 22, 1839, in *JSP*, D6:394 [D&C 121:43].

JOSEPH SMITH AND THE PERPLEXITY OF PANDEMICS

By Matthew J. Grow and Matthew C. Godfrey

Pandemics perplex. Long after the anxiety has receded, the suffering has subsided, and the dead have been buried, troubling questions remain. Epidemic disease often seems to strike indiscriminately, taking the young and the old, the healthy and the vulnerable, men and women, the righteous and the wicked.

"Where is God in a pandemic?" asked a Jesuit priest in a *New York Times* editorial in late March 2020 as COVID-19 bore down upon the city. "The honest answer," wrote Father James Martin, "is: We don't know." But he believed that Christians and non-Christians alike could find solace in the example of Jesus Christ, who chose to be fully human and enter into a world of suffering, who consistently sought out the sick and the suffering, and who blessed them throughout His ministry.[1]

Religious figures in past ages have not been as hesitant as Father Martin to answer the question as pandemics have ravaged humanity. Their answers often centered on the idea that pandemics strike to punish sinners. In an age saturated with religion and before germ theory and modern medicine, this idea had tremendous explanatory power.

Joseph Smith and the Saints faced these questions as a cholera epidemic swept the United States in the early years of the Church. The epidemic began in India in 1826, appeared in Canada in June 1832, and gradually made its way into the United States, traveling generally along waterways.[2] As thousands died, panic and anxiety spread among the public. "Every new story adds to the general stock of alarm; and under such feverish sensibility, much anxiety is created," one newspaper reported.[3] Although the pandemic had eased by 1834, smaller outbreaks continued.[4] Preachers were confident that the disease was sent by God to punish sinners.[5]

The Saints followed the news of the spread of cholera with deep concern. In July 1832, Joseph Smith wrote to William W. Phelps that "cholera is cutting down its hundreds in the city of New York" and was "raging" in other cities in the eastern United States. Joseph also relayed information from a letter he had received from his cousin Almira Mack Scobey, who was visiting friends in Detroit: "cholera is raging in that city to an alarming degree, hundreds of families are fleeing to the country and the country people have torn up the bridges and stopped all communication and even shot peoples horses down under them who attempt to cross the river on any express." The disease was "so malignant that it baffles the skill of the most eminent Phisicians."[6]

Americans had reason to fear. The disease struck quickly, violently, and ruthlessly. Those afflicted with it experienced "a torment of the bowels," as well as vomiting, "insatiable thirst, tension of the sinews and calves of the legs and arms," and fever.[7] Because of the diarrhea and vomiting, the disease could lead to severe dehydration and death in a matter of hours.

Joseph Smith and the Saints encountered cholera most tragically at the end of the Camp of Israel expedition (later known as Zion's Camp). In 1833, Church members had been driven from Jackson County, Missouri. In the early months of 1834, Joseph had led a group of over 200 men, accompanied by a smaller number of women and children, from Ohio to Missouri in an attempt to help the Saints return to their homes. After arriving in Missouri, Joseph received a revelation in June 1834, informing the camp that the Lord recognized their sacrifice but the time had not yet come to reclaim lands in Jackson County.[8]

As the expedition started to disband and prepare for their return, the cholera hit. According to Heber C. Kimball, "About 12 o clock at night we began to hear the cries of those who were seized with the cholera and they fell before the destroyer; even those on guard fell with their guns in their hands to the ground." The nightmarish scene continued the next day: "We had to exert ourselves considerable to attend to the sick for they fell on every hand."[9] Amasa Lyman found it difficult to describe the camp's condition: "This was a scene that can be more easily imagined than described, to see men stricken down in a moment, and in a short hour the ruddy glow of health displaced by the palor of death."[10]

For the next several days, members of the camp struggled with the sickness. It even spread into the community of Saints living in Clay County, Missouri. Thirteen members of the expedition perished from the disease; Sidney Gilbert, one of the Church's leaders in Missouri, also died. The youngest victim was six-year-old Phebe Murdock, a daughter of a Camp of Israel member, who was staying with the Gilberts.[11]

Most camp members responded to the outbreak with humility, faith, and service. Like religious leaders in other days who walked into sickrooms ridden with disease, putting themselves in peril, the men of Zion's Camp tended to the sick.[12] There was no social distancing here. Joseph Bates Noble remembered that he spent nearly two days "puking and purging powerfully then cramping from head to foot in the most powerful manner with a burning fever in my bowels." Seeing his intense suffering, Brigham Young, Joseph Young, Heber Kimball, and several others encircled him and prayed for his relief. "Never had I experenced before such a manifestations of the blessing of god as at this time," Noble stated. "Through the faith of my brethren that was in exercise for me, I got up and with there assistance put on my close [clothes]."[13]

Heber Kimball, after spending hours praying for those afflicted and burying several who died, also contracted the disease. In his suffering, he went to the home of Peter Whitmer in Clay County and found Vienna Jaques, another Church member, there. "I received great kindness" from the Whitmers, Heber recalled, as well as from Vienna, "who administered to my wants and also to my brethren." Reflecting back on their service to him, he noted, "May the Lord reward them for their kindness."[14]

Seeing the suffering of those who had selflessly joined the Camp of Israel to rescue the Missouri Saints, Joseph Smith was pained. When his teenage cousin Jesse Smith died from cholera, Joseph took it "very hard," according to James H. Rollins, a friend of Jesse's living in Missouri, "as he undoubtedly had been entrusted with his care by the boy's parents."[15] Even though Joseph himself contracted the disease, he still helped those in need. "Joseph Smith and others, strove with there mights to rebuke the destroyer," Joseph Bates Noble remembered, "and continued to do it, till the lord told him [cholera] to go away."[16]

Like most Christians in history who have faced pandemics, Joseph Smith and the Saints worried that the scourge had been sent by God to punish them. During the march to Missouri, the camp had suffered from constant complaining and bickering. On June 3, Joseph had stood on a wagon wheel and told the camp that the Lord was not pleased with their "murmuring, and fault finding and want of humility" and was preparing "a severe scourge." "I cannot help it," Joseph told the camp members. "By repentance and humility and the prayer of faith, the chastisement may be alleviated," he continued, "but cannot be entirely turned away."[17]

Trying to process this information, 16-year-old George A. Smith, cousin to the Prophet, first believed that the scourge would come at the hands of the Saints' enemies, who were threatening to attack the expedition seemingly at every turn. George came to believe, however, that Joseph's prophecy was fulfilled not by the sword but by the cholera. Other men in Zion's Camp, including Joseph at least for a time, agreed that the disease was a chastisement from the Lord.

But if Joseph believed that the Camp of Israel had been punished with cholera, he later gained additional insight. The following February, he told brothers Brigham and Joseph Young that he had seen a vision of those who had died of the disease. "The Lord knows, if I get a mansion as bright as theirs," Joseph Smith told them, "I ask no more." "At this relation he wept," Joseph Young recorded, "and for some time could not speak."[18]

Joseph Smith and the other Saints tried to understand what was happening to them, turning first to the idea of divine punishment. But, ultimately, Joseph's vision showed him the individuals who died were in heaven, suggesting that their suffering and deaths were not a punishment for sins. As in many issues in life, when facing a pandemic and trying to answer the question of "why," "we see through a glass, darkly."[19] We generally do not understand fully why pandemics come, what is the mix between germs and contingent human actions, and what is the role of the divine. But, even not knowing some things, we can (like Joseph and the early Saints) pray and seek priesthood blessings and serve others when faced with such challenges.

In the April 2020 general conference, Church leaders—facing an empty auditorium but speaking to Latter-day Saints around the world—sought to uplift their audience with expressions of sympathy and with messages of looking forward. Their themes were not apocalyptic, nor did they speak about the punishments of God. Rather, they pointed to the future and toward Jesus Christ. As President Russell M. Nelson said, "During times of deep distress, as when illness reaches pandemic proportions, the most natural thing for us to do is to call upon our Heavenly Father and His Son—the Master Healer—to show forth Their marvelous power to bless the people of the earth."[20] The members of the Camp of Israel had learned the importance of turning to God in their distress, just as we have been counseled today.

Matthew J. Grow is a general editor of the Joseph Smith Papers Project and the managing director of the Church History Department.

Matthew C. Godfrey is the managing historian and a general editor of the Joseph Smith Papers Project.

Notes

1. James Martin, "Where Is God in a Pandemic?" *New York Times*, Mar. 22, 2020, https://www.nytimes.com/2020/03/22/opinion/coronavirus-religion.html.
2. Charles E. Rosenberg, *The Cholera Years: The United States in 1832, 1849, and 1866* (Chicago: University of Chicago Press, 1962), 25–34; J. S. Chambers, *The Conquest of Cholera: America's Greatest Scourge* (New York: Macmillan, 1938), 64.

3. "The Cholera" and "Our City," *Detroit Courier*, July 12, 1832, [2].

4. G. F. Pyle, "The Diffusion of Cholera in the United States in the Nineteenth Century," *Geographical Analysis* 1, no. 1 (Jan. 1969): 59–65; John S. Bowron, *Observations on the Origin and Causes of Malignant Cholera* (New York: Charles S. Francis, 1835), 21–24.

5. Adam Jortner, "Cholera, Christ, and Jackson: The Epidemic of 1832 and the Origins of Christian Politics in Antebellum America," *Journal of the Early Republic* 27, no. 2 (2007): 233–64.

6. "Cholera Morbus," *The Evening and the Morning Star*, July 1832, 1:32; Letter to William W. Phelps, July 31, 1832, in *JSP*, D2:267–69.

7. T. H. Pollard, "Asiatic Cholera and Cholera Morbus," *Boston Medical and Surgical Journal* 57 (Sept. 10, 1857): 109.

8. Revelation, June 22, 1834, in *JSP*, D4:74 [D&C 105:9].

9. Autobiography of Heber C. Kimball, 16, CHL.

10. "Amasa Lyman's History," *Millennial Star*, Aug. 12, 1865, 27:502.

11. Max H Parkin, "Zion's Camp Cholera Victims Monument Dedication," *Missouri Mormon Frontier Foundation Newsletter* 15 (Fall 1997): 4–5.

12. An estimated 42–45 percent of priests during the black death (the bubonic plague) in Europe died, a percentage higher than the rest of the population because of the priests' service to the sick. See John Kelly, *The Great Mortality: An Intimate History of the Black Death, the Most Devastating Plague of All Time* (New York: Harper Perennial, 2006), 224. Cholera is a water-borne bacterial disease, and transmission generally occurs through drinking or eating contaminated water or food. The participants in the Camp of Israel likely did not understand the method of transmission.

13. Joseph Bates Noble, Autobiography, 8–9, in Reminiscences, 1836–66, CHL.

14. Autobiography of Heber C. Kimball, 15–17, CHL.

15. James H. Rollins, Reminiscences, 5, CHL.

16. Noble, Autobiography, 9.

17. George A. Smith, Memoirs, 26–27.

18. Joseph Young, *A History of the Organization of the Seventies* (Salt Lake City: Deseret News, 1878).

19. 1 Corinthians 13:12. Throughout their lives, many participants in the Camp of Israel understood the cholera pandemic as at least partly an expression of God's punishment. (See, for example, "Zion's Camp Festival," *Deseret News*, Oct. 13, 1866, 4.)

20. Russell M. Nelson, "Opening the Heavens for Help," General Conference, Apr. 2020, ChurchofJesusChrist.org.

THE EMOTIONAL WORK OF THE GATHERING

By James Goldberg

In the Church today, we tend to remember Joseph Smith in broad strokes. We remember teachings. A few key moments: Joseph praying in the Sacred Grove, shut in a Missouri prison, out preaching in the open air of Nauvoo. We remember the concept of gathering: that Joseph drew together people from here and there to build up cities and temples. But 200 years have left the lived details of that work fuzzy. We don't actually remember the stress and sweat it took to bring together the real, individual people who gathered.

It's there, where the rubber hits the road, that I am most fascinated by Joseph Smith. What sort of emotional work did it take just to keep the early Church together?

In principle, of course, we acknowledge Church members are not perfect. Years of being caught up in other people's lives in a branch or a ward are enough to teach anyone we all fall short of our ideals. But I still think we underestimate what the first generation of Latter-day Saints were up against.

A lot of early Latter-day Saints grew up *hard*. Many families, like the Smiths when Joseph was young, were poor and needed to move a lot. Many had fathers or other members who drank heavily: American alcohol consumption peaked in 1830 at three times today's rate.[1] Many early Saints had known physical violence in the home. Others experienced abuse in their formative years while working as apprentices or domestic servants. Most had watched loved ones die, often after nursing them through sicknesses and severe injuries. Many knew the pain of abandonment as a spouse, parent, or other relative simply walked away, off into the country's vast frontier.

Ideals may shape our goals, but baggage shapes our reflexes. As a rule, early Latter-day Saints were not easygoing. They got in each other's way. Since their culture primed them to be especially sensitive to questions of respect in public settings, their disagreements could rapidly spin out of control. And because the Church was still young and small, every explosion of personal drama was a threat to the faith's sustainability.

Records Joseph Smith left behind give us glimpses into the minefield of personalities and emotions he picked his way through day by day. We have only passing references to some of Joseph's visions,[2] but pages and pages, for example, dedicated to resolving an extended dispute that started with frayed tempers on the Camp of Israel (later Zion's Camp) march and an argument about Joseph's dog.[3] Hurt feelings among leaders inspired revelations that early Saints printed in the Doctrine and Covenants.[4] The emotional work of keeping the community together was real. Participants recognized it as important.

Years after I first read its minutes, I still find myself thinking about the Kirtland high council meeting held on October 29, 1835.[5] That's the day William Smith (an Apostle and Joseph's younger brother) brought a charge against David Elliott and his wife, Mary Elliott, for physically abusing David's oldest daughter, Lucina.

The weight of the situation still comes through in the written testimony. Aaron Lyon, a neighbor, testifies about whipping marks he saw on Lucina's body. His wife, Roxana, says Mary Elliott once threatened to kill Lucina with a broomstick. A Sister Osgood, who lived with the Elliott family a few years before, remembers Lucina being so distraught about her family situation she wanted to throw herself down a well. Erastus Babbitt remembers the family's troubles becoming a topic of public conversation at the time.

It's easy to identify with William for bringing charges. Surely something needed to be done.

And yet, what could be? Most child abuse laws and protection agencies in the United States date back only to the 1960s.[6] In the 1830s, people didn't worry yet about the dangers of physical discipline. William's charge was not that David Elliott had whipped his daughter but that he had done so "unreasonably."[7] The Church's options were limited. The high council could withdraw fellowship from David and Mary Elliott. But would that help Lucina when she went back home? Would a second round of public shaming change her father's and stepmother's behavior, or just increase their volatility?

We don't know exactly what the family dynamic was like, but it can't have been simple. Abuse tends to have a long history. David Elliott's early life was complicated. His mother died before he was two. When David was in his teens, his father had accepted a $100 payment to bind David in service for seven years to a blacksmith who David remembered as a "a perfect tyrant and a hard master."[8] As Latter-day Saints, we believe everyone has moral agency. But we can also recognize a person's experience limits the options he sees. What William Smith viewed as unreasonable abuse may have felt normal to David.

The dynamic between Mary and the Elliott children was also strained. The family had been through a lot. David's first wife abandoned the family shortly after Lucina was born. His second wife died, leaving four more children. By 1835, Mary had given birth to two more and was raising seven children altogether. Under the strain of their struggles, she might well have felt defensive about the repeated public scrutiny her parenting came under.[9]

The Church could rebuke the Elliotts, but rebuke alone might not produce change.

In the disciplinary council, Joseph Smith speaks instead in defense of David Elliott. I didn't love reading that in the minutes, but I also noticed the fine line the council's judgment walks. Joseph Smith and Oliver

Cowdery rule "that the complaint was not without foundation, yet the charge had not been fully sustained." They focus on David rather than Mary. Without condemning him, they note "he has acted injudiciously" and say "he ought to have trained his child in a way, that she should not have required the rod at the age of 15 years."[10] While taking care to allow the accused parents to save face, Joseph and Oliver find a way to discourage physical punishment for Lucina.

Is it enough? I don't know. Bad habits die hard. Broken family dynamics don't change easily: they rarely change at all. And deep despair like Lucina felt doesn't disappear even if the beatings stop.

Is it enough? Is gentle persuasion enough in the face of suffering?

And yet, what other options does the Church have in 1835?

Still, the day's trouble is not over. William Smith, ever passionate when he sees injustice, refuses to let the matter rest. After the council's recess, he returns with additional witnesses against Mary Elliott's treatment of the Elliott children.

There's soon a gap in the minutes. After introducing a Sister Childs as the first witness, the clerk, Orson Hyde, stops writing midsentence.

Joseph Smith's journal gives us the only indication of the tension playing out. Apparently, William also invited Lucy Mack Smith to testify. Joseph's journal notes she "began to relate circumstances that had been brought before the church and settled." As the presiding officer, and perhaps concerned about the Elliotts' emotional dynamics, Joseph objects. Things escalate quickly. "Br. William Smith arose and accused me of invalidating or doubting my mother's testimony," Joseph notes, "which I had not done nor did I desire to do." Joseph asks William to sit down, but an agitated William won't. "I finally ordered him," Joseph recounts. "He said he would not unless I knocked him down." Exasperated by his brother's attitude, Joseph almost walks out, staying only at their father's request. "The house was brought to order," the account concludes, "after much debate."[11]

Neither Joseph's journal nor Orson Hyde's minutes say what happened next. Somehow, when Hyde's notes resume, Mary Elliott is confessing to the council and seeking forgiveness. David Elliott, though already acquitted, confesses too.[12] Maybe something really is changing in Lucina's family. Maybe it will last.

Lucina doesn't kill herself. Genealogical records make clear she marries, has children.[13] She doesn't appear to stay in the Church, but it's not easy to separate a hard family experience from the religious world around it.

And we know deep wounds don't just disappear. In the weeks after the case, William still feels stung and slighted. Things get worse before they get better: the Elliott case begins the spiral that soon leads to William punching Joseph in a public meeting.[14]

It takes Joseph steady, persistent, anguished work through the rest of the year to restore good feelings in his own family.[15]

And it's that often anguished persistence I admire most in Joseph Smith. I don't know if he got the Elliott case right. I don't need him to get everything right, especially in a world where every choice seems to carry a different shade of wrong. I just need him to keep trying, keep working, to hold on through all the volatility of human nature to his belief that we can build something together, a Zion together, a place to welcome Christ when He returns to heal us all.

James Goldberg's plays, essays, and short stories have appeared in numerous publications; he currently writes for the Church History Department.

Notes

1. Jed Woodworth, "The Word of Wisdom: D&C 89," in *Revelations in Context: The Stories behind the Sections of the Doctrine and Covenants*, ed. Matthew McBride and James Goldberg, ChurchofJesusChrist.org.
2. For example, see "Minutes, 17 February 1834," pp. 29–30, josephsmithpapers.org. Joseph mentions having seen in a vision "the order of Councils in ancient days," but he doesn't give many details.
3. Minutes, Aug. 11, 23, and 28–29, 1834; Sept. 24, 1834, in "Minute Book 1," josephsmith papers.org.
4. See, for example, "Revelation, 1 June 1833 [D&C 95]," josephsmithpapers.org; and "Revelation, 23 July 1837 [D&C 112]," josephsmithpapers.org.
5. Minutes, Oct. 29, 1835, in "Minute Book 1," josephsmithpapers.org.

6. John E. B. Myers, "A Short History of Child Protection in America," in *The APSAC Handbook on Child Maltreatment*, 3rd ed., ed. John E. B. Myers (Thousand Oaks, CA: Sage Publications, 2010).

7. Journal, Oct. 29, 1835, in "Journal, 1835–1836," p. 11, josephsmithpapers.org.

8. "History Written by David Elliott," FamilySearch, https://www.familysearch.org/photos/artifacts/11839875.

9. See "David Elliott," FamilySearch, https://www.familysearch.org/photos/artifacts/98588290.

10. Minutes, Oct. 29, 1835, in "Minute Book 1," p. 128. While the high council estimated Lucina's age as 15, the transcript of David Elliott's personal history lists Lucina's birthdate as August 3, 1822, which would have made her 13 at the time of the council meeting. ("History Written by David Elliott.")

11. Journal, Oct. 29, 1835.

12. Minutes, Oct. 29, 1835, in "Minute Book 1," pp. 128–29.

13. "Lucina Elliott," FamilySearch, https://www.familysearch.org/tree/person/details/KJ44-LS8.

14. Journal, Dec. 16, 1835.

15. Joseph's attempts at reconciliation took place from the October council until January. For the moment of reconciliation, see Journal, Jan. 1, 1836.

"THE SPIRIT OF CONFESSION AND FORGIVENESS": JOSEPH SMITH'S 1835 RECONCILIATION WITH HIS BROTHER WILLIAM

By Anthony R. Sweat

Think of the latest difficulty you had with an immediate family member. Everyone experiences such conflicts, to varying degrees. Family DNA is a double helix, after all, joining spousal adoration with marital arguments, sibling loyalty and rivalry, and parent-child bonds with intense power struggles. Joseph Smith and his family were no different. They loved and raged, defended yet undermined, and fought and forgave. This essay examines these dual family dynamics through a violent fight in December 1835 between Joseph and his younger brother William, both young men in their twenties at the time. It shows how—despite the difficult aftermath—they chose to heal and maintain their family bonds through humble confession and divine forgiveness.

The Debate

In December 1833 Joseph pronounced a blessing on William that provides potential insight into his brother's character:

> Bro William is as the firce Lion who devideth not the spoil because of his strength and in the pride of his heart he will neglect the more weighty matters until his soul is bowed down in sorrow and

then he shall return and call on th[e] name of his God and shall find forgivness and shall wax valient therefor he shall be saved unto the utter most . . . the blessings of the God of Jacob shall be in the midst of his house notwithstanding his rebelious heart.[1]

Despite this rollercoaster character, William was chosen as one of the original Twelve Apostles in the latter days in February 1835.[2] Months later, in the late fall of 1835, William participated in a debate club, hosted in his home, in which some Church elders debated gospel subjects. Joseph Smith also attended and observed. He was impressed by the reasoning and points of view but was concerned that the debate caused the elders to argue in ways inconsistent with gospel principles.[3]

The elders resumed their meeting at William's home on Saturday, December 12, 1835. Joseph was again present, and even participated in the debate, but he was called away before it could conclude to attend to a sick member of the Church.[4] The meeting continued on Wednesday, December 16, again at William's home. This time the discussion wasn't cut short by someone who became sick but by someone who became enraged.

The Fight

As the December 16 meeting concluded, Joseph commented on the potential "impropiety of continueing the school fearing that it would not result in good." William "oposed these measures" and instead proposed that the club continue and that the elders pick a new subject.[5] Joseph harshly rebuked his brother, telling William he "manifisted, an inconciderate and stubourn spirit" and that in this state he "was as ugly as the Devil."[6] Joseph Smith Sr. was there (he lived in the same home with William) and, like a father trying to keep the peace, told everyone to be quiet. Joseph was about to leave, but his pride got the better of him after William insisted that he could say whatever he wanted in his own home. At this point, Joseph said that he had helped construct the home and that his father lived there as well as William. Thus, Joseph reasoned he had "the privilege of speaking in [his] fathers house." In hindsight, Joseph should have walked away. Instead, he said to William, "I will speak, for

I built the house, and it is as much mine as yours."[7] At this, William "bec[a]me much enraged" and physically attacked Joseph.[8]

Joseph would later write to William, describing the fight from his perspective:

> I saw that your indignation was kindled against me, and you made towards me, I was not then to be moved, and I thought, to pull off my loose coat, least it should tangle me, and you be left to hurt me, but not with the intention, of hurting You, but you was to[o] soon for me, and having once fallen into the hands of a mob, and now been wounded in my side, and now into the hands of a brother, my side gave way, and after having been rescued, from your grasp, I left your house, with, feelings that were indiscribale, the scenery had changed, and all those expectations, that I had cherished, when going to your house, of brotherly kindness, charity forbearance and natural, affection, that in duty binds us not to make eachothers offenders for a word.
>
> But alass! abuse, anger, malice, hatred, and rage with a lame side with marks, of violence heaped upon my body me by a brother, were the reflections of my disapointment, and with these I returned home, not able to sit down, or rise up, without help.[9]

These were two strong, full-grown brothers in a physical altercation. These were two Church leaders fighting!

The Letters

William wrote a letter to Joseph two days later, on December 18, humbly extending an olive branch of confession:

> Br. Joseph— Though I do not know but I have forfeited all right and title to the word brother, in concequence of what I have done. . . . When I reflect upon the ingury I have done you, I must confess that I do not know what I have been about— I feel sorry for what I have done and humbly ask your forgiveness— I have not confidence as yet to come and see you for I feel ashamed of what I have done, and as I feel now I feel as though all the confessions that I could make verbally or by writing would not be sufficient to atone for the

transgression— be this as it may, I am willing to make all the restitution you shall require.[10]

Joseph wrote in return, "In your letter you asked my forgivness, which I readily grant, but it seems to me, that you still retain an idea, that I have given you reasons to be angry or disaffected with me. . . . You know that it is my duty to admonish you when you do wrong this liberty I shall always take, and you shall have the same privilege."[11]

Although Joseph began by quickly granting forgiveness, it is hard not to read some lingering difficulty in Joseph's reply, and a desire to yet put William in check. Joseph concluded: "I desire brother William that you will humble yourself, I freely forgive you. . . . And now may God have mercy upon my fathers house, may God take away enmity, from betwe[e]n me and thee, and may all blessings be restored, and the past be forgotten forever."[12]

Despite the well-intended words, however, there were still unresolved emotions. The next day, December 19, Joseph wrote in his journal, "I have had many solemn feelings this day Concerning my Brothe[r] William."[13] The following day the internal turmoil continued, as Joseph recorded that he spent time with his family amid "many serious reflections."[14]

The Reconciliation

On New Year's Day 1836, a type of family intervention occurred to try to heal the breach. Joseph and William met along with their brother Hyrum, their father, their uncle John Smith, and their family friend Martin Harris. The Prophet recorded in his journal:

> [My father] expressed his feelings on the ocasion in a verry feeling and pathetic manner even with all the sympathy of a father whose feeling[s] were wounded deeply on the account of the difficulty that was existing. While he addressed us the spirit of God rested down upon us in mighty power, and our hearts were melted Br. William made an humble confession and asked my forgiveness for the abuse he had offered me and wherein I had been out of the way I asked his forgiveness, and the spirit of confession and forgiveness, was mutual among us all, and we covenanted with each other

in the Sight of God and the holy angels and the brethren, to strive from henceforward to build each other up in righteousness, in all things. . . . Gratitude swelled our bosoms, [and] tears flowed from our eys.[15]

It seems unlikely that this was the first Smith family council ever called to deal with difficulty. A culture of confession and forgiveness seems to have been cultivated by Joseph Smith Sr. and Lucy Mack Smith in their family. Brigham Young later remembered that when Joseph Smith made a mistake, "no man ever lived that was more ready and willing to repent of it and confess than he."[16] The Smith family may not have been perfect, but they knew how to perfectly forgive.

The Lesson

Although this encounter between Joseph and William may be painful to read about, it is also insightful. While this story has elements of pride, power, violence, justification, abuse, and malice, those characteristics are ultimately overcome by confession, forgiveness, love, repentance, and humility. And isn't that what Christianity is all about? Indeed, the Lord revealed through Joseph Smith in 1831 that His disciples are "required to forgive all men."[17] Although the double helix of family DNA inherently carries opposing experiences, the negative can always be outweighed by the positive if we will choose to live the gospel of love, the gospel of confession, the gospel of forgiveness—the gospel that can heal and seal eternal family ties.

Anthony R. Sweat is an associate professor of Church history and doctrine at Brigham Young University.

Notes

1. Journal, Dec. 18, 1833, in "Journal, 1832–1834," pp. 38–41, josephsmithpapers.org; see also "Blessing to William Smith, 28 September 1835," p. 10, josephsmithpapers.org.
2. "Minutes, Discourse, and Blessings, 14–15 February 1835," p. 149, josephsmithpapers.org.
3. Journal, Nov. 18, 1835, in "Journal, 1835–1836," p. 46, josephsmithpapers.org.
4. Journal, Dec. 12, 1835.
5. Journal, Dec. 16, 1835.

6. Letter to William Smith, Dec. 18 or 19, 1835, in "Journal, 1835–1836," p. 82.
7. Letter to William Smith, Dec. 18 or 19, 1835.
8. Journal, Dec. 16, 1835.
9. Letter to William Smith, Dec. 18 or 19, 1835.
10. "Copy of a Letter from Br. William Smith," in "Journal, 1835–1836," pp. 77–79. For the letter from William to Joseph, see also "Letter from William Smith, 18 December 1835," josephsmithpapers.org.
11. Letter to William Smith, Dec. 18 or 19, 1835.
12. Letter to William Smith, Dec. 18 or 19, 1835.
13. Journal, Dec. 19, 1835.
14. Journal, Dec. 20, 1835.
15. Journal, Jan. 1, 1836.
16. Brigham Young, Sermon, May 20, 1866, shorthand transcription by LaJean Purcell Carruth, CHL.
17. "Revelation, 11 September 1831 [D&C 64]," p. 109, josephsmithpapers.org.

IMAGINING A BETTER FUTURE: THE CONTEXT AND DEVELOPMENT OF JOSEPH SMITH'S VIEWS ON RACE AND SLAVERY

By Jessica M. Nelson

As is the case with any historical figure, those who research the life of Joseph Smith will find statements, behaviors, and political beliefs that can only be fully understood in the context of the time in which he lived. Understanding the political and social circumstances Joseph Smith lived in is not secondary information but is integral to the process of learning who he was. Approaching historical figures in a holistic way that encompasses the environment they lived in allows us to measure them within the parameters of their time and not standards that developed later. And while the situations that we face might be different, we can apply the principles we find when studying the lives of people who came before us. We can see that our own ideas about people and cultures can change based on experience, thought, and additional information.

The American Civil War did not start until almost 17 years after Joseph Smith's death, but he lived during the period of intense conflict in the United States that preceded the war. One of the reasons Missourians wanted to expel the Saints from Jackson County in 1833 was they believed that Church members would try to turn enslaved Black people against slaveholders. William W. Phelps had published an editorial in a Church newspaper giving direction on how free Black people might legally enter Missouri.[1] Slavery was legal in Missouri, and this editorial led some Missourians to believe that the Church was trying to recruit free Black people to come and convince enslaved people that they should be free.[2] Although Church members were not trying to encourage rebellions of enslaved people, Missourians used this imagined threat to justify violence and persecution against Church members. After the Saints had been driven from Jackson County, the Church printed a declaration in 1835 that restricted missionaries from preaching to enslaved people without permission from slaveholders and stated that it would not "meddle with, or influence [slaves] in the least to cause them to be dissatisfied with their situations in this life, thereby jeopardizing the lives of men."[3]

A year later, Joseph Smith wrote a letter to Oliver Cowdery affirming that the Church would not align itself with the abolitionist movement and that if slavery was immoral, the first people to realize it would be the Southerners: "If slavery is an evil, who, could we expect, to first learn it? Would the people of the free states, or would the slave states? All must readily admit, that the latter would first learn this fact." Joseph also stated that slaveholders should expect to stand before God and answer for how they treated their slaves, and therefore no one else could judge them. He recognized that those who opposed slavery would say that he was being "uncharitable, unfeeling, unkind, and wholly unacquainted with the Gospel of Christ." He answered that counterpoint by citing scriptures in the Bible commonly used by white Christians to support slavery, including scriptures in Genesis declaring that the descendants of Canaan were cursed and would be servants until the curse was lifted.[4]

Latter-day Saints might be surprised when they discover that someone who translated the Book of Mormon passage "he denieth none that come unto him, black and white, bond and free, male and female . . . all are alike unto God" could be a voice for slavery.[5] In that same letter to Cowdery, Joseph wrote that freeing the slaves would "lay waste the fair States of the South, and set loose, upon the world a community of people who might, peradventure, overrun our country and violate the most sacred principles of human society,—chastity and virtue."[6] In short, Joseph Smith absorbed and echoed the racism prevalent in his day that justified slavery on the grounds that abolition would destroy the South and that Black people should remain enslaved because of a supposed biblical curse. Such views were devoid of compassion and empathy. Latter-day Saints might expect that a prophet like Joseph Smith—someone who was *not* "unacquainted with the Gospel of Christ"—would align with the minority of American Christianity that opposed the violent enslavement of other human beings, but that was not the case in 1836. This was due, in part, to the Church trying to survive in Missouri without becoming targets of violent mob rage. Historians can supply more context to these points, but in essence, Joseph Smith in 1836 sounded no different than most white Americans who opposed radical abolitionism and who used the Bible to reinforce that political view.

Fortunately, these were not the last words that Joseph Smith spoke on the subject. His views developed over the next several years, perhaps because of his experience with persecution, state-sanctioned violence, and the loss of his own rights and liberties in Missouri during 1838–39. As a result of these experiences, Joseph became weary of the federal government's inability to protect the rights of its citizens. In early January 1843, while Joseph was in Springfield, Illinois, for a habeas corpus hearing in federal court, Apostle Orson Hyde asked him for his thoughts on the "situation of the Negro" in the United States. Joseph responded by saying Black people were enslaved mentally and physically from birth but had the same abilities as whites to be successful. Further, Joseph stated that a successful, educated Black man riding in a carriage, "risen by the power of his mind to his exal[te]d state. of r[e]spectability," could be found in a place like Cincinnati in the free state of Ohio. When Hyde countered by saying that Black people would try to "rise above" him if they were given equality, Joseph responded, "If I raised you to be my equal & then attempt to oppress you would you not be indignant, & try to rise above me?"[7] In this private setting with Hyde and other friends in 1843, Joseph Smith spoke about Black freedom differently than he had publicly in 1836. Living in a free state like Illinois may have played a role in how Joseph expressed his views, but this dialogue from 1843 shows a more empathetic position on the issue than he had previously expressed.

This is not to suggest that Joseph Smith was on the forefront of racial progress in the United States at that time. But he *did* progress and his views *did* evolve over time, even if he did not go further than a moderate antislavery position. His 1844 presidential campaign pamphlet outlined America's hypocrisy for claiming to be a land of liberty when millions of people were enslaved and many others were wasting away in prisons for debt or fabricated offenses. Joseph argued that the federal government could use the revenue from the sale of public lands to buy the freedom of enslaved people. He also supported an idea—popular among moderate circles of the time—that free Black people should be removed from the United States or in other ways kept segregated from white society.[8] However, in his personal life, Joseph did not live by a policy of segregation. In 1839, he sold land in Nauvoo to Elijah Able, a free Black convert, missionary, and priesthood holder.[9] In 1843, he warmly received Jane Manning James and her family of free Black converts in his home, told them they were "among friends," and applauded their faith.[10]

As a white man leading a persecuted religious minority group, racial equality and abolition were not Joseph Smith's causes. He was more concerned about securing his own freedom and protecting the civil rights he and the Latter-day Saints held claim to as American citizens. On this front, Joseph Smith's imagination was boundless. In the last several months of his life, Joseph was involved in creating two memorials (or petitions) asking the federal government to exercise power on the Saints' behalf.[11] Both petitions had very little chance of success but demonstrate that Joseph Smith was trying to create innovative solutions to the problems his community faced.

Joseph Smith's political views on the abolition of slavery and the rights of Black people belong in a larger discussion about the history of race and racism in America. However, there are principles that we can use when examining how Joseph viewed these issues over the course of his life. He demonstrated that our positions need not be fixed; if we can learn from life experience and remain open to new information, we can alter those positions. Joseph's question to Orson Hyde in 1843 is important: how might your perspective on an issue change if you switched places with someone from an oppressed or disadvantaged group? Can we, like Joseph, encourage our friends and family to be empathetic toward those who have struggles different than our own? It is much easier to identify problems and to advocate for solutions to the issues that we immediately face, like Joseph did when trying to figure out how to protect the Latter-day Saints. But by adding antislavery policies to his presidential platform, Joseph also showed his ability to change and to imagine a better America than the version he inherited. His life raises the question of how we might take the ambitious dreams we have for ourselves and include solutions that address wider problems.

Jessica M. Nelson is a historian and documentary editor with the Joseph Smith Papers Project.

Notes

1. "Free People of Color," *The Evening and the Morning Star* 2, no. 14 (July 16, 1833).
2. Letter from John Whitmer, July 29, 1833, in *JSP*, D3:192–93.
3. Declaration on Government and Law, ca. Aug. 1835 [D&C 134], in *JSP*, D4:484.
4. Letter to Oliver Cowdery, ca. Apr. 9, 1836, in *JSP*, D5:237–42.
5. 2 Nephi 26:33.
6. Letter to Oliver Cowdery, ca. Apr. 9, 1836, in *JSP*, D5:237–38.
7. Journal, Jan. 2, 1843, in *JSP*, J2:212.
8. *General Smith's Views of the Powers and Policy of the Government of the United States*, Feb. 7, 1844 (Nauvoo, IL), josephsmithpapers.org; Journal, Mar. 7, 1844, in *JSP*, J3:198.
9. Bond to Elijah Able, Dec. 8, 1839, in *JSP*, D7:81–85.
10. "Jane Manning James Autobiography, ca. 1902," [3], CHL.
11. "Memorial to the United States Senate and House of Representatives, 21 December 1843," pp. 16–17, josephsmithpapers.org; "Memorial to the United States Senate and House of Representatives, 26 March 1844," josephsmithpapers.org.

THE CHARACTER OF JOSEPH SMITH: INSIGHTS FROM HIS PAPERS

By Elizabeth A. Kuehn

After Joseph Smith's death, his friend William W. Phelps penned a poem memorializing the Prophet. One oft-quoted line from this poem, which is now a beloved hymn, expresses the hope that "millions shall know 'Brother Joseph' again."[1] To me, that does not mean that people will know simply that Joseph Smith existed but that they will know *him*—his personality, strengths, and weaknesses. One of the best ways I have found to really know Joseph Smith is through his papers.

I have had the opportunity for the last several years to study his papers as a writer, historian, and documentary editor for the Joseph Smith Papers Project. While the work of a writer and historian is self-evident, the role of a documentary editor is less obvious. Documentary editing is a field of scholarly editing for historical documents, with the objectives of preserving and transcribing texts.[2] Many notable women and men in history have documentary editing projects dedicated to collecting and publishing their papers. Some of the primary responsibilities of documentary editors include studying documents to understand when they were created, by whom, and for what purpose, and how they were received. Documentary editors study minute details that help answer these questions; they specialize in handwriting identification, understand the genres and language of a period, and track the close details of an individual's life.

An outgrowth of the Joseph Smith Papers Project has been a greater ability to personalize Joseph Smith. The project provides transparency into Joseph's life, revealing his mistakes and the personal quirks and foibles that make someone real and relatable. The project unveils Joseph's humanness by making the historical texts created by and for him central and accessible. A study of Joseph's papers provides readers with a multifaceted understanding of who he was as a religious and civil leader. Of more significance on the personal level, they reveal his character. A few of the traits that I have found meaningful as I have studied his papers are his humility and gratitude, his willingness to admit his imperfections, and his tender heart and compassion for others.

Humility and Gratitude

Joseph's papers reveal many instances of his humility and gratitude as he relied on others to provide for him, his family, or the fledgling Church. One of my favorite examples is his early interactions with Vienna Jaques, a convert from Boston who provided desperately needed financial relief to the Kirtland Saints through a sizable monetary donation in the early 1830s. Having decided to join the Church, she first moved to Ohio from Boston, then proceeded to follow the Prophet's direction to join the Saints in Jackson County, Missouri. Joseph wrote her a memorable letter in September 1833, shortly after she had arrived in Missouri. Joseph called himself her "unworthy brother in Christ" and reflected on spiritual promptings that urged him to remember her in his prayers and write to her. The letter referenced Vienna's generous donation, noting that it made her a "Savior of life." Joseph asked God to comfort and bless Vienna: "let thy handmaid live till her soul shall be satisfied in beholding the glory of Zion."[3] The letter captures not only Joseph's humility but also his immense gratitude for the Saints who supported him and the Church both spiritually and financially. The need for financial help—to expand the Church and care for the poor—was constant in Joseph's time as prophet, and his papers include other similar earnest and poignant blessings that convey his gratitude for the Saints' generosity.

Imperfection

Although sometimes held to an expectation of perfection then and now, Joseph Smith never characterized himself as a perfect person. His papers document many difficult moments where he faced public criticism. For example, in 1837, the Latter-day Saints in Kirtland experienced economic and spiritual crises amid a nationwide financial panic. This led some of the Twelve Apostles and other Church leaders to criticize the Prophet and question his leadership.[4] For his part, Joseph was quick to forgive the repentant but disappointed by those who moved from doubt to apostasy.[5] Among those who repented were Parley P. Pratt and Orson Pratt. A letter written by Latter-day Saint Eliza Carter in July 1837 reported the Pratts' confessions, as they admitted that their statements against the Prophet were false and that their "minds had ben darkened there hearts hardened."[6] Just as the Pratt brothers confessed their failings, so too did Joseph. According to Carter's letter, Joseph and Sidney Rigdon acknowledged that "they ware men Subject to Light [like] passions as other men and they had ured [erred] in some things as well as others."[7]

The doubt and dissent of the 1837 crisis in Kirtland deeply affected Joseph. But it may have let him better appreciate the expectations that his followers placed on him. Years later he cautioned the Saints in Nauvoo against unfair expectations: "If they expected perfection from him, he should expect it from them, but if they would bear with his infirmities and the infirmities of the brethren, he would likewise bear with their infirmities."[8] Speaking to the Relief Society in 1842, Joseph told them, "The wrong that I do is thro' the frailty of human nature like other men. No man lives without fault."[9]

I have come to admire Joseph Smith not because he was flawless but because he was flawed. Seeing his shortcomings increases my respect for him and my personal faith in him. I see a man striving to be better, sometimes failing, but giving his all—his comfort, his financial solvency, his reputation—for a higher purpose. It also gives me hope. Rather than seeing the Prophet Joseph as perfect and unreachable, I find that he had many of the same challenges and imperfections that you and I have. His imperfections help me relate to him and provide guidance as I too struggle through my weaknesses to become better.

Tenderheartedness

Perhaps the most poignant character trait of Joseph Smith's that I have found in his papers is his tender heart. His moments of compassion, love, and camaraderie are easy for me to relate to and are spread throughout his papers, especially his correspondence. In one such moment in 1832, he expressed empathy for his brother Hyrum Smith at the loss of a child, reflecting that he and Emma knew that pain well.[10] Another letter in 1836 highlights his joy at seeing Kirtland Church leaders, some of whom had struggled with pride and hierarchical concerns, come together in unity to prepare to dedicate the Kirtland Temple.[11] Also noteworthy are instances when he expressed frustration and despair at the unjust treatment his family and friends endured as they were forcibly exiled from Missouri while he was imprisoned and powerless to help them.[12]

Conclusion

Spending the last several years immersed in Joseph's history has brought him to life for me in ways I would never have imagined. It has made him become someone I feel I know. This familiarity comes through careful study of the documents that capture the course of his life, moments both simple and profound and the connection between them. Too often I think we understand Joseph's life in isolated events: the First Vision, the organization of the Church, his imprisonment in Liberty jail, the Martyrdom. These touchstones, though deeply meaningful, are not the full picture. A more comprehensive study of the Prophet Joseph's life, through analyzing his records, offers a deeper and more encompassing understanding of his character. Such study also provides the opportunity to see him develop and change over his lifetime, adding much-needed complexity and balance to our picture of him. He was a complex man, and when we allow ourselves to understand him as such, to see his imperfections, the moments of confidence and moments of frustration, it is then that we come to better know Joseph.

Elizabeth A. Kuehn is a historian and documentary editor for the Joseph Smith Papers Project and is lead editor of the project's Financial Records series.

Notes

1. William W. Phelps, "Praise to the Man," 1844; see *Hymns of The Church of Jesus Christ of Latter-day Saints* (Salt Lake City: The Church of Jesus Christ of Latter-day Saints, 1985), no. 27.
2. See Mary-Jo Kline and Susan Holbrook Perdue, *A Guide to Documentary Editing*, 3rd ed. (Charlottesville: University of Virginia Press, 2008), 1–34.
3. Letter to Vienna Jaques, Sept. 4, 1833, in *JSP*, D3:288–96.
4. Letter from Parley P. Pratt, May 23, 1837; Charges against Joseph Smith Preferred to Bishop's Council, May 29, 1837, in *JSP*, D5:386–91, 393–97.
5. See Historical Introduction to Revelation, July 23, 1837 [D&C 112], in *JSP*, D5:410–14.
6. Eliza Ann Carter to James C. Snow, July 22, 1837, Collection of Early Church Documents, 1816–44, CHL.
7. Eliza Ann Carter to James C. Snow, July 22, 1837.
8. Journal, Oct. 29, 1842, in *JSP*, J2:164.
9. Minutes and Discourse, Aug. 31, 1842, in *JSP*, D10:456.
10. Letter to Emma Smith, June 6, 1832, in *JSP*, D2:251.
11. Journal, Jan. 13, 1836, in *JSP*, J1:151; Minutes, Jan. 13, 1836, in *JSP*, D5:138–43.
12. Letter to the Church and Edward Partridge, Mar. 20, 1839; Letter to Emma Smith, Mar. 21, 1839, in *JSP*, D6:356–75.

"THOUGH I WAS HATED . . . YET IT WAS TRUE": DISSENT, PERSECUTION, AND JOSEPH SMITH'S UNWAVERING TESTIMONY

By Casey W. Olson

At a time when many of Joseph Smith's friends had turned against him, calling him a fallen prophet, Joseph gave the testimony of his First Vision now found in the Pearl of Great Price. While millions have read his account, perhaps few are aware that it was written during one of the most difficult periods of Joseph's life. This essay explores the vicious opposition Joseph experienced in the months just before he recorded his testimony of the First Vision in 1838.[1]

Difficulties in Kirtland and Far West

Following the dedication of the Kirtland Temple in the spring of 1836, some of the Saints shifted their focus from spiritual to temporal concerns. Eliza R. Snow wrote of Church members who "drank in the love and spirit of the world" and "were filled with pride and hatred toward those who maintained their integrity."[2] While some members concentrated primarily on personal gain, Joseph Smith was deeply concerned with how to pay the debts the Church had incurred while constructing the temple and purchasing lands for the settlement of the Saints. In November 1836, he, Sidney Rigdon, and others established the Kirtland

Safety Society, a banking institution they hoped would provide needed funds for the Church and stimulate Kirtland's economy.[3] However, a combination of local opposition and a severe national financial recession in 1837 led to the close of the Kirtland Safety Society only ten months after it had opened.[4] Because Joseph had encouraged the Saints to invest in the society, some blamed him personally for their losses when it failed.[5] For many Saints, resentment led to doubt and dissent.

Internal conflict and apostasy plagued the Church throughout the winter of 1837–38. While some of the Saints quietly held misgivings, others openly criticized the Prophet. Approximately 10 to 15 percent of the members in Kirtland withdrew from the Church. The Saints' long-standing enemies in Kirtland reveled in the discord, uniting with some dissenters to harass those who remained devoted to the Church. As opposition mounted, animosity toward Joseph Smith spread from Ohio to Missouri. Many of Joseph's closest friends and associates—including the Three Witnesses of the Book of Mormon, one of his counselors in the First Presidency, and several members of the Quorum of the Twelve Apostles—turned against him.[6]

Some of the more radical dissenters forcefully sought to overthrow the Church, denouncing Joseph and the Saints as heretics.[7] They threatened the Prophet and anyone who stood by him—particularly his loyal defender Brigham Young. On December 22, 1837, Brigham was forced to flee Kirtland to evade those "who had threatened to destroy him because he would proclaim publicly and privately that he knew by the power of the Holy Ghost that [Joseph] was a prophet of the most high God" and "had not transgressed and fallen as the apostates declared."[8]

As a new year dawned, opposition to Joseph and his supporters "continued to rage and grow hotter."[9] On January 12, 1838, the Prophet received a revelation directing the First Presidency to leave Kirtland. The Lord also assured them that He would be with them.[10] Joseph Smith and Sidney Rigdon acted immediately, mounting their horses and leaving Kirtland at ten o'clock that same night. Their families soon joined them on an 800-mile trek to Far West, Missouri.[11] One of the Saints wrote that "it is thought the lives of the presidents would have been taken" had they remained in Kirtland.[12] The timeliness of Joseph and Sidney's escape and the protection afforded them during their journey indicate the Lord indeed was with them. Joseph's history describes the intense journey to Far West:

> We were obliged to secrete ourselves in our wagons sometimes to elude the grasp of our pursuers who continued their race more than 200 miles from Kirtland armed with pistols and seeking our lives. They frequently crossed our track, twice they were in the houses where we stopped. Once we tarried all night in the same house with them, with only a partition between us and them, and heard their . . . threats concerning us if they could catch us. Late in the evening they came in our room and examined us, but decided we were not the men [they sought]. At other times we passed them in the streets, and gazed upon them and they on us, but they knew us not.[13]

About two months after Joseph had left Kirtland, he and his family were welcomed "with open arms and warm hearts" by the Saints in Far West. Although Joseph was temporarily safe, he was not free from challenges. He soon found that "various and many" falsehoods had been relayed from Kirtland to Far West.[14] In the months of March and April, several Church leaders in Missouri were excommunicated for actions ranging from the misuse of Church funds to "seeking to destroy the character of President Joseph Smith."[15] One of those leaders, John Whitmer, had been responsible for keeping the history of the Church. After withdrawing from the Church, John refused to give Joseph the records in his care.[16]

Joseph Smith's History and Testimony

In a rare moment of peace, Joseph began working on a new history on April 27, 1838.[17] Joseph opened the history by explaining that "the many reports which have been put in circulation by evil-disposed and designing persons" had created the need "to write this history, to disabuse the public mind, and put all inquirers after truth in possession of the facts."[18] But correcting misinformation was not the history's only purpose. Just one day earlier, the Lord had given Joseph a revelation instructing the Saints to "arise and shine forth, that thy light may be for a standard unto the nations."[19] Joseph's history would help fulfill that commandment by testifying to the world that God the Father and Jesus Christ had appeared to him in "a pillar of light . . . above the brightness of the sun," commencing the glorious latter-day Restoration of the gospel.[20]

In addition to testifying of his First Vision, Joseph highlighted the relentless opposition that had followed him since his boyhood. He noted that the "bitterest persecution and reviling" he experienced soon after his vision had "often caused [him] serious reflection both then and since." Joseph then observed: "I have thought since that I felt much like as Paul did when he made his defense before King Agrippa."[21] This reference to Paul's experience is insightful. Prior to Paul's appearance before Agrippa, he had boldly declared his willingness "to die . . . for the name of the Lord Jesus." Paul had then traveled to Jerusalem where he was nearly killed by a mob and imprisoned.[22] When he was brought before Agrippa, Paul recounted *his* first vision in which he saw "a light from heaven, above the brightness of the sun" and "heard a voice" speaking his name. Paul testified that the resurrected Lord had appeared to him and called him to be "a minister and a witness" of the gospel of Jesus Christ. When Paul was accused of madness, he held his ground, affirming that he spoke "the words of truth and soberness."[23]

In mentioning this account, the Prophet Joseph noted that "all the persecution under Heaven" could not destroy the reality of Paul's vision or prevent him from fulfilling his mission—not even if "they should persecute him unto death." Joseph then added these powerful words: "So it was with me."[24] From the time of his own First Vision, Joseph had faced the hostility of peers and "men of high standing."[25] Like Paul, he had been "in perils among false brethren."[26] He had been reviled, shunned, and hounded. On a cold night in March 1832, he had been dragged from his home, severely beaten, and tarred and feathered.[27] A little more than two months later, Joseph wrote to his wife, Emma: "God is my friend. In him I shall find comfort. I have given my life into his hands. I am prepared to go at his call." Joseph continued that 1832 letter by echoing the words of Paul: "I desire to be with Christ. I count not my life dear to me, only to do his will."[28]

Now, in the early months of 1838, Joseph's life had again been threatened. However, nothing could diminish his testimony or deter him from accomplishing the Lord's work. Looking back through 18 years of persecution, Joseph affirmed the reality of God's first revelation to him: "I had actually seen a light and in the midst of that light I saw two Personages, and they did in reality speak unto me . . . and though I was hated and persecuted for saying that I had seen a vision, yet it was true. . . . I knew it, and I knew that God knew it, and I could not deny it."[29]

Conclusion

Chosen by the Father and the Son to be Their premier witness in this final dispensation, Joseph Smith was fearless in testifying of Them. Joseph's 1838 account of his First Vision not only narrates his sacred experience but also affirms his unwavering commitment to the cause of the Restoration—no matter the opposition. To the end of his life, Joseph Smith continued to teach and testify of God the Father, the Lord Jesus Christ, and the sacred truths They revealed to him.[30]

Casey W. Olson holds a PhD in curriculum and instruction and has contributed to numerous publications on Latter-day Saint history, scripture, and doctrine.

Notes

1. "Primary Accounts of Joseph Smith's First Vision of Deity," josephsmithpapers.org.
2. Eliza R. Snow, *Biography and Family Record of Lorenzo Snow, One of the Twelve Apostles of The Church of Jesus Christ of Latter-day Saints* (Salt Lake City: Deseret News, 1884), 20.
3. Constitution of the Kirtland Safety Society Bank, Nov. 2, 1836, in *JSP*, D5:299; see also Articles of Agreement for the Kirtland Safety Society Anti-Banking Company, Jan. 2, 1837, in *JSP*, D5:324.
4. "Kirtland Safety Society" (glossary entry), josephsmithpapers.org.
5. Minutes, Sept. 3, 1837, in *JSP*, D5:420.
6. Historical Introduction to Journal, March–September 1838, in *JSP*, J1:227; John Corrill, *A Brief History of the Church*, 26, in *JSP*, H2:161; Milton V. Backman Jr., *The Heavens Resound: A History of the Latter-day Saints in Ohio, 1830–1838* (Salt Lake City: Deseret Book, 1983), 328. Backman noted that nearly half of those who dissented in this period later returned to full fellowship in the Church.
7. "History, 1838–1856, volume B-1 [1 September 1834–2 November 1838]," p. 779, josephsmithpapers.org.

8. "History, 1838–1856, volume B-1 [1 September 1834–2 November 1838]," p. 6 [addenda], capitalization standardized.
9. "History, 1838–1856, volume B-1 [1 September 1834–2 November 1838]," p. 780.
10. Revelation, Jan. 12, 1838–C, in *JSP*, D5:500.
11. "History, 1838–1856, volume B-1 [1 September 1834–2 November 1838]," p. 780.
12. Hepzibah Richards to William Richards, Jan. 22, 1838, in Journal History of the Church, Jan. 22, 1838, CHL.
13. "History, 1838–1856, volume B-1 [1 September 1834–2 November 1838]," p. 780, spelling and punctuation standardized.
14. Letter to the Presidency in Kirtland, Mar. 29, 1838, in *JSP*, J1:245–46, spelling standardized.
15. Synopsis of Oliver Cowdery Trial, Apr. 12, 1838, in *JSP*, J1:251–53, spelling and capitalization standardized; Editorial Note, in *JSP*, J1:250–51.
16. Revelation, ca. Mar. 8, 1831–B, in *JSP*, D1:284–86 [D&C 47:1–4]; Revelation, Nov. 11, 1831–A, in *JSP*, D2:129–32 [D&C 69:2–8]; Letter to John Whitmer, Apr. 9, 1838, in *JSP*, J1:249.
17. Journal, Apr. 27, 1838, in *JSP*, J1:260; Historical Introduction to History Drafts, 1838–ca. 1841, in *JSP*, H1:195. Sidney Rigdon and George W. Robinson assisted Joseph Smith in writing the first portion of this history. Although the original draft no longer exists, James Mulholland copied the 1838 material into "Draft 2" (the first part of volume A-1 of the multivolume history) in 1839. This essay thus quotes from Draft 2.
18. History, ca. June 1839–ca. 1841 (Draft 2), in *JSP*, H1:204 [Joseph Smith—History 1:1], spelling standardized.
19. Revelation, Apr. 26, 1838, in *JSP*, D6:113 [D&C 115:5].
20. History, ca. June 1839–ca. 1841 (Draft 2), in *JSP*, H1:214 [Joseph Smith—History 1:16], grammar standardized.
21. History, ca. June 1839–ca. 1841 (Draft 2), in *JSP*, H1:216 [Joseph Smith—History 1:23–24], spelling standardized.
22. Acts 21:13–14, 30–33.
23. Acts 25:24; 26:13–25.
24. History, ca. June 1839–ca. 1841 (Draft 2), in *JSP*, H1:218 [Joseph Smith—History 1:24–25].
25. History, ca. June 1839–ca. 1841 (Draft 2), in *JSP*, H1:216 [Joseph Smith—History 1:22].
26. 2 Corinthians 11:26.
27. "History, 1838–1856, volume A-1 [23 December 1805–30 August 1834]," pp. 205–7, josephsmithpapers.org.
28. Letter to Emma Smith, June 6, 1832, in *JSP*, D2:251, punctuation and capitalization standardized. Compare with Paul's words in Acts 20:24.
29. History, ca. June 1839–ca. 1841 (Draft 2), in *JSP*, H1:218 [Joseph Smith—History 1:25], capitalization standardized.
30. "History, 1838–1856, volume F-1 [1 May 1844–8 August 1844]," p. 172, josephsmithpapers.org.

"IN TRUTH AND RIGHTEOUSNESS": JOSEPH SMITH AS STORYTELLER

By Scott A. Hales

False or exaggerated stories plagued Joseph Smith throughout his life. In 1823, the angel Moroni warned him that his name "should be both good and evil spoken of among all people."[1] Early critics of the Prophet wasted no time in fulfilling these words. When Joseph began writing a detailed history of the Church in 1838, he did so "in truth and righteousness," hoping to put to rest the "many reports . . . by evil disposed and designing persons in relation to the rise and progress of the Church of Jesus Christ of Latter day Saints."[2]

Yet Joseph himself was an engaging storyteller, and he frequently drew on the power of story to teach principles, defend the Saints, and champion the cause of Zion. By definition, stories narrate events, both true and false, and people have long told them to engage, entertain, and instruct audiences. This was particularly so in Joseph's day, when preachers regularly supplemented their sermons with true stories and anecdotes to interest and inspire their congregations.[3] When Joseph incorporated traditional elements of storytelling into his everyday speech, he did so not to dabble in fantasy or imagination but to set the record straight.[4] For him, story was a vehicle for truth.

Joseph's talent for storytelling manifested at an early age, perhaps around the time Moroni began preparing him to translate the Book of Mormon narrative. Joseph's mother, Lucy Mack Smith, recalled how he used to tell his family "some of the most amusing recitals" about the history preserved on the gold plates: "He would describe the ancient inhabitants of this continent; their dress, mode of travelling, and the animals upon which they rode; their cities, and their buildings, with every particular; he would describe their mode of warfare, as also their religious worship. This he would do with as much ease, seemingly, as if he had spent his whole life with them."[5]

The Prophet's critics would later seize on Lucy's memory to claim that Joseph fabricated the Book of Mormon. But the Prophet's younger brother William, who was 16 at the time Joseph received the plates, remembered that the family "never doubted" Joseph's stories. "I suppose if he had told crooked stories about other things we might have doubted his word about the plates, but Joseph was a truthful boy," William recalled. "That father and mother believed his report and suffered persecution for that belief shows that he was truthful."[6]

Today the best-known stories Joseph told are those he revealed "by the gift and power of God." The Book of Mormon, like many books in the Bible, is story-based scripture. It chronicles the rise and fall of a people of God through a series of interwoven stories about great prophets, missionaries, warriors, and kings. Some of these stories, like the account of Nephi and his brothers returning to Jerusalem to retrieve the brass plates,[7] have strong, simple narrative arcs that build suspense and arrive at a satisfying resolution. Others, like the account of the people of Limhi or the so-called "war chapters,"[8] are complex, multilayered narratives that juggle several stories (and literary genres!) into one sophisticated whole.

The stories Joseph told in his daily life never reached the same level of complexity as the Book of Mormon narrative. The Prophet was an informal storyteller, who sometimes incorporated anecdotes into his everyday conversations and sermons. Most of these anecdotes were autobiographical. Unfortunately, since Joseph shared most of these stories orally, few detailed accounts of them exist. Contemporary records of his sermons, mostly from the 1840s, make only vague mention of his storytelling. In February 1843, for instance, William Clayton recorded that "President Joseph related some of his history" while instructing the Saints.[9] Another Latter-day Saint, Robert D. Foster, reported a sermon wherein "Gen. Smith . . . recited the many woes through which he had passed."[10] Sometimes the Prophet attached lessons or morals to these stories. Willard Richards once recorded that "Joseph spoke 5 minutes" and "told an anecdote of [how] Sidney Rigdon and A[lexander] Campbell got up a community at Kirtland." From this story, Joseph apparently concluded that "big fish eat up the little," a possible allusion to the successful efforts of Latter-day Saint missionaries among Campbell's flock in northeast Ohio in the early 1830s.[11]

Wilford Woodruff's journal provides one of the best views of Joseph Smith's talent for oral storytelling. On June 30, 1843, Woodruff recorded a discourse in which the Prophet vividly recounted his recent experience of being abducted by law enforcement officers attempting to bring him back to Missouri to stand trial. Joseph narrated the story with dramatic detail and dialogue, doubtlessly captivating his audience of 7,000 Saints.

In the story, Joseph told how two officers took him by surprise, shoved "two cocked pistols to [his] head," and "then dragged [him] away" from his family. He also re-created the officer's profane speech, contrasting it with his own cool comportment. When his captors threatened to shoot him "nearly fifty times," he heroically called their bluff. "I turned to him, opened my bosom, and told him to shoot away," Joseph told his audience, "and I did it frequently."

Unfortunately, Woodruff reported nothing about how the Prophet delivered his story. Did Joseph mimic his captors' voices? Did he pantomime the arrest or bare his chest to his audience as he spoke? All Woodruff noted was that Joseph thought the story might be "pleasing" to his audience, suggesting that he may have recounted it with a light or humorous tone. Indeed, Joseph told the story to mock the extradition attempt and celebrate the power of the Nauvoo charter, which had allowed him to secure the writ of habeas corpus that ultimately freed him. Throughout the story, he portrayed his captors as a witless set of brutes. Joseph also ended the story with an ironic, smile-inducing reversal: both captors were served "a writ . . . for unlawful proceedings towards [him] and cruel treatment." Evidently delighted by the twist, Joseph quipped, "They could not get out of town that night."[12]

Perhaps the Prophet's most ambitious efforts as a storyteller were his written histories of the Church. The Prophet's first-known attempt to write a long narrative history was extraordinarily bold considering his inexperience as a writer and the Church's youth and relatively small size. It was to be "A History of the life of Joseph Smith Jr., an account of his marvelous experience, and of all the mighty acts which he doeth in the name of Jesus Christ," as well as "an account of the rise of the church of Christ in the eve of time."[13] Joseph abandoned the history almost as soon as he began it, but it paved the way for what became known as the "History of the Church," which he began in 1838 with the help of his clerks. This history told the story of the First Vision, the visitation of the angel Moroni, the recovery and translation of the gold plates, the restoration of the priesthood, the publication of the Book of Mormon, the organization of the Church, and other early milestones of the Restoration.

In this history, Joseph's skill as a storyteller shines in his riveting account of the First Vision. Following a standard narrative arc, Joseph recounts his journey from confusion over the "different [religious] denominations" of his day to certainty "so far as the sectarian world was concerned." The story becomes especially gripping when Joseph narrates his effort to "ask of God" which church was "right": "After I had retired into the place where I had previously designed to go, having looked around me and finding myself alone, I kneeled down and began to offer up the desires of my heart to God, I had scarcely done so, when immediately I was seized upon by some power which entirely overcame me and had such astonishing influence over me as to bind my tongue so that I could not speak. Thick darkness gathered around me and it seemed to me for a time as if I were doomed to sudden destruction."

Joseph masterfully builds suspense as his fate becomes more and more uncertain. Then, "at this moment of great alarm," his story reaches its climax. "I saw a pillar of light exactly over my head above the brightness of the sun," he recounts. "It no sooner appeared than I found myself delivered from the enemy which held me bound." The rest of the account narrates the end of Joseph's confusion. The Father and Son appear, and he learns that he is to join none of the existing churches, "for they were all wrong." Joseph has his answer.[14]

Although Joseph began his 1838 history to counteract false stories about him and the Church, it has since acquired a greater and more lasting significance as the founding narrative of the Latter-day Saints. Until the recent, groundbreaking work of the Joseph Smith Papers Project, subsequent histories of the Church depended primarily on the 1838 history to understand the Church's early history. Through its stories, Joseph Smith and those who helped him write it gave generations of Latter-day Saints a sense of their sacred past and the divine origins of the Church and the authority that governed it. They also helped the Saints understand and appreciate their place in human history and God's great plan of happiness. Most important, these stories showed Latter-day Saints what it meant to be a community united in the common cause of Zion. It should be no surprise that Latter-day Saints now recognize a portion of this history as sacred scripture (Joseph Smith—History 1:1–75).

Joseph Smith was not the most gifted or polished of storytellers. But he was an earnest storyteller who understood the unifying and refining power of story. "In this history I will present the various events in relation to this Church in truth and righteousness as they have transpired," Joseph declared at the start of his 1838 history.[15] In telling his story, he set out not only to give an accurate account of his life and the rise of the Church of Jesus Christ but also to produce a record that would be an immense force for good. Millions of Latter-day Saints throughout the world can now testify of his success.

Scott A. Hales is a general editor and writer for *Saints: The Story of the Church of Jesus Christ in the Latter Days.*

Notes

1. "History, circa June 1839–circa 1841 [Draft 2]," p. 5, josephsmithpapers.org.

2. "History, 1838–1856, volume A-1 [23 December 1805–30 August 1834]," p. 1, joseph smithpapers.org. Punctuation and spelling standardized in this and all subsequent quotations.

3. David S. Reynolds, "From Doctrine to Narrative: The Rise of Pulpit Storytelling in America," *American Quarterly* 32, no. 5 (Winter 1980): 481–91.

4. Both fictional and nonfictional storytelling rely on the same basic elements. In general, these elements are character, setting, conflict, plot, point of view, and theme. In *Storycraft: The Complete Guide to Writing Narrative Nonfiction* (Chicago: University of Chicago Press, 2011), journalist Jack Hart identifies structure and plot, point of view, voice and style, character, scene, action, dialogue, and theme as important elements of any strong narrative.

5. "Lucy Mack Smith, History, 1845," p. 87, josephsmithpapers.org.

6. J. W. Peterson, "Wm. B. Smith's Last Statement," *Zion's Ensign,* Jan. 13, 1894, 6.

7. See 1 Nephi 3–5.

8. See Mosiah 7–25; and Alma 43–63.

9. "Instructions, 9 February 1843 [D&C 129], as Reported by William Clayton," p. 53, josephsmithpapers.org.

10. "Remarks, 3 October 1843, as Reported by Robert D. Foster," p. [3], josephsmithpapers .org.

11. "Discourse, 14 September 1843, as Reported by Willard Richards," p. [94], josephsmith papers.org.

12. "Discourse, 30 June 1843, as Reported by Wilford Woodruff," p. [61], josephsmithpapers .org.

13. "History, circa Summer 1832," p. 1, josephsmithpapers.org.

14. "History, 1838–1856, volume A-1 [23 December 1805–30 August 1834]," pp. 2–4.

15. "History, 1838–1856, volume A-1 [23 December 1805–30 August 1834]," p. 1.

"OUR GREATEST OBJECT": BUILDING ZION ON EARTH

By Sharalyn D. Howcroft

Governor Lilburn Boggs's expulsion order in 1838 sanctioned the forcible removal of Latter-day Saints from the state of Missouri. The Prophet Joseph Smith, who was imprisoned on charges of treason and other crimes in the Clay County jail in Liberty, Missouri, anguished over the expulsion of the Saints from their Zion and his powerlessness to assist them. To all outside appearances, the Latter-day Saint concept of Zion had evaporated and its literal space in Missouri was no more, but to Joseph, God's grander conceptualization of Zion was still a reality. Recognizing the plausibility of his imminent death, Joseph acknowledged the work of God would continue. Church members were to gather in pockets of refuge between Kirtland, Ohio, and Far West, Missouri, and await further instruction from the Lord. In the meantime, the Saints were to gather information about their sufferings and losses in Missouri so they could appeal to the federal government for reparation. America would remain Zion to all who chose to gather there.[1]

Throughout his prophetic ministry, Joseph used the term *Zion* to mean different things. The process of building up Zion took different forms depending on context. He used *Zion* or *build up Zion* to describe an exact gathering location in the United States for Latter-day Saints, the general process of gathering the Saints, and the effort to build up the Church and to spread the gospel through missionary work. When describing Zion, Joseph also elaborated on the collective and individual characteristics of its inhabitants that were necessary so they could receive Jesus Christ at His Second Coming. This essay explores the meaning of Zion in each of these contexts using the revelations, translations, teachings, and writings of Joseph Smith.

Zion as a Location

Joseph Smith used *Zion* to identify an exact site of gathering for Latter-day Saints. Book of Mormon passages referenced God establishing Zion in America, and subsequent revelation through the Prophet identified Missouri as the gathering place for the Lord's people.[2] According to a July 1831 revelation, the center place for the City of Zion (or the New Jerusalem) was in Independence, Jackson County, Missouri.[3] The revelation also identified the location of a future temple there, provided instructions on purchasing land for distribution to Church members, and commanded that a printing establishment be built. Within a month of this revelation, Joseph, Sidney Rigdon, and others dedicated the City of Zion and a site for the temple in Independence.[4] Plans for the city were ambitious. It was slated to hold 2,600 residential lots, with 24 temples at its center and farms and fields for livestock on the city's periphery.[5] Approximately a thousand Latter-day Saints flocked to this literal Zion, eager to fulfill a revelation from God. Outlying Latter-day Saint settlements, including Kirtland, were called "stakes" of Zion.[6]

Less than two years after the center place had been identified, however, tensions erupted between the Saints and their Missouri neighbors. The printing press was destroyed, Bishop Edward Partridge was tarred and feathered, and Church members were expelled from Jackson County. The immediate hope for a temple and a Zion community was lost, yet the intention to redeem Zion persisted in revelation.[7] Hearing of the expulsion, Joseph and several Church leaders recruited volunteers and formed an expedition called the Camp of Israel (Zion's Camp) to travel to Missouri to assist in "redeeming Zion," meaning to help restore the Saints' lost lands.[8]

After traveling nearly a thousand miles in May and June 1834, the camp was disbanded; the redemption of Zion would not occur until after the Lord had bestowed an "endowment of power" in a house of the Lord in Kirtland.[9] With the Zion in Jackson County unredeemed, Joseph counseled the Saints to form another Zion community in Far West, Missouri. Missourians thwarted that Zion as well, leading Joseph and the Saints to start over again in Nauvoo, Illinois. In the meantime, Joseph's ideas about where Zion could be expanded, and by 1840, he defined the "land of Zion" as "all North and South America." He added that "any place where the Saints gather is Zion."[10]

Zion as a Cause

In addition to teaching about Zion as an actual physical location, Joseph Smith instructed the Saints that Zion was a cause that involved building up the Church and preaching the gospel. The elect of God were to be gathered from the world to build Zion and its stakes. These points of gathering would provide the Saints refuge from worldly destruction prior to the Second Coming.[11] "We ought to have the building up of Zion as our greatest object," Joseph stated.[12] It was an effort to be performed "by the counsel of Jehovah; by the revelations of heaven."[13] Revelations instructed individual Church members to "seek to bring forth and establish the cause of Zion"[14]—a commandment that became an invitation to "all those who have desires to bring forth and establish his work."[15] Though the plan to build the City of Zion in Missouri was frustrated by the expulsion of the Saints from Jackson County in 1833, the edict to build up the cause of Zion remained in force in its stakes. Efforts to build a temple in Kirtland accelerated. Saints were instructed to sanctify and purify themselves prior to being "endowed with power from on high" in the temple.[16] The endowment of power was an essential preparatory step for elders of the Church who were going on missions to preach the gospel and gather the elect to the stakes of Zion.[17]

The cause of Zion relied on saving ordinances for the living and the dead. Once the Saints were gathered and had built up Zion, they could become "Saviors on Mount Zion" by constructing temples, performing baptisms for the dead, and "receiving all the ordinances, baptisms, confirmations, washings, anointings ordinations, & sealing powers upon [their] heads in behalf of all [their] progenitors who are dead."[18] Though baptism for the dead was the only proxy ordinance performed during Joseph's lifetime, Joseph's prophetic foresight pointed to ordinances for the dead yet to come. He instructed the Saints that creating binding links between generations connected them to God and forged an unbroken priesthood link through the generations.[19]

Zion as a People

Joseph Smith also described Zion as a community of believers who were united in purpose. The notion of a latter-day Zion was rooted in a description of the ancient inhabitants of the city of Enoch who "were of one heart and one mind, and dwelt in righteousness; and there was no poor among them."[20] In a January 1831 Church conference, the Lord admonished the attendees by revelation that "if ye are not one, ye are not mine."[21] Joseph underscored this message, stating that the vigilant cultivation of unity would result in "the most glorious blessings" among individuals and the whole Church.[22] The highest blessings Heavenly Father has in store for His children and His Church required unity.

Latter-day revelation defined Zion as "the pure in heart."[23] Purity and righteousness, according to Joseph Smith, were essential components of Zion. "So long as unrighteous acts are suffered in the Church," he taught, "it cannot be sanctified, neither can Zion be redeemed."[24] The Prophet instructed Church members that the redemption of Zion was an individual and collective responsibility that required effort and obedience and a willingness by all to do their part. He said: "Let every one labor to prepare himself for the vineyard, sparing a little time to comfort the mourners; to bind up the broken-hearted; to reclaim the backslider; to bring back the wanderer; to re-invite into the kingdom such as have been cut off, by encouraging them to lay to while the day lasts, and work righteousness, and with one heart and one mind, prepare to help redeem Zion, that goodly land of promise, where the willing and the obedient shall be blessed."[25]

Conclusion

Just as was the case in the early Church, unity, purity, and a collective effort to build Zion are essential characteristics today of the inhabitants of Zion. Missionary work, the building up of the Church, and temple ordinances remain vital. We must prepare ourselves and help others prepare to serve in the Lord's cause. Building up Zion is not a to-do list of things that we systematically check off. Rather, it is a bold and exciting opportunity to witness the fulfillment of prophecy and scripture, to be part of a cause that binds the past, present, and future into one great whole. When we act in faith and earnestly strive to fill our role in the kingdom of God, God will expand our capacities, and we ourselves will become a vehicle for the fulfillment of prophecy. And as we build Zion in our stakes and purify ourselves to become a Zion people, we can be assured that when He comes again, "we shall be like him; for we shall see him as he is."[26] We will be a Zion people worthy to inherit the kingdom of heaven.

Sharalyn D. Howcroft is the project archivist for the Joseph Smith Papers Project.

Notes

1. Letter to Heber C. Kimball and Brigham Young, Jan. 16, 1839, in *JSP*, D6:310; Letter to the Church and Edward Partridge, Mar. 20, 1839, in *JSP*, D6:356.
2. 3 Nephi 20:22; Ether 13:3–6; Revelation, June 6, 1831, in *JSP*, D1:328 [D&C 52:3, 5].
3. Revelation, July 20, 1831, in *JSP*, D2:5 [D&C 57:3].
4. See "Volume 2 Introduction: Joseph Smith Documents Dating from July 1831 through January 1833," in *JSP*, D2:xix–xx; and "Part 1: Missouri, Summer 1831," in *JSP*, D2:3–4.
5. Plat of the City of Zion, ca. Early June–June 25, 1833, in *JSP*, D3:121; Revised Plat of the City of Zion, ca. Early Aug. 1833, in *JSP*, D3:243.
6. Journal, May 18, July 8, and Sept. 1, 1838, in *JSP*, J1:270, 282, 311.
7. Revelation, Dec. 16–17, 1833, in *JSP*, D3:390 [D&C 101:17, 55–57, 75]; Revelation, Feb. 24, 1834, in *JSP*, D3:461, 462–63 [D&C 103:21–22, 30, 37–40]; Letter to the Saints Scattered Abroad, June 1835, in *JSP*, D4:469; Council of Fifty, "Record," Mar. 11, 1845, in *JSP*, CFM:295.
8. Minutes, Feb. 24, 1834, in *JSP*, D3:453.
9. Revelation, June 22, 1834, in *JSP*, D4:69.
10. Discourse, ca. July 19, 1840, in *JSP*, D7:333.
11. See "Volume 1 Introduction: The 1830s Journals," in *JSP*, J1:xlix–l.
12. "Discourse, between circa 26 June and circa 4 August 1839–A, as Reported by Willard Richards," p. 70, josephsmithpapers.org.

13. "The Government of God," in Selections from *Times and Seasons*, July 15, 1842, in *JSP*, D10:278.

14. Revelation, Apr. 1829–A, in *JSP*, D1:34 [D&C 6:6]; Revelation, May 1829–A, in *JSP*, D1:50 [D&C 11:6]; Revelation, May 1829–B, in *JSP*, D1:55 [D&C 12:6].

15. Revelation, May 1829–A, in *JSP*, D1:50 [D&C 11:3]; Revelation, May 1829–B, in *JSP*, D1:55 [D&C 12:7].

16. Revelation, June 22, 1834, in *JSP*, D4:69 [D&C 105:11].

17. See "Part 1: 2 October–1 December 1835," in *JSP*, D5:4.

18. "Discourse, 21 January 1844, as Reported by Wilford Woodruff," p. [182], josephsmith papers.org.

19. "Discourse, 12 May 1844, as Reported by George Laub," p. 21, josephsmithpapers.org.

20. Moses 7:18.

21. Revelation, Jan. 2, 1831, in *JSP*, D1:229 [D&C 38:27].

22. Letter to the Quorum of the Twelve, Dec. 15, 1840, in *JSP*, D7:463.

23. Revelation, Aug. 2, 1833–A, in *JSP*, D3:198 [D&C 97:21].

24. Letter to Lyman Wight and Others, Aug. 16, 1834, in *JSP*, D4:102.

25. Letter to the Saints Scattered Abroad, June 1835, in *JSP*, D4:469.

26. 1 John 3:2; Moroni 7:48.

THE LONELY SOUL OF JOSEPH SMITH

J. Chase Kirkham

Latter-day Saints think of Joseph Smith as a visionary, and rightly so. During his life, he received heavenly manifestations, including visits from God, Jesus Christ, and angels. He introduced translated records of humanity's past and received visions of the afterlife. If improperly interpreted, however, these experiences can turn Joseph into a caricature of himself, a man who was constantly tuned into heaven. Although Joseph received striking visions and visitations, he was a lonely soul who struggled to understand how to fulfill God's will. But this loneliness—his experience of the absence of God's presence or direction—was formative. It shaped his prophetic voice, possibly even more so than the heavenly encounters did. But how did this work? How did Joseph's inner isolation foster his visionary worldview? When he found himself alone, Joseph reflected on and explored his inner world, which paradoxically was an experience tantamount to communing with God.[1] Three moments from Joseph's life demonstrate how loneliness fostered a rich communion with deity: his experiences before his First Vision, his time in Liberty jail, and his instruction during the April 1844 conference.

Prologue to the First Vision

Joseph recalled that as a boy he, at times, experienced great anxiety. He worried about his soul and the world—as if the fates of both were somehow connected.[2] The idea of joining a church also concerned him because his choice carried "eternal consequences"—deep thoughts for a child.[3] Finding no guidance in his religious culture, which was embroiled in a "war of words, and tumult of opinion," Joseph turned inward.[4] His mother, Lucy Mack Smith, recalled that Joseph differed from her other children because he was inclined to "reflection and deep study" over book learning.[5] One, however, should not assume from his mother's observation that Joseph never read. Hers, instead, was a statement about how Joseph preferred to learn. Consider how he engaged with the scripture James 1:5, "If any of you lack wisdom, let him ask of God, that giveth to all men liberally, and upbraideth not; and it shall be given him." When Joseph read this passage, it impressed him deeply. "It seemed to enter with great force into every feeling of my heart," he said. Joseph's account indicates that he first focused on how the scripture affected him, after which he returned to the text, which he read not once but "reflected on . . . again and again."[6] For Joseph, the act of thinking was not divorced from his emotions. This scripture first spoke to his heart and then to his mind.[7]

Thinking about this verse, however, was only one of "many things" he reflected on during the lengthy period before his First Vision, which was a time of inner struggle. He said his "feelings were deep" and used phrases such as "exceedingly distressed" and "great uneasiness" to describe his mental state. His lonely reflection, however, was fruitful, for it was during this time that he first discovered God. It is a mistake to assume that Joseph's first encounter with deity occurred during the First Vision. Before his prayer in the grove, he had already found God by observing nature, reading scripture, and pondering.[8] Joseph's First Vision from God, then, was not triggered alone from a passage in the New Testament but was the culmination of years of deep and solitary reflection.

Incarcerated Isolation

When today's Latter-day Saints reflect on the defining aspects of Joseph Smith's life, four events are often mentioned: the First Vision, the translation of the Book of Mormon, priesthood restoration, and the introduction of saving ordinances. These events were crucial aspects of Joseph's mission, but an undertaking just as central to his prophetic identity was his attempt to build the New Jerusalem in Missouri, a city where the Saints would gather to prepare for Christ's Second Coming. Indeed, it cannot be overemphasized just how important building Zion was for Joseph Smith. It was one of his defining projects until the Saints were expelled from Missouri during the winter of 1838–39. After the Saints gathered in Illinois, Joseph spent the rest of his life seeking justice for their losses.[9]

Joseph never built the New Jerusalem; instead, he ended up in prison, charged with treason for participating in the "Mormon War," the conflict with Missourians that led to the Saints' expulsion.[10] Even though he was incarcerated with others, Joseph experienced a deep loneliness in Liberty jail, for he did not know where God was. As he had done as a boy, Joseph approached God for wisdom, this time petitioning his creator to explain his absence—"O God, where art thou[?]" God responded by comforting Joseph and offering him perspective. This exchange appeared in a letter written to Church members on March 20, 1839, portions of which were later canonized in the Doctrine and Covenants. This and a letter written approximately two days later offer insights into Joseph's theological response to loneliness. Part of the March 20 letter captures Joseph's reflections on salvation, which include his instruction that one must think deeply and carefully to save a soul: "Thy mind O Man, if thou wilt lead a soul unto salvation must stretch as high as the utmost heavens, and search into and contemplate the lowest considerations of the darkest abyss, and expand upon the broad considerations of eternal expanse, he must commune with God." While in Liberty jail, Joseph found himself twice incarcerated: his body was bound by visible walls, while his mind was imprisoned in a seemingly boundless chasm. But this isolation was not without meaning. Stretching the mind, contemplating *both* heaven and hell, was an inner activity, Joseph wrote, that would bring one into the presence of God. Finding salvation and encountering God therefore required one, at times, to consider the abyss.

In a follow-up letter to the Saints, Joseph returned to this theme of deep contemplation. He recorded more of God's words, which transformed hell and the experience of darkness into a monster with a wide maw—"if the very jaws of hell shall gape open her mouth wide after thee." God informed Joseph that encountering this beast would provide him experience. In his March 20 letter, Joseph had indicated that comprehending God's designs required "time and *experience* and careful and ponderous and solemn thoughts." Thus, the experiences associated with Joseph's incarcerated isolation would help him to better understand God. While imprisoned, Joseph was also told that Jesus had contemplated the abyss, descending lower than anyone.[11] As a boy, Joseph had encountered God in the light; now, he was encountering God in the darkness. God seemed to be present in both heaven and hell, and to commune with him, one had to discover him in both places.

A Lonely Heart

"You never knew my heart," Joseph told the Saints during the April 1844 semiannual conference. He continued, "No man knows my history; I cannot tell it. I shall never undertake it." As many as 20,000 people heard Joseph declare that his inner world was incommunicable. But one aspect of it could be shared—his views on God. He believed the validity of his prophetic enterprise hinged on his ability to teach about God's character: "if I fail [to explain his nature], it becomes my duty to renounce all my pretensions to revelations." Known as the King Follett sermon, this April 7 discourse is remembered for Joseph's teaching that God is an exalted human being. This striking doctrine, however, is not the most remarkable aspect of the sermon and distracts from Joseph's more profound teaching that God has a character, which can be known. According to Joseph, to have eternal life is to live with a certain worldview, to have insight into God's being.[12]

The way to access this knowledge came through careful thoughts coupled with God's inspiration. However, the problem with humanity was that they did not comprehend God's designs; instead, they were given over to "a fanciful and flowery and heated imagination."[13] "Few beings in the world," Joseph said, "understand rightly the character of God." He, therefore, asked his listeners to "lift your minds into a more lofty sphere, a more exalted understanding; that [than] what the human mind generally understands." Joseph challenged the crowd, asking them if they knew who God was: "have any of you seen him, heard him, *communed* with him?"[14] Joseph had. But the encounter occurred within a lonely heart that no one knew.

The moments of loneliness that Joseph Smith experienced during his life were real. God's absence was palpable. But this inner isolation was not without purpose. Loneliness, with its anxieties and worries, led the Prophet to commune with God, a being he found in a grove and a dungeon. It was because of and during the lonely moments of his life that Joseph learned about his God. Loneliness forced Joseph to question, to doubt, and to reflect, which, for him, led to deeper insights about the nature of divinity. During his life, Joseph came to know God through visions and visitations as well as during the moments when he felt separated from the being he worshipped.

J. Chase Kirkham is a historian and documentary editor with the Joseph Smith Papers Project.

Notes

1. This essay is influenced by some of Richard Bushman's observations on this topic. See Bushman, *Joseph Smith: Rough Stone Rolling* (New York: Vintage Books, 2007), 63, 185–86, 225, 237.
2. History, ca. Summer 1832, 2, in *JSP*, H1:11–12; History Drafts, 1838–ca. 1841, Draft 2, in *JSP*, H1:208, 210.
3. Journal, Nov. 9, 1835, in *JSP*, J1:87.
4. History Drafts, 1838–ca. 1841, Draft 2, in *JSP*, H1:210.
5. "Lucy Mack Smith, History, 1844–1845," bk. 4, p. [1], josephsmithpapers.org.
6. History Drafts, 1838–ca. 1841, Draft 2, in *JSP*, H1:210, 212.
7. Compare Revelation, Apr. 1829–B, in Doctrine and Covenants 34:1, 1835 ed. (D&C 8:2).

8. History, ca. Summer 1832, 2–3, in *JSP*, H1:11–12; History Drafts, 1838–ca. 1841, Draft 2, in *JSP*, H1:208, 210.
9. For the importance of Zion, see "Volume 1 Introduction: Joseph Smith Documents Dating through June 1831," in *JSP*, D1:xxxiv–xxxvi; and "Volume 2 Introduction: Joseph Smith Documents Dating from July 1831 through January 1833," in *JSP*, D2:xvii–xxi; for examples of Joseph's attempts at redress, see Memorial to the United States Senate and House of Representatives, ca. Oct. 30, 1839–Jan. 27, 1840, in *JSP*, D7:138–74; and JS et al., Memorial to U.S. Senate and House of Representatives, Nov. 28, 1843, Record Group 46, Records of the U.S. Senate, National Archives, Washington, DC.
10. "Volume 6 Introduction: Joseph Smith Documents from February 1838 through August 1839," in *JSP*, D6:xix–xxix.
11. Letter to the Church and Edward Partridge, Mar. 20, 1839, in *JSP*, D6:362–63, 365–66, 368–69, emphasis added; Letter to Edward Partridge and the Church, ca. Mar. 22, 1839, in *JSP*, D6:395 [see D&C 121:1–46; 122:1–9], spelling and mechanics standardized.
12. "Conference Minutes," *Times and Seasons*, Aug. 15, 1844, 5:617, 613; for the crowd size, see "Conference," *Nauvoo Neighbor*, Apr. 10, 1844, [2]; for "insight," see Elaine Pagels, *Beyond Belief: The Secret Gospel of Thomas* (New York: Random House, 2003), 33.
13. Letter to the Church and Edward Partridge, Mar. 20, 1839, in *JSP*, D6:368.
14. "Conference Minutes," *Times and Seasons*, Aug. 15, 1844, 5:613, emphasis added.

JOSEPH SMITH AS A HUSBAND

By Mary Jane Woodger

Joseph Smith once told the Quorum of the Twelve Apostles, "A man filled with the love of God, is not content with blessing his family alone, but ranges through the whole world, anxious to bless the whole human race."[1] Joseph's prophetic legacy as seen in his papers shows that he blessed all humanity as he restored doctrine regarding the role of husbands. As a husband, Joseph fulfilled his responsibility to love and care for Emma Hale Smith.

Joseph Smith approved Paul's teaching from Ephesians about a husband's responsibility. These verses were repeated by Joseph in a letter to the elders published in the *Messenger and Advocate* in 1835. "Wives, submit yourselves unto your own husbands, as unto the Lord, for the husband is the head of the wife, even as Christ is the head of the Church; and He is the Savior of the body. Therefore, as the Church is subject unto Christ, so let the wives be to their own husbands, in everything. Husbands, love your wives, even as Christ also loved the Church and gave Himself for it. . . . (Ephesians 5:22–31)."[2]

Joseph not only taught husbands to love their wives as Christ loves the Church, but he exemplified this principle in his own marriage. His marriage to Emma, which began on January 18, 1827, was an affectionate relationship. Emma was willing to marry Joseph at a time of persecution from his claims of visions and golden plates—persecution and hardship that never ceased. Early in their marriage, Joseph was blessed with the support, assistance, and strength of a wife while translating the Book of Mormon. On one morning, Joseph tried to translate after a disagreement with Emma but could not. David Whitmer recalled, "Going into the Whitmer orchard where he could be alone, Joseph spent an hour in supplication with the Lord. When he returned to the house, he asked Emma's forgiveness. He was then in the proper [spirit] to continue the translation."[3] Joseph learned through this experience and others that the Lord felt it was a solemn responsibility to be a husband. Things had to be right with Joseph as a spouse before things were right with him as a prophet.

Entries in the Prophet's journal and letters to Emma reveal that Joseph valued her counsel. In 1832, Joseph confided to Emma, "[I wish to] converse with you on all the subjects which concern us, things . . . [that are] not prudent for me to write. I omit all the important things which could I see you I could make you acquainted with."[4] Joseph sought Emma's opinion on important issues.

During 1838, Joseph was arrested and incarcerated in Missouri. Letters back and forth reveal the strength of the Smiths' relationship as Joseph expressed trust in Emma's ability to make good decisions in his absence. On November 12, 1838, the Prophet wrote, "Act according to your own feelings, and best Judgment."[5] In another letter on April 4, 1839, he complimented Emma, saying, "I find no fault with you at all, I know nothing but what you have done the best you could." After spending five months in prison, he wrote, "The contemplations of the mind under these circumstances defy the pen, or tongue, or angels to describe, or paint, to the human being, who never experienced what we experience." In this letter, he crossed out "I" and replaced it with "we," suggesting that Joseph was mindful of Emma's part in his persecutions.[6]

Joseph seems to have been consistently cognizant of Emma's contribution. Jesse S. Crosby recalled observing Joseph doing what he called "women's work" and concluded that Joseph was "mismanag[ing] Emma." Crosby argued, "Brother Joseph, my wife does much more hard work than does your wife." The Prophet gave Crosby a "terrible reproof" that "if a man cannot learn in this life to appreciate a wife and do his duty by her, in properly taking care of her, he need not expect to be given one in the hereafter."[7]

Such instances of Joseph honoring his wife were common. On one occasion, while having dinner at the Nauvoo Mansion, Joseph remarked to William W. Phelps that Emma was "a kind, provident wife," and if he just "wanted a little bread and milk, she would load the table with so many good things, it would destroy [his] appetite." Emma walked in on the conversation as Phelps replied, "You must do as Bonaparte did—have a little table, just large enough for the victuals you want yourself." Emma quipped, "Mr. Smith is a bigger man than Bonaparte: he can never eat without his friends." Joseph, complimenting his wife, responded, "That is the wisest thing I ever heard you say."[8]

Joseph often expressed love for his wife, addressing her as "Dear and Affectionate Wife," "My dear Emma," and "My dear and beloved companion."[9] This sentiment written in 1839 would make any wife's heart tender: "If you want to know how much I want to see you . . . I would gladly walk from here to you barefoot, and bareheaded, and half naked, to see you and think it great pleasure, and never count it toil."[10] Joseph felt his heart was "entwined" around Emma's.[11] Such tender feelings were also expressed through physical affection. In a November 1838 letter, he wrote of wanting to press his wife and children to his bosom and to "kiss their lovely cheeks."[12] Reflecting on his responsibility of caring for his wife and children when denied this opportunity in prison, he expressed, "If God will spare my life once more to have the privilege of taking care of you, I will ease your care and endeavor to comfort your heart."[13]

Others noticed Joseph's consideration for Emma. Mercy Rachel Fielding Thompson recalled the Prophet "exhibiting all the solicitude and sympathy possible for the tenderest of hearts and the most affectionate of natures to feel" toward his wife.[14] During 1842, Joseph's journal reports his concern over a severe illness Emma contracted even though he was not feeling well either. Joseph stayed by her bedside for several days. She worsened, and his extreme anxiety for her becomes evident in these excerpts from his journal, kept by William Clayton:

Wednesday 5th [October] Sister E. [Emma Smith] is worse. Many fears are entertained that she will not recover. . . . President Joseph does not feel well, and is much troubled on account of Sister E's sickness.

Thursday 6th This day sister Emma is better . . . she appears considerably easier. . . .

Friday 7th Sister E. is some better. Prest Joseph is cheerful and well.

Monday 10th Sister E. is yet gaining slowly.

November Tuesday 1st President & sister E. rode up to Temple for the benefit of her health. She is rapidly gaining.[15]

The Smiths' strong connection can also be seen even in their greatest trial: the commandment that Joseph marry additional women. The experience was heart-wrenching for both Joseph and Emma and at times strained their relationship. Emma had difficulty accepting the principle and occasionally was vexed with Joseph over it. She gave approval for at least some of Joseph's plural marriages, but she likely knew nothing about other such sealings.[16] But not even this greatest trial destroyed their marriage. In the summer of 1842, after the principle of plural marriage had been instituted, Joseph was in hiding to avoid extradition to Missouri. He reflected on the important people in his life, including his parents and some of his staunchest supporters. His mind turned to Emma and "the fatigues, and the toils, the sorrows, and sufferings, and the joys and consolations" they had experienced. "Again she is here, even in the seventh trouble," he reflected. "Undaunted, firm and unwavering, unchangeable, affectionate Emma."[17] For her part, Emma continued to defend her husband even after his death and after her own remarriage.[18]

Joseph and Emma's marriage was not perfect, and they experienced problems and trials, just as all marriages do. But the above examples reveal that Joseph tried his best to love and care for his wife. He expressed affection for her, he sought her opinion, and he cared for her when she was sick. In other words, he treated her with the love and charity that the

Apostle Paul counseled Saints to have in their marriages. These and so many other records found in the Joseph Smith Papers give us a wonderful glimpse into Joseph Smith as a husband and also show how he exemplified his teachings about the sacred role of husbands.

Mary Jane Woodger is a professor of Church history and doctrine at Brigham Young University.

Notes

1. "History, 1838–1856, volume C-1 [2 November 1838–31 July 1842]," p. 1115, josephsmith papers.org.
2. "Letter to the Elders of the Church, 16 November 1835," pp. 211–12, josephsmithpapers.org.
3. David Whitmer, interviews by William H. Kelly and G. A. Blakeslee, Jan. 15, 1882, in *David Whitmer Interviews: A Restoration Witness*, ed. Lyndon W. Cook (Provo, UT: Grandin Book, 1991), 86.
4. "Letter to Emma Smith, 6 June 1832," p. [3], josephsmithpapers.org, grammar and punctuation standardized.
5. "Letter to Emma Smith, 12 November 1838," p. [2], josephsmithpapers.org.
6. "Letter to Emma Smith, 4 April 1839," pp. [1], [3], josephsmithpapers.org; spelling, grammar, and punctuation standardized.
7. Martha Cragun Cox, "Stories from the Notebook of Martha Cox, Grandmother of Fern Cox Anderson," typescript, CHL.
8. "History, 1838–1856, volume E-1 [1 July 1843–30 April 1844]," p. 1853, josephsmith papers.org.
9. "Letter to Emma Smith, 4 April 1839," p. [1]; "Letter to Emma Smith, 4 November 1838," p. [1], josephsmithpapers.org.
10. "Letter to Emma Smith, 4 April 1839," p. [2].
11. Letter to Emma Smith, Jan. 20–25, 1840, in *JSP*, D7:136; spelling standardized.
12. "Letter to Emma Smith, 12 November 1838," p. [1].
13. "Letter to Emma Smith, 21 March 1839," p. [1], josephsmithpapers.org.
14. "Recollections of the Prophet Joseph Smith," *Juvenile Instructor* 27 (July 1, 1892): 399.
15. "Journal, December 1841–December 1842," pp. 206–7, 209, josephsmithpapers.org.
16. "Plural Marriage in Kirtland and Nauvoo," Gospel Topics, ChurchofJesusChrist.org.
17. "Journal, December 1841–December 1842," p. 164, josephsmithpapers.org.
18. See, for example, "Last Testimony of Sister Emma," *Saints' Herald*, Oct. 1, 1879, 289–90.

PART 3

NAUVOO, 1839–1844

TO "MOURN WITH THOSE THAT MOURN": JOSEPH SMITH AND CONVERSATIONS OF CONSOLATION

By Claire M. Haynie

The Book of Mormon prophet Alma taught the people of God at the waters of Mormon that they should "mourn with those that mourn . . . and comfort those that stand in need of comfort."[1] Joseph Smith demonstrated one way of fulfilling the disciples' duty of comforting those "that stand in need." That salve for those in mourning came in the form of prophetic teaching. Into the darkly lit glass of the afterlife, Joseph shone light, and in his conversations of consolation with those in mourning, he revealed three of the most pivotal and defining doctrines related to the character of God.

Death had followed the Saints from Missouri to western Illinois and eastern Iowa Territory in 1839. In the sweaty summer heat, the banks on both sides of the Mississippi River were covered with belongings and makeshift shelters. Within these fragile walls, the newly arrived Saints fell prey to malaria. They had survived the horrors of the Missouri exodus only to suffer grave illness in their new settlements. Zina Diantha Huntington, just 18 years old when she first arrived in Illinois, had been an eager and committed member of the Church since her baptism in 1835. As her mother, also named Zina, lay dying, accounts of the Prophet Joseph's miraculous healing of other Saints along both shores of the river must have met her ears.[2] Perhaps she felt robbed of a miracle as her mother trembled from the malarial fever. With her sister Presendia married and occupied with her sixth pregnancy, Zina was the lone Huntington daughter available to care for her dying mother. Her mother had been a pillar of faith since their family's conversion in their hometown of Watertown, New York, and had been a close associate of Joseph and other Church leaders.[3] As her mother passed from life in July 1839, Zina was distressed. In later years, she told of a conversation with Joseph shortly after the death of her mother, which marked the beginning of a deeply held belief in Zina and other members of the Church. As Susa Young Gates recorded,

> One day, when . . . Zina was speaking with the Prophet Joseph Smith concerning the loss of her mother and her intense grief, she asked the question: "Will I know my mother as my mother when I get over on the Other Side?" "Certainly you will," was the instant reply of the Prophet. "More than that, you will meet and become acquainted with your eternal Mother, the wife of your Father in Heaven." "And have I then a Mother in Heaven?" exclaimed the astonished girl. "You assuredly have. How could a Father claim His title unless there were also a Mother to share that parenthood?"[4]

As a loved one passed beyond the limits of mortality, Joseph provided comfort in the form of a doctrine clarifying in one way the mystery-shrouded afterlife. In this conversation of consolation Joseph oriented Zina to the family of heaven, presided over by the Divine Couple. Key to the nature of God was the fact that He was not alone, that at His side stood a Mother in Heaven, and that Their power was derived from Their togetherness. This knowledge, coupled with the idea that her own relationship with her mother would be unchanged by death, must have offered Zina comfort and peace. She shared this recollection with close associates many times during her lifetime.[5]

While no contemporary record of this conversation exists, this revealed doctrine has persisted in part because of a poem written by Zina's dear friend Eliza R. Snow. Originally published in 1845 in the Latter-day Saint newspaper *Times and Seasons*, "My Father in Heaven" speaks of the same doctrine that had been shared with Zina in the sorrowful summer of

1839. The poem was soon put to music and has become one of the most beloved Latter-day Saint hymns, "O My Father."

> *In the heav'ns are parents single?*
> *No, the thought makes reason stare;*
> *Truth is reason—truth eternal*
> *Tells me I've a mother there.*
> *When I leave this frail existence—*
> *When I lay this mortal by,*
> *Father, mother, may I meet you*
> *In your royal court on high?*[6]

Earlier revelation to Joseph Smith had made clear that many others would populate the heavenly realms. The Vision, a name given to the vast 1832 revelation received by Joseph Smith and Sidney Rigdon on the afterlife, which is now canonized as Doctrine and Covenants section 76, offered in some detail the contours of heaven, the degrees of glory, and the means of attaining each one.[7] This rich detail, initially confusing to some Saints who misinterpreted it to mean a Universalist vision of heaven, gained further clarification in later years.[8] If baptism, the first ordinance of the gospel, was the eternal gate by which all people must enter the strait and narrow path leading back to God, Joseph taught at Nauvoo how such a gate could be opened to more than just those who had accepted the gospel during their lifetime.

In a sermon given at the August 1840 funeral service of Seymour Brunson, a member of the Nauvoo high council,[9] Joseph further described the heavens in his consoling words to those in mourning. In a letter to the members of the Twelve then preaching in England, Joseph described his sermon. "I presume the doctrine of 'Baptizm for the dead' has ere this reached your ears," he wrote. He explained that the Saints were now engaged in being baptized on behalf of their dead relatives who "they feel to believe would have embraced the gospel if they had been priviledged with hearing it."[10]

Heaven suddenly became a reflection of the community of Zion then being formed by the ever-expanding gospel family.[11] God's merciful and unchanging nature was further revealed, offering the hope of salvation to all people, regardless of whether they had lived when the fulness of the gospel was present on the earth. Heaven seemed less of a foreign place with the promise of loved ones among its ranks. The Saints flocked to the Mississippi River and began performing baptisms on behalf of deceased relatives.[12] God's merciful nature was unfolding before their very eyes.

In a final funeral sermon, just over two months before his own death, Joseph revealed a key piece of the nature of God: His familiarity. The April 1844 sermon was given at the funeral of King Follett, a devout Church member who had been "crushed to death in a well."[13] Here is yet another moment of mourning when Joseph revealed more about heaven and God's relationship to His children. He assured listeners that beyond this mortal realm, one would find a Father in Heaven, enthroned and yet familiar, "a man like unto one of yourselves."[14] The assurance of such familiarity, to see a God so like ourselves in form, not only made Him knowable but also promised to infuse the potential to become like our Heavenly Parents within each of Their children. Heaven became a place with Parents, with family and friends, coupled with eternal glory.

Why would the Prophet Joseph have shared these doctrines at these times of mourning and loss? Clearly, Joseph understood an important role he inhabited, and among his many prophetic responsibilities, he took seriously the call to "comfort those who stand in need of comfort" and ministered to individual needs. In his sermon at King Follett's funeral, he said that "to speak for the consol[ation] of those who mourn for the loss of their friend it is nec[essary] to understand the char[acter] & being of God."[15] At these three instances of loss and mourning, Joseph offered concrete information he had regarding life after death. He illuminated important aspects of the character of God. While it seemed that God's will had not provided a lifesaving miracle for Zina Huntington's mother, Seymour Brunson, or King Follett, Joseph instead offered pure revelation on the nature of God and the structure of His heavens as a lasting and faith-building salve. These conversations of consolation ordered and populated heaven in a way that seemed intimately familiar and also infinitely glorious.

Claire M. Haynie is a historian with the Church History Department.

Notes

1. Mosiah 18:9.
2. See, for example, Wilford Woodruff, Journal, July 22, 1839, Wilford Woodruff Journals and Papers, 1828–98, CHL.
3. Benjamin F. Johnson, Biographical Sketch of Zina D. Young, 1896, Zina Card Brown Family Collection, 1806–1972, CHL; "Young, Zina Diantha Huntington" (biographical entry), josephsmithpapers.org.
4. Susa Young Gates, *History of the Young Ladies' Mutual Improvement Association of The Church of Jesus Christ of Latter-Day Saints* (Salt Lake City: Deseret News, 1911), 15–16.
5. Gates, *History of the Young Ladies' Mutual Improvement Association*, 16.
6. Eliza R. Snow, "My Father in Heaven," *Times and Seasons*, Nov. 15, 1845, 6:1039; "O My Father," in *Hymns of The Church of Jesus Christ of Latter-day Saints* (Salt Lake City: The Church of Jesus Christ of Latter-day Saints, 1985), no. 292.
7. "Vision, 16 February 1832 [D&C 76]," josephsmithpapers.org.
8. See Matthew McBride, "'The Vision': D&C 76," in *Revelations in Context: The Stories behind the Sections of the Doctrine and Covenants*, ed. Matthew McBride and James Goldberg, ChurchofJesusChrist.org; Historical Introduction to "Vision, 16 February 1832 [D&C 76]," josephsmithpapers.org.
9. "Brunson, Seymour" (biographical entry), josephsmithpapers.org.
10. "Letter to Quorum of the Twelve, 15 December 1840," p. [6], josephsmithpapers.org.
11. See "Appendix 2: William Clayton, Journal Excerpt, 1–4 April 1843," p. 67, josephsmith papers.org. A portion of this report of Joseph's teachings was later canonized as section 130 of the Doctrine and Covenants.
12. See "Part 6: 3 October 1840–30 January 1841," in *JSP*, D7:417.
13. "Discourse, 7 April 1844, as Reported by Thomas Bullock," p. 14, josephsmithpapers.org; see also "Follett, King" (biographical entry), josephsmithpapers.org.
14. "Discourse, 7 April 1844, as Reported by Thomas Bullock," p. 16.
15. "Discourse, 7 April 1844, as Reported by Thomas Bullock," p. 16.

"A CLOAK OF CHARITY": JOSEPH SMITH AND FORGIVENESS

By Jeffrey D. Mahas

Just one month before he was killed, Joseph Smith reportedly pleaded with a gathering of the Saints in Nauvoo, "I can go to the cross, I can lay down my life, but don't forsake me. I want the friendship of my brethren."[1] In his religious, political, and personal endeavors, Joseph was motivated by his desire for friends and friendship. For Joseph, friendship and its accompanying charity perfectly encapsulated the message of the gospel and his religious teachings. As he once declared, "Frie[n]dship is the grand fundamental prin[c]iple of Mormonism."[2] Growing out of this desire and reverence for friendship, Joseph developed a remarkable capacity to forgive. While Joseph could be very quick to anger, he was at times even quicker to forgive his friends.

The most famous example of this attribute is Joseph's relationship with early Latter-day Saint William W. Phelps. Beginning in 1837, Phelps and other Church leaders in Missouri became enveloped in a conflict with Joseph and others over authority and Church finances. During the 1838 conflict between Latter-day Saints and Missourians, Phelps turned against the Church and submitted testimony against Joseph and others. After two years of estrangement and hostility toward Joseph and the Church, Phelps wrote to Joseph saying, "I have Seen the folly of my way and I tremble at the gulf I have passed. . . . I ask forgiveness in the name of Jesus Christ of all the saints for I will do right God helping me, I want your fellowship: If you cannot grant that, grant me your peace and friendship, for we are brethren, and our communion used to be Sweet."[3] To this humble letter, Joseph graciously replied, "I shall be happy once again to give you the right hand of fellowship, and rejoice over the returning prodigal." He closed his letter with a paraphrase from a Methodist poem: "Come on dear Brother since the war is past, For friends at first are friends again at last."[4] Phelps returned to the Church, joined the Saints in Nauvoo, and eventually began working as one of Joseph's scribes.[5]

While Phelps's experience is the most well-known story of Joseph forgiving someone, it is far from unique. Many early Church leaders publicly split away from Joseph or the Church and were eventually welcomed back, including William Smith, Parley P. Pratt, Orson Hyde, Sidney Rigdon, and Orson Pratt. Others who left the Church never returned, yet Joseph seems to have often tried to regain their friendship if not their religious fellowship. During the tumultuous years of 1837–38, many senior Church leaders abandoned their faith, and many of them never returned to the Church during Joseph's lifetime. Statements and actions of these men contributed to the threats and violence Joseph and the Saints experienced in Ohio and Missouri.

Yet, once the Saints found temporary peace in Illinois, Joseph's anger subsided into forgiveness as it had toward Phelps. In a letter to her husband, Heber C. Kimball, Vilate Kimball noted her surprise when Joseph brought former apostles John F. Boynton and Lyman Johnson back to Nauvoo with him after a riverboat excursion. Both had left the Church during the 1837–38 difficulties, and although the two men and their families had not returned to the Church, they temporarily moved in with Joseph and planned to make Nauvoo their home. When they arrived, Kimball stated, "I never saw Joseph appear more happy. Said he, I am going to have all my old friends around me again."[6] Two years later, Boynton returned Joseph's hospitality by stalling law officers who had come to arrest Joseph in the Smith home, giving him enough time to escape out the back door.[7]

Joseph's forgiving nature was reflected by his fellow Church members. In April 1843, Joseph instructed the Quorum of the Twelve Apostles to write to Oliver Cowdery, who had been excommunicated in 1838, and invite him to return to the Church.[8] The nine Apostles then present immediately wrote a letter informing Cowdery that the Saints were "ready to receive" him should he ever return to the Church. Regardless, they remained Cowdery's "*unchangeable* friends *in* the Gospel."[9] Cowdery responded kindly, reasoning "ought not old friends—long tried in the furnace of affliction, to be friends still, even laying out of view any and all religious considerations?"[10] Although Cowdery did not return to the Church for several years, ties of friendship were rekindled. Phelps, himself a recipient of Joseph's forgiveness, reached out to prominent Kirtland dissenter Warren Parrish with a similar message. "We are all Little Children as to the great things of eternity," Phelps wrote, "and when we begin to play and hurt one another we ought to have humanity and good sense enough, not to always act foolish, but to settle the matter by forgiveness, and '*be friends*.'"[11]

Joseph's ability to forgive was one of his most admirable characteristics and greatest strengths. Ironically, it was at times also a weakness. Joseph sometimes erred on the side of mercy with some unscrupulous men, leading to challenging issues that were not easy to solve. For example, as early as the summer of 1841, Joseph learned about the sexual improprieties of John C. Bennett and others. Joseph rebuked Bennett and his followers several times in private, but because they pleaded for mercy and forgiveness, they were not formally disciplined until May 1842. When he was finally excommunicated, Bennett became one of Joseph's bitterest enemies, touring the nation lecturing against the Church and facilitating legal prosecution against Joseph.[12]

Similarly, Joseph forgave powerful preacher and missionary George J. Adams after Joseph confronted him over his adultery as a missionary and Adams begged for forgiveness. Only when Joseph learned that Adams had fathered a child out of wedlock did he recall Adams to Nauvoo and privately rebuke and discipline him.[13] When other Church leaders subsequently questioned Adams's standing in the Church, Joseph explained that Adams "had confessed all wharein he had done wrong & had asked for mercy & he had taken the right course to save himself that he would now begin new in the church."[14] When public knowledge of Adams's adultery created a scandal in Nauvoo during 1843, Joseph—relying on Adams's previous confession—publicly stood by him and testified on his behalf.[15] Adams was finally excommunicated nearly a year after Joseph's death, after reports of adultery and embezzlement of Church funds reached Brigham Young. Likewise, when Joseph learned that his longtime friend Orrin Porter Rockwell had privately taught others that it was no sin to steal from nonmembers, he publicly condemned stealing but took no action against Rockwell.[16]

Some of Joseph's followers, then and since, have wondered why he maintained relationships with these and other disreputable men. I have come to believe that the answer to this problem lies in the value Joseph placed on friendship and his willingness to forgive those loyal to him. He was not blind to people's faults. For example, when he hired Joseph H. Jackson, a drifter with a sketchy background, Joseph explained that "Jackson appears a fine and noble fellow but is reduced in circumstances"; Joseph felt "disposed to employ him and give him a chance in the world." Although Joseph quickly changed his mind about Jackson's character—denouncing him as "rotten hearted" just days later—he kept Jackson employed for nearly a year, until Jackson began plotting against Joseph's family.[17] So long as men like Jackson, Bennett, Adams, and others remained loyal to him, Joseph was willing to forgive and overlook their faults, just as he was willing to forgive men like Phelps who had turned against him but then sought to rekindle ties.

Beyond his personal actions, Joseph preached his understanding of forgiveness and friendship as part of his gospel message. In an 1841 sermon, Joseph described his style of forgiveness as being associated with biblical charity. If the Saints "would throw a cloak of charity over his sins," Joseph reportedly offered, he would throw one over theirs, "for charity coverd a multitude of sins."[18] In the same 1843 discourse in which he taught that "frie[n]dship is the grand fundamental prin[c]iple of Mormonism," Joseph likewise said, "I beli[e]ve in a principle of reciprociprocity [reciprocity] . . . dont care what a character is if he's my frie[n]d.——— a fri[e]nd a true friend. & I will be a f[r]iend to him."[19]

For good and sometimes for ill, Joseph Smith valued extending mercy and forgiveness to his friends. At times, this characteristic led Joseph to exhibit a remarkable Christlike capacity for dispensing grace and forgiveness, while at other times, it left him and the Church vulnerable to unscrupulous individuals. In either case, Joseph was governed by a fundamental principle of forgiveness in his personal relationships.

Jeffrey D. Mahas is a historian with the Joseph Smith Papers Project.

Notes

1. "Discourse, 26 May 1844, as Compiled by Leo Hawkins," p. 7, josephsmithpapers.org.
2. "Discourse, 23 July 1843, as Reported by Willard Richards," p. [13], josephsmithpapers.org.
3. Letter from William W. Phelps, with Appended Letter from Orson Hyde and John E. Page, June 29, 1840, in *JSP*, D7:304–5.
4. Letter to William W. Phelps, July 22, 1840, in *JSP*, D7:347–48.
5. See Samuel M. Brown, "The Translator and the Ghostwriter: Joseph Smith and William Phelps," *Journal of Mormon History* 34, no. 1 (Winter 2008): 26–62.
6. Vilate Kimball to Heber C. Kimball, Dec. 8, 1840, CHL.
7. Journal, Sept. 3, 1842, in *JSP*, J2:125.
8. Journal, Apr. 19, 1843, in *JSP*, J2:370.
9. Quorum of the Twelve Apostles to Oliver Cowdery, Apr. 19, 1843, CHL, emphasis in original.
10. Oliver Cowdery to Brigham Young et al., Dec. 25, 1843, CHL.
11. William W. Phelps to Warren Parish, Mar. 22, 1843, CHL, emphasis in original.
12. See Letter to the Church and Others, June 23, 1842, in *JSP*, D10:178–87.
13. Letter from George J. Adams and David Rogers, Oct. 11, 1842, in *JSP*, D11:143–48; Letter from Caroline Youngs Adams, ca. Jan 15, 1843, in *JSP*, D11:320–26; Minutes, Feb. 10, 1843, in *JSP*, D11:413.
14. Wilford Woodruff, Journal, May 27, 1843, CHL.
15. Minutes, Nauvoo High Council, Sept. 1, 1843, CHL; Journal, Sept. 1, 1843, in *JSP*, J3:91.
16. Journal, Mar. 10, 1843, in *JSP*, J2:302; "Proclamation," Mar. 25, 1843, in *Wasp* (Nauvoo, IL), Mar. 29, 1843.
17. William Clayton, Journal, May 10, 1843, in *An Intimate Chronicle: The Journals of William Clayton*, ed. George D. Smith (Salt Lake City: Signature Books, 1991), 105–6; Journal, May 27, 1844, in *JSP*, J3:264.
18. Discourse, Nov. 7, 1841, in *JSP*, D8:358.
19. "Discourse, 23 July 1843, as Reported by Willard Richards," p. [13].

"I SAW . . . MY BROTHER ALVIN": THE RESTORATION OF THE DOCTRINE OF THE REDEMPTION FOR THE DEAD

By Norman W. Gardner

The summer of 1842 had been an unusually difficult period in Joseph Smith's life. One of his trusted associates, John C. Bennett, had not only proven to be an adulterer and an impostor but was also intent on having Joseph extradited to Missouri on false charges of involvement in an assassination attempt on former governor Lilburn W. Boggs.[1] In hiding as he evaded the law officers holding the arrest warrant, Joseph reflected on those who had greatly influenced him. His thoughts rested on his oldest brother, Alvin, who had died nearly 19 years earlier at the age of 25. "I remember well the pangs of sorrow that swelled my youthful bosom and almost burst my tender heart, when he died," Joseph recalled. "He lived without spot from the time he was a child."[2] But Alvin had died before the fulness of the gospel had been restored, leaving his family to wonder what his condition would be in the afterlife. Perhaps because of Joseph's concern for Alvin, the Lord had revealed over the years truths that brought great comfort to Joseph's soul—and to the Latter-day Saints as a whole.

Alvin's death in 1823 came at a key time in Joseph's life. Joseph had been visited in September 1823 by a heavenly messenger named Moroni, who told him about an ancient record buried in a hill near his home.

Alvin "manifested a greater zeal and anxiety" about the plates than other members of the family.[3] However, less than two months after Moroni's visit, Alvin became sick and suffered greatly. Sensing that he was nearing death, Alvin called individual family members to his bedside. To Joseph, Alvin said, "I want you to be a good boy & do everything that lays in your power to obtain the records be faithful in receiving instruction and keeping . . . every commandment that is given you."[4]

Lucy Mack Smith recorded that, upon Alvin's death, the family members were "for a time almost swallowed up in grief so much so that it seemed impossible for us to interest ourselves at all about the concerns of life."[5] This grief became more poignant when the Presbyterian minister who officiated at Alvin's funeral commented in his sermon "that [Alvin] had gone to hell, for Alvin was not a church member" and thus could not be saved.[6]

Alvin's death, along with the deaths of other family members, provided Joseph reason to seek greater spiritual understanding. During the Prophet's ministry, the Lord gradually brought forth significant truths regarding the status of those who have died and how they could be redeemed.

The contrast between the bitterness experienced by the Smith family at Alvin's death and the comments Joseph made in 1844 at the funeral of his friend King Follett illustrate how restored truth brings understanding and comfort: "What have we to console us in relation to our dead? We have reason to have the greatest hope and consolations for our dead of any people on the earth."[7]

In Moroni's first visit to Joseph, the angel quoted the words of Malachi, the Old Testament prophet, with a few modifications: "Behold I will reveal unto you the Priesthood by the hand of Elijah the prophet before the coming of the great and dreadful day of the Lord. . . . And he shall plant in the hearts of the Children the promises made to the fathers, and the hearts of the children shall turn to their fathers, if it were not so the whole earth would be utterly wasted at his coming."[8]

As Joseph's understanding developed, he came to know that Malachi was referring to the preservation of essential family relationships. At this early stage, Joseph probably did not comprehend that Elijah's promised return would unite generations of families for eternity. The heavenly communication given through Moroni was the first of several revelations that gradually defined the way that God had prepared to make salvation available to all of His children.

At the time of the Church's organization, members were taught that baptism was essential to salvation. They largely accepted the common view of their day that, at death, the righteous who had been baptized would be saved in heaven while the wicked and the unbaptized would be consigned to hell.[9]

On February 16, 1832, Joseph and Sidney Rigdon experienced a vision showing them that the afterlife consisted of more than just heaven and hell. Instead, there were three degrees of glory that God had prepared.[10] Joseph and Sidney learned that hell was temporary for all but a few (the sons of perdition). Yet, additional truth was needed for the Saints to have a clear understanding regarding the destiny of those individuals who died before having an opportunity to accept the gospel and be baptized.

Despite what the Presbyterian minister had said at Alvin's funeral, and perhaps with hope generated by his vision of the afterlife, Joseph was optimistic that his family, including Alvin, might someday be found together in God's presence. Writing to his brother William in 1835, Joseph closed the letter with a prayer to heaven: "may humble repentance bring us both to thee O God and to thy power and protection, and a crown, to enjoy the society of father mother Alvin Hyrum Sophron[i]a Samuel Catharine [Katharine] Carloss [Don Carlos] Lucy the Saints and all the sanctif[ie]d in peace forever."[11]

Joseph's hopes for Alvin were strengthened when Church leaders assembled in the nearly completed Kirtland Temple on January 21, 1836. During this meeting, the Prophet had a vision of the celestial kingdom. He stated, "I saw . . . my brother Alvin that has long since slept, and marvled how it was that he had obtained an inheritance in that kingdom, seeing that he had departed this life, before the Lord had set his hand to gather Israel the second time and had not been baptized for the remission of sins."[12]

As Joseph pondered this thrilling discovery, the Lord provided him with the next significant step in comprehending the doctrine of redemption for the dead. The voice of the Lord taught him that "all who have died with[out] a knowledge of this gospel, who would have received it, if they had been permited to tarry, shall be heirs of the celestial kingdom of God."[13] The vision of the celestial kingdom gave Joseph and the early Saints a new perspective on God's mercy. But it was still unclear how the requirement of baptism would be satisfied in cases like Alvin's.

On April 3, 1836, in the Kirtland Temple, Joseph Smith and Oliver Cowdery were visited by Jesus Christ. Moses, Elias, and Elijah then appeared bringing keys of the priesthood. Elijah committed unto Joseph and Oliver the same keys given to righteous servants in previous dispensations to seal on earth and in heaven.[14] Elijah's long-awaited visit in the latter days would soon enable the sealing of the fathers to the children and the children to the fathers for the living and for the dead.

Joseph later explained that these keys of the priesthood empowered him to obtain further heavenly knowledge: "For him, to whom these keys are given there is no difficulty in obtaining a knowledge of facts in relation to the salvation of the children of men, both as well for the dead as for the living."[15] With priesthood keys restored, Joseph Smith continued to search out greater understanding of the salvation of the dead.

The final piece to the puzzle of how someone who had not been baptized in this life could still receive salvation came in 1840. At a funeral sermon in August of that year, Joseph Smith preached that members of the Church could be baptized for their dead relatives, thus providing them with the essential ordinance. Soon afterward, baptisms for the dead began to be performed.[16] This development confirmed that God was prepared to save all people, living or dead, who desired salvation. Shortly after this announcement, Joseph Smith Sr., with his health failing and near death, insisted that a baptism be performed for Alvin. Hyrum Smith served as proxy for the baptism.[17] Just before he died, Joseph Sr. declared to his family, "I see Alvin."[18]

While in hiding in Nauvoo in the late summer of 1842—and at the same time that he remembered his brother Alvin and what he meant to him—Joseph prepared a letter to be read aloud in a meeting of the Saints. He taught that the work to save deceased family members is "essential to our salvation" and that "the earth will be smitten with a curse, unless there is a welding link of some kind or other between the fathers and the children."[19] Joseph identified baptism for the dead as this welding link.

The gospel principles relating to the redemption of the dead, restored by the Lord through Joseph, are the foundation for today's temple and family history efforts. They show that Heavenly Father and Jesus Christ have provided the way for all worthy individuals, living or dead, to receive the ordinances of salvation and for families to be sealed together, eternally linked with previous generations. The coming forth of the truths and ordinances related to the redemption of the dead are powerful evidence of Joseph Smith's prophetic mission. And they came perhaps because of Joseph's concern for the fate of his own family, including his brother Alvin, in the afterlife.

Norman W. Gardner is an instructional designer with Seminaries and Institutes of Religion.

Notes

1. *Saints: The Story of the Church of Jesus Christ in the Latter Days*, vol. 1, *The Standard of Truth, 1815–1846* (Salt Lake City: The Church of Jesus Christ of Latter-day Saints, 2018), chap. 38.
2. "Reflections and Blessings, 16 and 23 Aug. 1842," p. 180, josephsmithpapers.org.
3. "Lucy Mack Smith, History, 1844–1845," bk. 4, p. [7], josephsmithpapers.org.
4. "Lucy Mack Smith, History, 1844–1845," bk. 4, p. [4].
5. "Lucy Mack Smith, History, 1844–1845," bk. 4, p. [7].
6. William Smith, interview by E. C. Briggs and J. W. Peterson, Oct. or Nov. 1893, originally published in *Zion's Ensign*; reprinted in *Deseret Evening News*, Jan. 20, 1894, p. 2.
7. "History, 1838–1856, volume E-1 [1 July 1843–30 April 1844]," p. 1977, josephsmith papers.org.
8. "History, 1838–1856, volume A-1 [23 December 1805–30 August 1834]," pp. 5–6, josephsmithpapers.org [D&C 2:1–3].
9. "Articles and Covenants, circa April 1830 [D&C 20:25]," p. [4], josephsmithpapers .org; Grant Underwood, "'Saved or Damned': Tracing a Persistent Protestantism in Early Mormon Thought," *BYU Studies* 25, no. 3 (1985): 87–88.

10. "Vision, 16 February 1832 [D&C 76]," josephsmithpapers.org.

11. "Letter to William Smith, circa 18 December 1835," p. 87, josephsmithpapers.org.

12. "Journal, 1835–1836," p. 136, josephsmithpapers.org [D&C 137:5–6].

13. "Journal, 1835–1836," pp. 136–37 [D&C 137:7].

14. "Visions, 3 April 1836 [D&C 110:13–16]," p. 193, josephsmithpapers.org.

15. "Letter to the Church, 7 September 1842 [D&C 128:11]," p. 4, josephsmithpapers.org.

16. Simon Baker, Statement, Joseph Smith Collection, CHL; Jane Harper Neyman and Vienna Jaques, Statement, Nov. 29, 1854, Historian's Office, Joseph Smith History Documents, ca. 1839–60, CHL.

17. Larry C. Porter, "Alvin Smith: Reminder of the Fairness of God," *Ensign*, Sept. 1978, 67.

18. "Lucy Mack Smith, History, 1845," p. 301, josephsmithpapers.org.

19. "Letter to the Church, 7 September 1842 [D&C 128:15, 18]," pp. 5–6, josephsmith papers.org.

JANE NEYMAN, JOSEPH SMITH, AND THE GOSPEL OF INCLUSION

By Patricia Lemmon Spilsbury

On a warm August morning in 1840, thousands gathered in a grove close to the Mississippi River in Nauvoo, Illinois, for the funeral of Seymour Brunson.[1] An early convert to The Church of Jesus Christ of Latter-day Saints, Brunson was a missionary and a stake high council member described as "a lively stone in the building of God."[2] Joseph Smith gave the funeral sermon at Brunson's earlier request.[3]

Joseph read from 1 Corinthians 15 and mentioned the "glad tidings of great joy" found in the gospel of Jesus Christ. He saw a widow in the congregation who, in light of Jesus's teaching in John 3:3–5, was concerned about the fate of her son who had died without being baptized. Joseph promised the widow "glad tidings" and "went on to say that people could now act for their friends who had departed this life" and that "the plan of salvation was calculated to save all who were willing to obey the requirements of the law of God."[4]

Jane Neyman was one of many widows in the congregation that day.[5] Her son Cyrus Livingston Neyman had died before Jane and her husband, William, found the Church in 1838. Jane and William had frequently discussed their great concern for their son, who didn't have the opportunity to hear the "glad tidings."[6] As Jane listened to Joseph's funeral sermon, she heard him introduce the doctrine of baptism for the dead. In speaking directly to the concern of Jane and of so many others in the congregation, Joseph demonstrated he empathized with the Saints' anxiety for their deceased loved ones, an example of his sincere concern and interest in his followers.

In 1836, Joseph learned through a vision that those who died without a knowledge of the restored gospel, but who would have received it, could still be saved in the celestial kingdom.[7] However, that vision did not reveal to Joseph that the Saints themselves would be the means of salvation for their deceased friends and family members. That knowledge was unveiled dramatically four years later at Brunson's funeral, as Joseph reiterated Paul's teachings: "For as in Adam all die, even so in Christ shall all be made alive. . . . Else what shall they do which are baptized for the dead, if the dead rise not at all? why are they then baptized for the dead?"[8]

Jane resolved years of heartache by receiving Joseph's teaching and acting on it. After hearing of the doctrine of baptism for the dead, she "immediately applied to the Elders" to perform a proxy baptism. When "they hesitated," Jane was patient. While waiting for permission, she spoke about her desire with her friend Vienna Jaques. Finally, nearly a month after Joseph's sermon, Harvey Olmstead agreed to baptize Jane for her son Cyrus. Vienna witnessed the event, riding "into the River on horseback to get close so as to hear what the Ceremony would be."[9] Jane's baptism for Cyrus was the first recorded baptism for the dead in this dispensation.[10]

Joseph Smith heard about the baptism that evening and affirmed that the correct wording had been used in the prayer.[11] Later, Jane was baptized for her deceased parents, father-in-law, two brothers, and a daughter.[12] The Lord restored the doctrine of the redemption of the dead "line upon line." It was not until 1845 that Brigham Young instructed that proxy baptisms should occur along gender lines, with men being baptized for men and women for women.[13]

Jane's entire life is an example of persistence, patience, charity, and love for the gospel of Jesus Christ as restored by the Prophet Joseph Smith. Jane was born in southwestern Pennsylvania on September 21, 1792. She was baptized a member of the Church in 1838, and she and her husband gathered with the Saints in Nauvoo in 1840. Her life in Nauvoo would present immense challenges, both economic and social. A few months later, Jane's husband died, leaving her a widow with nine children.[14] Jane also lost several children to death. She married again, but after caring for Thomas G. Fisher through a lingering illness, he also died.[15]

The Nauvoo Relief Society minutes for April 28, 1842, describe "widow Nighman" (Jane Neyman) as "destitute." On May 12, Jane's oldest daughter, Mary Ann Nickerson, was admitted to the newly organized society. In the Nauvoo Relief Society, women applied for admission, rather than being automatically accepted as members. Nearly all who applied were granted admission, but surprisingly, when Jane requested membership on July 14, objections were raised and she was not admitted.[16]

The denial of Jane's membership came at a time of uproar in Nauvoo regarding several men who had seduced or attempted to seduce women, claiming Joseph Smith's authorization. By 1842, Joseph had been commanded to begin the practice of plural marriage. Though this practice was kept confidential, some unscrupulous men used rumors about plural marriage to pursue extramarital relationships. In April, Joseph preached against "fornicators & unvirtuous persons. & those who had made use of his name to carry on their iniquitous designs."[17] Late in May, three women, including two of Jane's younger daughters, testified to being victims.[18] Emma Smith, president of the Nauvoo Relief Society, recommended that some sisters visit Jane "to inquire if she was dispos'd to reform the order of her house."[19]

One can only imagine Jane's distress. Trusted men in authority had broken that trust in insidious ways—and now *her* reputation was being called into question. How did Jane react? She certainly had reason to leave Nauvoo and the society of the Saints because of death, poverty, deceit, and slander toward her family. But, according to a eulogy of Jane given decades later, Joseph Smith continued to be "her unvarying friend; he rebuked those who falsely slandered her."[20]

Though Jane could not join the Nauvoo Relief Society, her daughter Mary Ann surely shared Joseph's teachings with her. In his addresses to the sisters, Joseph often preached on the power of mercy, charity, and repentance. On May 26, 1842, he encouraged them to "be arm'd with mercy" and reminded them they held "the keys of pow'r which will influence to virtue and goodness." He admonished them to "be pure in heart" and reminded them of Jesus's teaching "Ye shall do the work which ye see me do." To that he added, "These are the grand key words for the Society to act upon."[21]

Jane migrated to the Salt Lake Valley in 1850 along with her daughter Rachel Neyman, her daughter Mary Ann Nickerson, and the Nickerson family. Cholera raged as they traveled, and Jane cared for the ill. Louisa Barnes Pratt later described her service: "Mother Neyman shrank not from the hazardous task of administering to the victims of that disease, both temporally and spiritually, believing that if she did all in her power to save others, the Lord would spare her, and thus it proved."[22] Upon their arrival in the valley, Jane and Rachel settled with the Nickersons in the Cottonwood area. But Jane and others were soon called to settle Beaver, 200 miles south in Utah Territory.[23]

When the Beaver Relief Society was organized in 1868, Jane was called to be its first president. Though she had been rejected by the Nauvoo Relief Society, she accepted this call. Reflecting Joseph's teachings to the Nauvoo Relief Society, Jane preached unity among the sisters in Beaver. She invited them "to unite with us in this great and good work," namely "for the relief of the poor and afflicted among us and the mutual benefit of each other."[24] The following year, Jane addressed the Beaver Relief Society on charity. She encouraged "all to be forbearing and forgiving, refraining as much as possible from scrutinizing the conduct of our neighbors, remembering always that we are human and must therefore err."[25]

In March 1869, Jane resigned as president, "thinking the burden too great for her being far advanced in life" (she was nearly 80). Her bishop commended her service: "Her energies and faithfulness have been tested the past year; they have been untiring, both physically and spiritually."[26]

Jane died in Beaver on May 3, 1880. In her obituary, Louisa Barnes Pratt, her friend and counselor in the Beaver Relief Society, described her continued service to her community and to her Savior: "She lived to do good, to wash[,] anoint and nurse hundreds of her sex, to soothe and comfort their hearts, to which office she was set apart by the holy priesthood and in many instances, through her faith, was the power of God manifested in a marvelous manner."[27]

From her promptness to responding to the call to do proxy work for her kindred dead to the care and compassion she extended to all, Jane's life reflected her personal witness of the truthfulness of the gospel and her internalization of Joseph Smith's teaching to the Relief Society: "Let kindness, charity and love, crown your works."[28] Is she unique? I submit that she is not. Many who have gone before and many among us now understand and exemplify the same principles of faith and charity. It isn't easy, and it takes more than a little practice, but it's a degree of faith and service we can achieve, as did Jane.

Patricia Lemmon Spilsbury is a Church service missionary and the team leader of the Church History Department biographical research team.

Notes

1. "Part 6: 3 October 1840–30 January 1841," in *JSP*, D7:417; Vilate Kimball to Heber C. Kimball, Sept. 6, 1840, p. [3], Heber C. Kimball Letters, CHL; Minutes and Discourse, Apr. 6–8, 1840, in *JSP*, D7:242; Minutes and Discourse, Oct. 3–5, 1840, in *JSP*, D7:418.
2. "Brunson, Seymour" (biographical entry), josephsmithpapers.org; "Obituary," *Times and Seasons*, Sept. 1840, 1:176.
3. Vilate Kimball to Heber C. Kimball, Sept. 6, 1840, p. [3].
4. Simon Baker, Minutes of Recollection of Joseph Smith's Sermon on Baptism for the Dead, Aug. 15, 1840, Joseph Smith Collection (Supplement), 1833–44, box 4, folder 4, CHL.
5. Lyndon W. Cook, in *Nauvoo Marriages, Proxy Sealings, 1843–1846* (Provo, UT: Grandin Book, 2004), identifies the widow Joseph addressed as Jane Neyman. He gives no source for the identification.
6. Jane Neyman Statements, Nov. 29, 1854, image 3, CHL.
7. Visions, Jan. 21, 1836, in *JSP*, D5:157–60 [D&C 137].
8. Cook, *Nauvoo Marriages, Proxy Sealings*, ix; 1 Corinthians 15:22, 29.
9. Neyman Statements, Nov. 29, 1854, images 1, 3.
10. "Baptism for the Dead," Church History Topics, ChurchofJesusChrist.org.
11. Neyman Statements, Nov. 29, 1854, image 1.
12. Nauvoo Temple, Baptisms for the Dead, 1840–45, vol. A, 1840–41, pp. 69–70, 114–15, 203, microfilm 183376, Family History Library, Salt Lake City.
13. Matthew McBride, "Letters on Baptisms for the Dead: D&C 127, 128," in *Revelations in Context: The Stories behind the Sections of the Doctrine and Covenants*, ed. Matthew McBride and James Goldberg, ChurchofJesusChrist.org.

14. Historical Introduction to "Be Forbearing and Forgiving," in *At the Pulpit: 185 Years of Discourses by Latter-day Saint Women* (website), churchhistorianspress.org; "The Rachel Neyman Story," in Jane Harper (KVFB-RX4), Memories, FamilySearch, https://www.familysearch.org/tree/person/details/KVFB-RX4.

15. Lyndon W. Cook, comp., *Nauvoo Deaths and Marriages, 1839–1845* (Orem, UT: Grandin Book, 1994), 112; Fred E. Woods, "The Cemetery Record of William D. Huntington, Nauvoo Sexton," *Mormon Historical Studies* 3, no. 1 (Spring 2002): 150; "Rachel Neyman Story."

16. Nauvoo Relief Society Minute Book, Apr. 28, May 12, and July 14, 1842, in *The First Fifty Years of Relief Society: Key Documents in Latter-day Saint Women's History*, ed. Jill Mulvay Derr et al. (Salt Lake City: Church Historian's Press, 2016), 61, 63, 89.

17. Journal, Apr. 10, 1842, in *JSP*, J2:50.

18. Derr et al., *First Fifty Years*, 67, note 175.

19. Nauvoo Relief Society Minute Book, Apr. 28, 1842, in Derr et al., *First Fifty Years*, 61.

20. Louisa Barnes Pratt, "Obituaries," *Woman's Exponent* 9, no. 1 (June 1, 1880): 4.

21. Nauvoo Relief Society Minute Book, May 26, 1842, in Derr et al., *First Fifty Years*, 69–71.

22. "Jane Neyman," Pioneer Database, 1847–68, history.ChurchofJesusChrist.org/overland travel; Pratt "Obituaries," 4.

23. 1850 U.S. Census, Great Salt Lake City, Utah Territory, 102.

24. Beaver 1st Ward Relief Society Minutes, 1868–78, Jan. 11, 1868, 1, CHL.

25. Beaver 1st Ward Relief Society Minutes, Nov. 4, 1869, 25–26, quoted in "Be Forbearing and Forgiving," in At the Pulpit (website), churchhistorianspress.org.

26. Beaver 1st Ward Relief Society Minutes, Mar. 4, 1869, 13–14.

27. Pratt, "Obituaries," 4–5.

28. Nauvoo Relief Society Minute Book, Apr. 28, 1842, in Derr et al., *First Fifty Years*, 59.

"A DAY OF DARKNESS": HOW JOSEPH SMITH DEALT WITH DEATH IN 1841

By Brett D. Dowdle

Compared to many of the other years of Joseph Smith's prophetic tenure, 1841 ranks among the calmest. But the absence of violent persecutions did not prevent 1841 from having its own special challenges. Throughout that year, Joseph struggled as he worked to meet debt payments on the lands the Latter-day Saints had purchased in Nauvoo. More significant, the month of August brought four painful deaths that tried Joseph enormously. The intimacy of these moments of loss, and Joseph's efforts to continue the work of the Lord during these times, provide not only important insights into his heart but also a greater understanding of how we can fulfill our covenants to "mourn with those that mourn."[1]

Joseph was certainly not unacquainted with death and mourning prior to August 1841. He had already experienced the death of his father, Joseph Sr. (1840), brothers Ephraim (1810) and Alvin (1823), a son born in 1828, a son and a daughter born in 1831, and an adopted son named Joseph Murdock (1832), to say nothing of the deaths of close friends. Indeed, death marked Joseph's life in profound ways, raising important questions that yielded revelatory answers, underscoring the deep significance of his prophetic ministry.[2] But the deaths in August 1841 were significant because they came at a time when Joseph had learned or was beginning to learn many of the important principles that define the Latter-day Saint view of death.

Beginning in July 1841, members of the Quorum of the Twelve Apostles began to trickle back into Nauvoo, concluding their lengthy mission to the British Isles.[3] Their return, together with the growing emigration of British converts to Nauvoo, gave the Saints added enthusiasm about their "beautiful place" overlooking the Mississippi River.[4] On July 25, soon after his return home, Apostle George A. Smith married Bathsheba W. Bigler, with George's cousin Don Carlos Smith performing the ceremony. Following the wedding, George A., Bathsheba, and Don Carlos attended a meeting in a grove where they heard Sidney Rigdon preach "a general funeral address" that was "designed to comfort and instruct the saints, especially those who had been called to mourn the loss of relatives and friends." Joseph Smith then preached on the resurrection.[5] The sermons would prove sadly anticipatory of events in the month to follow.

On August 7, just two weeks after performing the marriage, Don Carlos died at the age of 25, becoming the third of Joseph's brothers to die during his lifetime. Speaking to the unexpected nature of his death, the *Times and Seasons* explained, "He was just in the bloom of manhood . . . but just as the sun was shining with its lustre, and sheding a radiance all around, it set in a moment."[6] Despite the tragic event, Joseph spent the day following the funeral in council with five members of the Quorum of the Twelve, instructing them to call a special conference six days later on August 16.[7]

Unexpectedly, that conference was marred by another passing, as Joseph and Emma's 14-month-old son, Don Carlos, died on August 15 and was buried the following day.[8] While Joseph missed the morning session of the conference to be at the burial, he arrived around 2:00 p.m. and gave an address that transformed Church governance. He explained that "the time had come" for the Twelve "to stand in their place next to the first presidency" and to "assist in managing the affairs of th[e] kingdom." In this way, the Prophet would be enabled to "attend to the business of translating."[9] But while Joseph strove to carry on in his responsibilities, he was not unaffected by these deaths. On August 25, while writing to creditor Horace Hotchkiss, Joseph was unable to contain his feelings, providing a glimpse into his grief. He described his "beautiful city" as "a *deathly sickly hole*" and explained that the illnesses and deaths had made it difficult for the Saints to make their payments on land in Nauvoo. Concluding the letter, he wrote, "In fact we are in the midst of death."[10]

At the end of August, Joseph lost two of his most helpful associates. Eleven days after Joseph and Emma buried their son, the Prophet's clerk and friend Robert B. Thompson died at the age of 29 from a lung infection.[11] Thompson had been a trusted record keeper for Joseph, who took his loss hard.[12] Unbeknownst to Joseph and the Saints, just days before Thompson's death, Oliver Granger had died at Kirtland, Ohio. Granger had been integral to Joseph's efforts to settle his debts dating back to the Kirtland period.[13]

In less than a month, the Prophet had lost a baby son, a brother, and two vital associates. In a letter to Granger, written on August 30 when Granger's own passing was still not known to those in Nauvoo, Joseph and Hyrum described this as "an Eventful Period[,] a Day of Darkness & of thick darkness & Mourning[,] weeping & L[a]mentation."[14] Yet there were lessons to be learned from this heartache. Despite his personal grief, Joseph used it as an opportunity to teach the Saints.

In that same letter to Granger, Joseph reflected upon the importance of preparing for life's unexpected experiences, including untimely deaths.[15] Joseph also urged the Saints to be wise in their use of the various medicines of the day. On Sunday, September 5, he counseled a large congregation to "trust in God when Sick" and to "live by faith" rather than using the bogus medicines peddled by the newspapers and the often fraudulent doctors of the day.[16] Thus he encouraged the Saints to reject the supposed cure-all remedies in favor of greater wisdom.

Additionally, Joseph taught further truths about baptism for the dead, a doctrine he had only begun teaching in August 1840.[17] During the October 1841 conference of the Church, the Prophet taught that it was "no more incredible that God should *save* the dead, than that he should *raise* the dead." Through this ordinance, the Saints could "appear as saviors on mount Zion," helping to "release the spirit of the dead" from the bondage of the grave and becoming "instrumental in bringing multitudes of their kin into the kingdom of God." Through this doctrine the Saints could clearly see "the wisdom and mercy of God" and that "all are within the reach of pardoning mercy, who have not committed the unpardonable sin."[18]

This period of "Mourning[,] weeping & [Lamentation]" reminded Joseph and the Saints of the tenuousness of mortality and the need for wisdom. Furthermore, this season of death prompted them to place greater trust in God and underscored the urgency of their work for the dead, with the coming years bringing even greater insight into that doctrine.

In our own lives, as we respond to the deaths or severe illnesses of loved ones, the lessons learned by Joseph and the Saints are not unworthy of our attention. Just as Joseph found it hard to contain his emotions at times, so too will our seasons of encountering sickness and death bring moments and perhaps even outbursts of emotional exhaustion. As we experience those times, we should give voice to our pain in conversation, letter, journal entry, or some other way. And as others express their distress and perhaps even direct it toward us, as Joseph did toward Horace Hotchkiss, we can be patient, kind, and understanding while they navigate their grief.

When grief and mourning come, they can paralyze us and bring life to a standstill. While we must take proper time to mourn, we must also follow Joseph's example and press forward in such moments. Like Joseph, we can share the weight of responsibility with the trusted ones around us, while at the same time finding ways to continue to magnify our callings and responsibilities. With greater understanding and empathy, we can use the lessons of these moments to testify and teach of gospel truths. Through our sadness, we must learn to see "the wisdom and mercy of God," and then we must stand as witnesses for those truths.[19] In this way, we will come to know, as Joseph did, that "God [has] not designed all this for nothing" but that there are eternal insights and strength that we and others may gain through our grief.[20]

Brett D. Dowdle is a historian with the Church History Department.

Notes

1. Mosiah 18:9.
2. See Samuel Morris Brown, *In Heaven as It Is on Earth: Joseph Smith and the Early Mormon Conquest of Death* (New York: Oxford University Press, 2012).
3. Joseph Smith, History, July 1, 13, and 19, 1841, in "History, 1838–1856, volume C-1 [2 November 1838–31 July 1842]," pp. 1213–14, 1219, josephsmithpapers.org.
4. Richard M. Young to Elias Higbee, Apr. 22, 1840, in "Letterbook 2," p. 135, josephsmith papers.org.
5. Joseph Smith, History, July 25, 1841, in "History, 1838–1856, volume C-1 Addenda," p. 9, josephsmithpapers.org; George A. Smith, Journal, June 25, 1841, George A. Smith Papers, CHL.
6. "Death of General Don Carlos Smith," *Times and Seasons*, Aug. 16, 1841, 2:503.
7. Joseph Smith, History, Aug. 10, 1841, in "History, 1838–1856, volume C-1 [2 November 1838–31 July 1842]," p. 1220.
8. Obituary for Don Carlos Smith, *Times and Seasons*, Sept. 1, 1841, 2:533; George A. Smith, Diary, Aug. 16, 1841, CHL.
9. Discourse, Aug. 16, 1841, in *JSP*, D8:228; Minutes, Aug. 16, 1841, in *JSP*, D8:224–27.
10. Letter to Horace Hotchkiss, Aug. 25, 1841, in *JSP*, D8:237–40, emphasis in original.
11. Letter to Oliver Granger, Aug. 30, 1841, in *JSP*, D8:245; "Death of Col. Robert B. Thompson," *Times and Seasons*, Sept. 1, 1842, 2:519–20.
12. Letter to Oliver Granger, Aug. 30, 1841, in *JSP*, D8:244–47.
13. Obituary for Oliver Granger, *Times and Seasons*, Sept. 15, 1841, 2:550; Revelation, July 8, 1838-E, in *JSP*, D6:191–94 [D&C 117:12–15].
14. Letter to Oliver Granger, Aug. 30, 1841, in *JSP*, D8:246.
15. Letter to Oliver Granger, Aug. 30, 1841, in *JSP*, D8:246.
16. Joseph Smith, History, Sept. 5, 1841, in "History Draft [1 January–31 December 1841]," p. 15, josephsmithpapers.org.
17. Simon Baker, Statement, Joseph Smith Collection, CHL.
18. Minutes and Discourse, Oct. 1–5, 1841, in *JSP*, D8:287–89, emphasis in original.
19. See Mosiah 24:14.
20. Minutes, Discourse, and Blessings, Feb. 14–15, 1835, in *JSP*, D4:225.

JOSEPH SMITH: APPOINTED TO LEAD US

By Julie A. Russell

Until recently, I had not been interested in studying the history of The Church of Jesus Christ of Latter-day Saints. Twenty years ago, when I was learning about the Church from the missionaries, I received a profound and undeniable testimony from the Holy Spirit that the Book of Mormon is truly the word of God. At the time, that was enough for me. My personal feelings were that if the Book of Mormon is legitimate, then all other doctrine, history, and organization falls into place no matter how challenging or alien—or alienating. Fast forward a couple of decades. Just when I thought nothing could shake my testimony that The Church of Jesus Christ of Latter-day Saints is God's Church restored in the latter days, I began to encounter one Latter-day Saint after another who shared his or her doubts about Joseph Smith's character and status as a true prophet of God. It seemed more than coincidence that unconnected people from different parts of my life would all converge upon me at once with the message that Joseph Smith was a fallen prophet.

What was most disconcerting to me was not so much the message my friends shared as the confidence with which the message was shared. It was shared by educated, grounded, and even-minded folks whom I (continue to) respect. I knew that I would need to discover Joseph's character for myself if I wanted to quiet the nagging questions that my friends' assertions began to cultivate in my mind. Intuitive to me is the reality that *where* you get your information is more important than the *quantity* of information you find. Naturally, I turned to the primary sources— the Doctrine and Covenants and *The Joseph Smith Papers.* I also explored the Gospel Topics Essays, *Saints: The Standard of Truth,* and Richard L. Bushman's *Rough Stone Rolling*—making sure to refer to the sources cited in the footnotes as often as possible. I read these texts with an open mind, a mind that would hopefully allow me to understand more perspectives than my own.

When I read about the failed bank called the Kirtland Safety Society,[1] I wondered how a prophet of God could have been so unsuccessful in his endeavors to serve the people God had called him to serve. When I read through different accounts of men challenging Joseph's authority as a prophet,[2] I thought to myself, "Did Joseph not have enough of the Holy Spirit that these men could feel it when they were near him? What kinds of things did he do that would have caused these men to doubt him?" The succession crisis at Joseph's death disturbed me as I read about all the fractures within the upper echelons of the Church's government and the various accounts of different men claiming to have received authority from Joseph Smith to assume leadership after he was gone.[3] But perhaps, most challenging—to me and many others—is Joseph Smith's practice of plural marriage.[4]

There are accounts of Emma Smith vacillating between acceptance of the practice and publicly censuring it.[5] I can certainly empathize with Emma. The practice was as taboo then as it is now, and while we have several accounts of other women having received spiritual witnesses and even angelic visitations to confirm the holiness of the practice,[6] I could not find a record of Emma saying she had received such a witness. But I did read letter after letter of Joseph expressing sincere and heartfelt love to Emma and concern for her emotional and physical well-being.[7] I read accounts of Joseph's struggle with the commandment to practice plural marriage and his reluctance to obey and share it with others, including his closest friends and associates.[8]

The most compelling documents to me, though, are the ones that demonstrate that even after Joseph began practicing plural marriage in earnest in 1841, he was still receiving revelation from God—the kind of revelation we still teach and discuss in our regular curriculum and study. In other words, after he introduced plural marriage, he was still allowed to lead and guide the Church, which is, according to our own doctrine, guided by Christ Himself through His called prophets. The King Follett sermon, delivered in April 1844, was a powerful address that annihilated conventional concepts about the nature of God the Father and Jesus Christ. In it Joseph asserted his hope that the Saints could know God for themselves—that they could receive personal revelation so they could know what Joseph already knew.[9] This desire is far from the approach of a tyrant who would demand the ignorance and disunity of his subjects to maintain absolute control.

In May 1842, God revealed the sacred ordinance of the temple endowment to Joseph Smith.[10] In September 1842, Joseph Smith received revelation for the Church clarifying the practice of baptism for the dead—a sacred practice in which we continue to participate—now found in section 127 of the Doctrine and Covenants.[11] Again, to me this is clear evidence that Joseph Smith was still operating as God's mouthpiece, still possessing authority, still a prophet of God. I could continue to enumerate evidences of Joseph Smith's enduring right to lead the Church, but the most powerful and indisputable of all evidences is the testimony of the Holy Spirit. I would submit that nothing I nor anyone else may say will convince another of the truth as effectively as the Holy Spirit, whose personal witness all members of God's Church have a right to.

There have been many times throughout my adult life that I have questioned the truthfulness of the Book of Mormon and whether Joseph Smith really was a prophet. These doubts scare me. I can't imagine my life without the Book of Mormon, the gift of the Holy Ghost, and all other blessings that come from honoring my membership in The Church of Jesus Christ of Latter-day Saints. Ultimately, I have had to search my own mind and heart for the undeniable and real experiences I have had with the Holy Spirit as He has borne testimony to me of the truthfulness of doctrine, the Book of Mormon, and temple ordinances and as He has helped me understand that policy and practice come from inspiration. I have realized that the individual parts of the gospel make up a synergistic whole, and if I can develop a firm testimony in one of those parts, I can use that to build my testimony of the other parts. In that way I have brought myself back from the brink of a ruptured testimony more than once. When my or others' concerns or incorrect assertions have threatened my testimony, I have practiced an exercise in chronology.

In studying the Church's history, I sometimes questioned Joseph Smith's motives and veracity. In those moments, I would return to that first, singular experience when the Holy Spirit testified of the Book of Mormon so tangibly that had I been standing, I would have fallen. From there I would walk forward through time, cataloging each spiritual experience, letting the sum of them reinforce my faith in the goodness of God—the same God who allowed His Holy Spirit to convince me to accept the invitation to be baptized a member of The Church of Jesus Christ of Latter-day Saints. I had studied many different denominations before I found the Church. Not until I investigated the Church did God allow His Spirit to fill up the emptiness inside me. I believe that this experience was meant to help me learn to trust the doctrinal teachings of the Church.

Ultimately, if—as the Holy Spirit has confirmed to me—the Book of Mormon is true, then Joseph Smith must be a prophet. God promises us that we "shall not be moved out of [our] place" when we "hearken unto . . . the voice of my servants whom I have appointed to lead my people."[12] Joseph Smith was "appointed to lead" us. Plural marriage was practiced for decades after Joseph's death. It was sustained and perpetuated by successive prophets who also were "appointed to lead" us. Those early Saints who heeded the prophets' voices were not moved out their places.

I have had the opportunity to research Relief Society minute books dating from 1868 until 1887 to locate Eliza R. Snow's sermons for publication. In the course of my research, I read time and again the testimonies of plural wives who had received for themselves a spiritual manifestation of the divine origin and necessity of plural marriage. One of those women, Eliza R. Snow, a plural wife of Joseph Smith and then of

Brigham Young, consistently defended this "most holy Principle"[13] over the nearly 20 years she traveled and preached to wards and branches throughout Utah Territory. She "knew [Joseph Smith] to be a man of God," and, therefore, she "held the doctrine of plural marriage as sacred as any other principle of salvation." She believed it elevated the spirituality of women, and, in her own words, she at no time felt degraded, oppressed, or debased.[14]

It is given to us to judge for ourselves, to know by the fruits of our fellow humans, whether they be of God or the devil. But that judgment must come from a prayerful and pliable heart, a firm testimony that God is good and trustworthy, and a willingness to accept that we may not like or understand the answers God gives us—or that He may not answer all of our questions. Otherwise, we are simply judging a nineteenth-century man from a twenty-first-century perspective.

Julie A. Russell is a project manager supporting the Discourses of Eliza R. Snow and *Saints*, volume 4.

Notes

1. See "Kirtland Safety Society" (glossary entry), josephsmithpapers.org.
2. See, for example, "Minutes, 28–29 August 1834," pp. 58–61, josephsmithpapers.org; and Wilford Woodruff, Journal, Jan. 3–4, 1844, Wilford Woodruff Journals and Papers, 1828–98, CHL.
3. For an account of the succession crisis, see *Saints: The Story of the Church of Jesus Christ in the Latter Days*, vol. 1, *The Standard of Truth, 1815–1846* (Salt Lake City: The Church of Jesus Christ of Latter-day Saints, 2018), 553–68.
4. Joseph Smith entered his first plural marriage in the mid-1830s and reintroduced the practice in Nauvoo in 1841. ("Plural Marriage in Kirtland and Nauvoo," Gospel Topics, ChurchofJesusChrist.org.)
5. "Joseph and Emma" section in "Plural Marriage in Kirtland and Nauvoo."
6. See, for example, Zina Huntington Jacobs, Autobiographical Sketch, Zina Card Brown Family Collection, CHL.
7. For a summary of such letters, see Carol Cornwall Madsen, "My Dear and Beloved Companion," *Ensign*, Sept. 2008.
8. See, for example, Historical Introduction to "Letter from Oliver Cowdery, 21 January 1838," josephsmithpapers.org; and Richard Lyman Bushman, *Joseph Smith: Rough Stone Rolling* (New York: Knopf, 2005), 437–38.
9. "Accounts of the 'King Follett Sermon'" (featured topic entry), josephsmithpapers.org.
10. "Endowment" (glossary entry), josephsmithpapers.org.

11. "Letter to 'All the Saints in Nauvoo,' 1 September 1842 [D&C 127]," josephsmithpapers .org.

12. "Revelation, 19 January 1841 [D&C 124]," josephsmithpapers.org; see Doctrine and Covenants 124:45.

13. Cottonwood 1st Ward Relief Society Minutes and Records, 1868–1971, May 17, 1870, vol. 1, p. 50, CHL.

14. Eliza R. Snow, "Degradation of Woman in Utah," *Deseret News*, Apr. 27, 1870.

"HE WEPT AS THOUGH HIS HEART WOULD BREAK": JOSEPH SMITH AS A MAN OF DEEP AND TENDER FEELINGS

By Jay A. Parry

In August 1842, Joseph Smith was hiding from authorities who sought to extradite him from Illinois to Missouri for a crime he didn't commit. Missing his family and friends, he arranged for a friend to row him from his hiding place to an island in the Mississippi River, where he met secretly with his wife and several others. A few days later, he wrote, "How glorious were my feelings when I met that faithful and friendly band. . . . With what unspeakable delight, and what transports of joy swelled my bosom."[1]

Joseph Smith was a man of deep and tender feelings, and he often let those feelings rise to the surface. This is evident from many of his teachings and writings and from reminiscences of those who loved him—and it is significant for several reasons.

First, recognizing and expressing feelings is godly behavior. When Enoch had his remarkable vision of God and His creations, he learned that God Himself is a being of deep and tender feelings. He saw God weep over the wickedness of His children on the earth. Enoch himself then "wept . . . , and his heart swelled wide as eternity; and his bowels yearned; and all eternity shook."[2]

Second, Church leaders are more effective when they feel genuine empathy for their people. Alma observed that Jesus would "go forth, suffering pains and afflictions and temptations of every kind." In doing so, "his bowels [would] be filled with mercy, according to the flesh," which would help him "succor his people."[3] As with the Master, so with the servant. Prophets and others are able to minister better as they feel and understand the struggles and difficulties and *feelings* of those they serve.

I have personally experienced the power of empathy in both local and general Church leaders. When I see the compassion in their eyes and hear in their voices that they understand my feelings, I feel a connection—which in turn more completely blesses me than otherwise would have occurred. I recall once sharing a personal challenge with a priesthood leader, and he wept with me. And when one of the Brethren speaks with emotional intensity—as President Russell M. Nelson or Elder Jeffrey R. Holland have done—their words reach deeply into my soul.

Third, the Spirit often speaks to us through our feelings. Nephi chastised his rebellious brothers by saying that the Lord had "spoken unto you in a still small voice, but ye were past feeling, that ye could not feel his words."[4] In our dispensation, the Lord said that revelation often comes as the Spirit speaks "in your mind and in your heart."[5]

Men and women of God, then—including prophets—are more able to represent the Lord when they are open to emotions and when they let those feelings have place in their lives. Such a man was Joseph Smith.

Joseph was emotionally sensitive even in his youth. In his canonized account of the First Vision, he spoke of the extreme feelings he and others felt during a period of "unusual excitement on the subject of religion." There was "no small stir and division" among the people in the area; it was an "extraordinary scene of religious feeling, . . . a scene of great confusion and bad feeling" involving "a strife of words and a contest about opinions." Again and again he emphasized the strong feelings in the Palmyra area around the year 1820: "confusion and strife," "cry and tumult," and a "war of words, and tumult of opinions."

Young Joseph expressed his own "great uneasiness" about religion and the state of his soul. "My feelings were deep and often poignant," he wrote. He was "greatly excited" by the whole question. In that mental and emotional state, he read James 1:5, inviting those who lacked wisdom to ask God. James's promise of an answer from God entered "with great force into every feeling of my heart." Given all his "anxieties," he determined to pray vocally, offering "up the desires of [his] heart to God." When Satan temporarily intervened, Joseph said, his power was "astonishing." Joseph was filled with "great alarm," and he was "ready to sink into despair." But as Joseph persisted in his prayer, the light and power of God drove away the darkness and power of Satan, and Joseph then received a marvelous manifestation of the Father and the Son,[6] "one of the most significant events in the history of the world."[7]

Joseph freely shared his deep feelings in personal letters to his wife, Emma, and others. In 1832, Joseph wrote to Emma from Indiana, telling her that nearly every day he had visited a grove near town where he could "give vent to all the feelings of [his] heart in meditation and prayer." As he contemplated his mortal weaknesses, he was "left to mourn and shed tears of sorrow." Still, he was grateful that "God is merciful" and had forgiven his sins. He learned a few days earlier that Hyrum Smith's young daughter had tragically died. In the letter to Emma, Joseph said he was "grieved to hear that Hiram had lost his little child" and then added (as one who had similarly been bereaved), "I think we can in some degree sympathise with him."[8]

In early November 1838, writing from imprisonment in Missouri, he conveyed his "great anxiety" for his family and said, "My heart mourns and bleeds for the brethren and sisters." Poignantly, he asked Emma to tell his "little children . . . that Father is yet alive," and added, "God grant that he may see them again." He expressed his fears that they might not meet again in this life and concluded by writing, "I cannot express my feelings, my heart is full."[9]

A few months later, Joseph wrote to a friend from the jail in Liberty. "Oh, what a joy it would be to us to see our friends. It would have gladdened my heart. . . . What inexpressible joy it gives a man to see the face of . . . a friend after having been enclosed in the walls of a prison for five months. It seems to me that my heart will always be more tender after this than ever it was before. My heart bleeds continually when I contemplate the distress of the Church."[10]

Reminiscences of those who knew Joseph support what we find in his writings. Daniel Tyler attended a meeting in Kirtland at a time when some of the elders were rebelling against the Prophet's authority. "I perceived sadness in his countenance and tears trickling down his cheeks." Joseph knelt to pray, but he turned his back to the congregation "to hide his sorrow and tears." Tyler recalled that never before had he heard such a prayer, as Joseph addressed "his Maker as though He was present listening as a kind father would listen to the sorrows of a dutiful child." When Joseph stood to speak, "he wept as though his heart would break."[11]

Edward Stevenson recalled the occasion when Joseph, after escaping from captivity in Missouri, spoke to a group of Saints in Quincy, Illinois. "His soul was filled with emotion, and it seemed as though relief could . . . [come] only with a flood of tears." When Joseph finally spoke, he explained his emotions. While he was imprisoned, the Saints had been driven from their homes. Yet they had remained true to the faith. "To realize that my life has been spared to behold your faces again seemed to be so great a pleasure that . . . words seemed only a vague expression of my soul's gratitude."

Stevenson added, "The Prophet was of a tender heart, as well as of a stern and firm disposition when occasion required it. I have known the Prophet to weep with tender affection, and I have seen him . . . when he was mighty as well as powerful."[12]

The death of Robert B. Thompson, Joseph's close friend and secretary, deeply grieved Joseph. Robert's wife, Mercy, noted: "I saw him [Joseph] stand in sorrow, . . . while the tears of love and sympathy freely flowed. This was indeed a time of sorrow, but I can never forget the tender sympathy and brotherly kindness he ever showed toward me and my fatherless child."[13]

George A. Smith, a cousin of Joseph Smith and an Apostle, recalled that after a meeting with the Prophet, "he wrapped his arms around me and squeezed me to his bosom and said: 'George A., I love you, as I do my own life.'" George was "so affected [he] could hardly speak" but finally responded in kind.[14]

By seeing Joseph Smith as a man of deep and tender feelings, we can begin to know him as his own contemporaries did. His feelings of sorrow and rejoicing alike were close to the surface. His expressions of feeling give us a model of a godly man who knew how to receive guidance from on high while remaining truly empathetic with others.

Jay A. Parry is an editor for the Church Historian's Press as well as a published author; his most recent book is *A Treasured Testament: The Miraculous Coming Forth of the Book of Mormon* (American Fork, UT: Covenant Communications, 2019).

Notes

1. "Reflections and Blessings, 16 and 23 August 1842," p. 164, josephsmithpapers.org. Joseph was particularly anxious to avoid extradition to Missouri because he feared for his life there.
2. Moses 7:41.
3. Alma 7:11–12.
4. 1 Nephi 17:45.
5. "Revelation, April 1829–B [D&C 8:2–3]," p. 13, josephsmithpapers.org, punctuation and spelling standardized.
6. "History, circa June 1839–circa 1841 [Draft 2]," pp. [1–3], josephsmithpapers.org, punctuation and spelling standardized.
7. Russell M. Nelson, "Opening Message," General Conference, Apr. 2020, Churchof JesusChrist.org.
8. "Letter to Emma Smith, 6 June 1832," p. [1], josephsmithpapers.org, punctuation and spelling standardized.
9. "Letter to Emma Smith, 4 November 1838," pp. [1–2], josephsmithpapers.org, punctuation and spelling standardized.
10. "Letter to Presendia Huntington Buell, 15 March 1839," p. [1], josephsmithpapers.org, punctuation and spelling standardized.
11. Daniel Tyler, in "Recollections of the Prophet Joseph Smith," *Juvenile Instructor* 27, no. 4 (Feb. 15, 1892): 127–28.
12. Autobiography of Edward Stevenson, typescript, 55, CHL, punctuation and spelling standardized.
13. Mercy Fielding Thompson, in "Recollections of the Prophet Joseph Smith," *Juvenile Instructor* 27, no. 13 (July 1, 1892): 399.
14. George A. Smith, Journal, May 15, 1843, in *Ancestry, Biography, and Family of George A. Smith,* comp. Zora Smith Jarvis (Provo, UT: Brigham Young University Press, 1962), 86–87.

"AS FREE FROM DISSIMULATION AS ANY MAN": THE AUTHENTIC JOSEPH SMITH

By Ronald O. Barney

In every circumstance, for as long as humans have gathered, leaders have emerged in one way or another. Their effectiveness, contribution, and durability often stem from how they are perceived by those who follow. One need not have exhibited perfection to have been respected and honored among the people. But there are integrities that, for the individual to qualify for enduring greatness, must be clearly shown and recognized by the followers. There has to be no mystery among them regarding the person's core character and designs. He or she has to be "real" to the people. As a modern American journalist wrote, "A person is either himself or not himself; is either rooted in his existence or is a fabrication; has either found his humanhood or is still playing with masks and roles and status symbols."[1] It requires a long-term demonstration of authentic openness displaying one's true nature to capture yearning hearts. Should the person, over time, merit the collective devotion of his or her adherents is evidence the person surpassed the hurdle of authenticity demanded by most followers.

The result is the creation of a bond that fosters perpetuity of the leader's influence and his or her long-term objectives. As the noted historian Arnold Toynbee stated, "A society cannot maintain its social cohesion unless a decisive majority of its members hold in common a number of guiding ideas and ideals. One of the necessary social ideals is a symbolic hero to embody, in a personal form, the recognized goal of the society's endeavors."[2] In The Church of Jesus Christ of Latter-day Saints and to its people, that symbolic hero is Joseph Smith.

There were, it is well known, measures of uncertainty among Church members in the beginning about how the restored gospel of Jesus Christ would be administered. But within months of the Church's organization, the revelations of Jesus to the Prophet made clear that he was the *one* appointed to lead the kingdom. That he had the designation of prophet, seer, and revelator, however, was not enough to lastingly impress those who had grasped the missionaries' message. Joseph won the people, the evidence reveals, because of his genuine expression of humanity to which all of them could relate. A later commentator wrote, "They loved him because he was to them so human and so like themselves, and yet, when necessary, his dignity was ready, and his mission became divine in their wondering eyes."[3]

Another who recognized the genuine nature of Joseph Smith was a physician who led the New York City congregation of the Latter-day Saints before immigrating to Nauvoo in 1843. Being single, John M. Bernhisel lodged with Joseph and Emma Smith for the last nine months of Joseph's life. He observed them up close. Two weeks before the Martyrdom, Bernhisel, who later became the territorial delegate to Congress from Utah, wrote to Illinois Governor Thomas Ford attempting to mitigate the momentum of injustice enveloping Joseph. Besides emphasizing the "gentle charities" of Joseph's "domestic life, as the tender and affectionate husband & parent, the warm and sympathising friend," he emphatically stated that it was "almost superfluous to add that the numerous rediculous and scandilous reports in circulation respecting him, have not the least foundation in truth." He underscored that Joseph was "honest, frank, fearless, and independent" and "as free from dissimulation as any man to be found."[4] Dissimulation defined someone who was a pretender—a person who was actually not what he represented himself to be. The matter was particularly salient to nineteenth-century Americans familiar with underhanded characters who preyed upon all classes of people.

When new converts responded to the call to join with the Saints, many were impressed upon meeting Joseph Smith that he presented himself as an ordinary man. George Washington Taggart, who complied with the missionaries' challenge to gather, arrived in Nauvoo in the late summer of 1843. Writing to family in New Hampshire about the man whom he most desired to see, he stated, "He does not pretend to be a man without failings and follies," and "neither is He puffed up with His greatness as manny suppose but on the contrary is familiar with anny decent man."[5] Similarly, Jonah Randolph Ball, who also arrived in Nauvoo in 1843, wrote to a friend: "I found Joseph familiar in conversation, easy and unassuming. I found no syconphancy. there is those that came in or went out not even taking their hats or caps off their heads." Ball continued, "He is what the Mormons represent him to be & the stories about him are false . . . this I tell you as the Truth of a Friend & Brother."[6]

Over the course of his life, Joseph Smith was, perhaps surprisingly, freely open about his human limitations. Instead of being fearful that he might be exposed, as would a pretender, he readily acknowledged his weakness. From Nauvoo in March 1843, one Church member wrote to a Boston newspaper to explain, "He said he did not profess to be a *very good man*, but acknowledged himself a sinner like other men, or as all men are, imperfect; and it is necessary for all men to grow into the stature of manhood in the gospel."[7] A New York journalist who heard Joseph speak in Washington, DC, in early 1840 wrote to his wife about the Latter-day Saint prophet: "Towards the close of his address, he remarked that he had been represented as pretending to be a Saviour, a Worker of Miracles, &c. All this was false. He made no such pretensions. He was but a man, he said—a plain untutored man; seeking what he should do to be saved."[8]

Perhaps most telling was Joseph's inclusion of Jesus's reproofs to him for all to see in the revelations he received. As he was the one to dictate to his scribes his spiritual impressions, he easily could have eliminated the reprimands that would eventually be published. Instead he included the rebukes. The first recorded revelation he received, for example, stated, "And behold how oft you [Joseph Smith] have transgressed the Laws of God & have gone on in the Persuasions of men for behold you should not have feared men more then God. . . . behold thou art Joseph & thou wast chosen to do the work of the Lord but because of transgression thou mayest fall."[9] Some months later he heard: "& now I command my Servant Joseph that he repenteth & walketh more uprightly before me & yield to the perswations of men no more."[10] Over the course of his ministry, he continued to include the Lord's admonishment to him in the revelations he dictated.[11]

As Joseph explained to the Twelve Apostles in November 1835, "I am determined to do all that I can to up-hold you, although I may do many things invertaintly [inadvertently] that are not right in the sight of God."[12] Those who knew him best recognized his earnest sincerity. His prophetic ministry and how he represented himself proved to be a model to the Church for human authenticity.

Ronald O. Barney is a former archivist and historian in the Church History Department, a former associate editor with the Joseph Smith Papers, and the author of *Joseph Smith: History, Methods, and Memory* (Salt Lake City: University of Utah Press, 2020).

Notes

1. Sydney J. Harris, *The Best of Sydney J. Harris* (Boston: Houghton Mifflin, 1976), 30.
2. Arnold Toynbee, *An Historian's Approach to Religion* (London: Oxford University Press, 1956), 220.
3. T. B. H. Stenhouse, *The Rocky Mountain Saints: A Full and Complete History of the Mormons, from the First Vision of Joseph Smith to the Last Courtship of Brigham Young* (New York: D. Appleton, 1873), 159.
4. John M. Bernhisel to Thomas Ford, June 14, 1844, in Joseph Smith Office Papers, CHL.
5. George W. Taggart to [his brothers in New Hampshire], Sept. 10, 1843, Albert Taggart Correspondence, 1842–60, CHL.
6. Jonah Randolph Ball to Harvey Howard, Jan. 15, 1843, Jonah R. Ball, Letters, 1842–43, CHL.
7. "Mormonism," *Boston Bee*, Mar. 24, 1843, reported in *Times and Seasons*, May 15, 1843, 4:199–200, emphasis in original.
8. Matthew L. Davis to Mary Davis, Feb. 6, 1840, in *JSP*, D7:179.
9. Revelation, July 1828, in *JSP*, D1:8 [D&C 3:6, 9].
10. Revelation, Mar. 1829, *JSP*, D1:17 [D&C 5:21].
11. See also these other examples of Joseph exhibiting his weaknesses as included in the revelatory texts: Doctrine and Covenants 1:17–19, 24; 6:19; 9:1; 10:2, 37; 20:5; 29:3; 35:17–18; 64:5, 7; 67:5; 90:1, 6, 17–18; 93:47; 111:1; 124:1; 128:18; and 132:45.
12. Journal, Nov. 12, 1835, in *JSP*, J1:97.

A DAY IN THE LIFE OF JOSEPH SMITH

By Nathan N. Waite

Wednesday, February 8, 1843, was not a significant date in Joseph Smith's life.[1] The excitement had come a month before, when Joseph stood in front of a federal judge in Springfield, Illinois. Missourians had been trying to get their hands on the Latter-day Saint prophet ever since he had escaped them in 1839. Now they wanted to haul him back to Missouri to face new charges. Joseph had been in and out of hiding for months, evading lawmen and bounty hunters. Had he been caught, his life would have been in grave peril.

Instead, the judge threw the charges out, and a triumphant group of Saints traveled back to Nauvoo, laughing and composing celebratory songs all the way.[2] But now the cheering and feasts were past, and it was back to everyday life.

For Joseph, everyday life meant filling a dizzying number of roles: He was prophet and president of a growing church. He was mayor of Nauvoo, having been reelected on February 6. He was also a municipal judge, registrar of land deeds for the city, and head of the local militia.[3]

Aside from these roles, he was in the middle of finding and buying more land for Church members to settle on. The land transactions went on despite the fact that money was extremely scarce in Nauvoo (a fact

Joseph was all too familiar with as a local store owner) and the Church was deeply in debt (a fact that must have hounded him every day as the one responsible for Church finances). He had personally filed for bankruptcy a year earlier and was still awaiting the verdict. Lawsuits were piling up. And all too often he had to settle some squabble or other among the men building the temple, or plead for more donations to ensure that the stone walls up on the hill kept rising.[4]

Meetings of all sizes, scheduled and unscheduled, seemed to fill every hour. In the first week of February alone, Joseph attended three political gatherings and spoke at (at least) one of them, held a municipal court session, witnessed citizens swearing affidavits, went to a meeting of the Freemasons, performed a wedding, attended and likely spoke at a meeting of the Quorum of the Twelve, and counseled privately with multiple Church members.[5] An observation by Wilford Woodruff several months earlier was still true: "I have never seen Joseph as full of business as of late; he hardly gets time to sign his name."[6]

Joseph was father to four living children at this time, and he was an attentive husband to Emma. The Prophet would not record the revelation on plural marriage, now Doctrine and Covenants section 132, for five more months, but for years he had felt the Lord's command to put the doctrine in practice. We don't know how much he was involved in the lives of the women, or even the nature of these marriages, but by February 1843 he had been sealed to at least nine plural wives.[7]

All of this must have been a constant, heavy psychological burden.

The first thing noted in Joseph's journal on February 8 is that he had a lesson in German. For several weeks, apostle Orson Hyde had been tutoring Joseph at his two-story log home.[8] Orson had learned the language during his recent mission in Europe. Joseph, meanwhile, had been interested in languages ever since he unearthed the gold plates. In the mid-1830s, he had dedicated significant time to studying Hebrew and Egyptian. He studied English grammar and participated in debating societies. He liked to throw a little Latin into letters to give them some pizzazz.[9]

After morning language class, Joseph stepped out of the role of student and into the role of leader and gatherer, as he greeted and counseled a company of Church members recently arrived from Michigan. Perhaps he had a moment beforehand to gather his thoughts and offer a silent prayer for inspiration. Perhaps he didn't.

His ordinary appearance and lack of decorum sometimes surprised visitors, but he had a ready reply. A year earlier, Willard Richards had recorded, "He said he was but a man and they must not expect him to be perfect; if they expected perfection from him, he should expect it from them, but if they would bear with his infirmities and the infirmities of the brethren, he would likewise bear with their infirmities."[10] His words to the Michigan Saints were briefer, but still memorable: "A prophet is not always a prophet, only when he is acting as such."

After that it was noon and time for dinner, likely prepared by Emma and enjoyed together by the entire Smith family. Then Parley P. Pratt arrived for a visit. Joseph and Parley's friendship was a strong one, forged by years of consecrated service together—and by words of anger and tears of reconciliation. They had even been chained together in a Missouri jail. But they had not seen each other in three and half years, ever since Parley left on a mission to England. The journal's one-word description, "Conversati[o]n," leaves us with little sense of the excitement and emotion that must have accompanied such a reunion.

Joseph's journal often obscures as much as it clarifies, in fact. By the 1840s, the journals were two steps removed from the Prophet—not only did he not write entries himself, but in a lot of cases he wasn't even telling his scribe Willard Richards what to write. Instead, Willard stayed by the Prophet's side and wrote down the things that happened. In his own journal, Joseph often shows up not as "I" but as "he." In his very earliest journal, begun in 1832, Joseph put pen to paper himself, and readers get a glimpse into his mind and heart. In 1840s Nauvoo, we see him acting, but most often at a distance.

Willard recorded that Joseph spent time that afternoon catching up on recent events. A local newspaper reported that his brother William, a delegate to the Illinois House of Representatives, had defended the Saints before the state legislature, arguing that Nauvoo had the right to self-governance. Joseph clearly approved.[11]

From there Joseph's thoughts turned to the persecution he and the Church had continually suffered, and it didn't take long for those thoughts to settle on John C. Bennett, the man who had been the biggest thorn in his side in recent years. Bennett had burst on the Nauvoo scene in 1840, a talented, well-connected convert who was given prominent Church leadership positions and was elected mayor. Then, just as suddenly, he had been found out as a philanderer and con man and was excommunicated from the Church. He fled Nauvoo, only to turn to newspaper columns and the lecture circuit to denounce "Joe Smith" and the "Mormons" with lies and exaggerations.[12] Joseph was frustrated that Bennett was still getting so much attention, and the journal entry records a metaphor he came up with: Bennett was "Jonah's gourd," which miraculously grew in a single day to shade an Old Testament prophet and then the next day withered away into nothingness. Joseph hoped the same for Bennett.[13]

All of this—the land and finances, the migrants and returned missionaries, the meetings and the persecutions—swirled around Joseph as the day wore on. Too often the press of business encroached on his family time. On another evening not long after, he was out "shaking hands & conversing freely" among the Saints until nine o'clock, perhaps after his younger children went to sleep.[14]

But on February 8, Joseph went home at four o'clock. It must have been hard sometimes for him to cast aside all the other roles and be mentally and emotionally present with his family. On this day, though, he zeroed in on six-year-old Frederick. Maybe Emma nudged him in that direction. Maybe Frederick was being a handful, annoying his older siblings, Julia and Joseph, or teasing his younger brother, Alexander. Whatever the case, the journal records the simple fact that as the sun dipped low over the Mississippi River, Joseph "went out. with Frederic to slide on the ice."

Joseph's children do not show up very often in his papers. At the end of every day, Willard Richards the scribe went off to his own house, so we don't catch many glimpses of Joseph's evenings at home. In this instance, though, the window into Joseph's family life is perfectly clear. In the 200,000 or so words that make up Joseph's journals, these nine—telling of a father's one-on-one time with his little boy—are some of the most meaningful.

There is one more insight worth pointing out, one that can only be realized by looking at the original journal page. The writing before those nine words is in brown ink, while the line about sliding on the ice with Frederick is in blue. What that means is that there was a gap between the recording of the previous events and this one. It could very well be that when Willard saw Joseph the next day, he asked, "Anything worth writing down from last evening?" And it's easy to imagine the Prophet pausing for a moment and reflecting on the time with his son. That one line about Joseph and Frederick speaks as a voice from the past, telling us not to get too caught up in the busyness of life and hinting at what is really going to matter when there are no more pages left to write.

Nathan N. Waite is an associate editorial manager of the Church Historian's Press, where he contributes to the Joseph Smith Papers Project and the four-volume history *Saints: The Story of the Church of Jesus Christ in the Latter Days*.

Notes

1. I owe much of the analysis in this essay to Andrew H. Hedges, Alex D. Smith, and the late Richard Lloyd Anderson, editors of *Journals, Volume 2* of the Joseph Smith Papers. The events of February 8, 1843, are reported in Joseph Smith's journal, reproduced in *JSP*, J2:256–57.
2. See "Joseph Smith Documents from September 1842 through February 1843," in *JSP*, D11:xxii.
3. See "Organizational Charts," in *JSP*, D11:571–86.
4. See, for example, Letter to Richard M. Young, Feb. 9, 1843, in *JSP*, D11:397–401; Letter to Horace Hotchkiss, Nov. 26, 1842, in *JSP*, D11:233; Letter to "Hands in the Stone Shop," Dec. 21, 1842, in *JSP*, D11:295–98; and Discourse, Feb. 21, 1843, in *JSP*, D11:460.
5. Journal, Feb. 1–7, 1843, in *JSP*, J2:254–56; Calendar of Documents, Feb. 1843, josephsmith papers.org.
6. Wilford Woodruff to Parley P. Pratt, June 18, 1842, Parley P. Pratt, Correspondence, CHL, punctuation standardized.
7. See "Kimball, Presendia Lathrop Huntington," "Young, Zina Diantha Huntington," "Kimball, Martha McBride," "Lightner, Mary Elizabeth Rollins," "Parry, Patty Bartlett," "Snow, Eliza Roxcy," "Kimball, Sarah Ann Whitney," "Young, Louisa Beman (Beaman),"

and "Babbitt, Delcena Diademia Johnson" (biographical entries), josephsmithpapers.org; and "Nauvoo Journals, December 1841–April 1843," in *JSP*, J2:xxiv–xxvii.

8. Journal, Feb. 3, 1843, in *JSP*, J2:254.
9. See, for example, Letter to John C. Bennett, Mar. 7, 1842, in *JSP*, D9:224; and Letter to the Church, Sept. 7, 1842 [D&C 128], in *JSP*, D11:62–63.
10. Discourse, Oct. 29, 1842, in *JSP*, D11:190.
11. "House of Representatives," *Sangamo Journal*, Feb. 2, 1843, [2].
12. See "Joseph Smith Documents from May through August 1842," in *JSP*, D10:xxxi–xxxiv.
13. Compare Jonah 4:6–7.
14. Journal, Apr. 12, 1842, in *JSP*, J2:352.

JOSEPH SMITH AND THE CREATION OF ETERNAL FAMILIES

By Laura Harris Hales

Sometimes our most important insights come through innocent exchanges. A casual word may spur ponderings that lead to a softening of the heart and deeper understanding. Recently, I had one of those moments. It began when my sister-in-law, a genealogy enthusiast, was showing my husband and me her latest project. She pointed to her husband's name, carefully inscribed on a diagram next to hers. Above were their ancestors, and below were their children. "Look," she said as she turned to my husband, "All you need to do is substitute your name here and add your children." Smiling at each other, we inwardly shook our heads. For us, things were a bit more complicated. The biological links were clear, but not the eternal ones. Kinship dynamics that were straightforward for my sister-in-law appeared muddy for us. Although our temple marriage offered us future companionship, we mulled over our eternal ties to my five children and his four. Could there, perhaps, be blended families in heaven?

I wonder if our musings would have surprised Joseph Smith, who spent much of the last decade of his life addressing our concerns. As early as 1835, he began alluding to relationships that persisted after death. We find the first hint in a letter William W. Phelps wrote to his wife, Sally, in May of that year. At the time, William was assisting the Church in Kirtland. Meanwhile, Sally was in Missouri, caring for their children following the expulsion from Jackson County. Their separation was temporary but challenging. Though displaced, William felt fortunate to lodge with Joseph and Emma Smith, and he filled his correspondence to his wife with references to concepts learned from Joseph. In one memorable message, he wrote, "A new idea, Sally. If you and I continue faithful to the end, we are certain of being one in the Lord throughout eternity. This is one of the most glorious consolations we can have in the flesh."[1]

On April 3, 1836, the angel Elijah appeared to the Prophet in the Kirtland Temple and conferred upon him the sealing authority.[2] We celebrate that event now, but Joseph may not have immediately appreciated the full importance of those priesthood keys. Still, over the next half-decade, he developed a deeper understanding of the blessings this power could bestow, as well as the conditions required to receive those benefits. The priesthood, the Prophet learned, could bless husbands, wives, and children beyond their earthly existences. In Nauvoo, Joseph began sharing this discovery as he secretly taught of celestial marriages that endured for this life and the next. William Clayton, his clerk, noted that during the last year of Joseph's life, he spoke of it on nearly every occasion they were together.[3]

It is hard for me to fully appreciate what Joseph's revelations meant for his primary audience. Death touched their lives more than it does mine. Approaching childbirth wondering if my newborn will survive and facing my children's sniffles with dread are experiences spared me as a parent. Many illnesses that are now easily treated once whisked beloved companions into silence. Life in the nineteenth century was not more precious, but it was more fragile. That may have influenced the receptiveness of his first listeners to a doctrine that promised the perseverance of family. The Saints clung to Joseph's novel teachings, for they, like us, yearned to secure their cherished relationships for the eternities. The promises accessible through priesthood ordinances offered them a chance to sketch a future of their choice despite the cruelties of mortality.

Joseph C. Kingsbury's loss mirrors that of many others of the period. At the age of 24, Joseph married Caroline Whitney, then 20, in 1836. Like many other Saints, they moved to Missouri in 1838.[4] While there, they mourned the death of their toddler son and suffered many hardships because of persecution. Though Caroline remained cheerful, she experienced physical infirmities after they moved to Nauvoo. Soon after giving birth to a second son who did not survive, she died on October 16, 1842.[5] This double blow weighed on Joseph Kingsbury as he mourned the absence of his young wife. The soothing words of a blessing given to him by Joseph Smith in March 1843 illustrate how the Prophet's message encouraged hope in times of despair. Kingsbury recorded in his diary that Joseph promised him the "full desire of his heart." Though death had robbed them of life together, he and Caroline would reunite with their sons in the celestial kingdom.[6]

Death also deprived Hyrum Smith of a lifetime with the bride of his youth. While living in Kirtland, his wife, Jerusha, died in 1837 shortly after giving birth to their sixth child.[7] Hyrum was hundreds of miles away at the time on Church business, and his absence likely added to his distress. Mourning while managing a household proved difficult for the Prophet's brother. Seeing the devastating toll of Jerusha's death on Hyrum, Joseph's solution was to arrange a marriage between Hyrum and Mary Fielding, an English immigrant by way of Canada. The two were married just a few weeks after Hyrum had returned home to his motherless children. Over the years, the couple grew to love each other deeply, and the family increased with first a son and then a daughter.[8]

When learning of the new and everlasting covenant of marriage in 1843, Hyrum reflected on Jerusha. If the only marital bonds that persisted in heaven were the ones sealed upon living couples through priesthood authority, then his connection to Jerusha was severed at her death. This realization disturbed Hyrum. Speaking to Joseph, Hyrum learned that through a proxy ceremony, they could share an eternal marriage. But then, he wondered about Mary. The Prophet explained that Hyrum could be sealed to her as well. When Hyrum took the matter to Mary, she volunteered to stand for Jerusha before her own ceremony. Mary said, "I love you, and I do not want to be separated from you nor be forever alone in the world."[9]

The statements of William Phelps, Joseph Kingsbury, and Hyrum Smith discuss the celestial bonding of *spouses*. Strangely, only Kingsbury refers to the status of *children* or eternal *family* relationships. To confuse matters, several of the women Joseph Smith taught recalled the ambiguity between the celestial marriage covenant and infinite connections to their children, their parents, and even their grandparents in heaven. Lucy Walker, Helen Mar Kimball, and Sarah Ann Whitney reported that the Prophet discussed marital sealings nearly in the same breath that he discussed being part of a continuous priesthood chain back to Adam. Sealings, he instructed, would bring eternal blessings both to these women and their extended families. Nevertheless, Joseph did not elaborate on how their fathers, their mothers, and their offspring benefitted.[10]

The Prophet was not outlining the fabric of heaven with a fountain pen. Instead, he was using watercolors that bleed on porous parchment with each brushstroke. Joseph did not have time to complete the depiction, though, leaving the Saints without a clear vision of how all sealing covenants reverberate through time. He had defined the bond between husband and wife, but details for binding children to parents were left blurry. In fact, he died without being sealed to his children, his mother Lucy (still living at his death), or his deceased father. According to historian Richard Bushman, Joseph was more concerned about expanding his eternal family through priesthood connections rather than biological ones.[11] His attitude could reflect the fact that nineteenth-century family ties were often complex with affinity and necessity playing roles as much as genetics. Maybe if he had lived longer, he would have explained the doctrine more fully.

Over the years, subsequent Church leaders have filled in more of the missing pieces. When the St. George Temple opened in 1877, members performed child-to-parent sealings for the first time since Nauvoo. Some sealed themselves to their biological parents, but only if the parents had accepted the gospel. Others received ordinances binding them eternally to nonrelatives, usually Church leaders. In 1894, President Wilford

Woodruff answered some of the questions the Saints had been asking for 50 years. He announced that he had received a revelation that Church members should seal themselves to their ancestors, as far back as they could discover.[12] Emphasizing that revelations about the eternal family doctrine were ongoing, he declared, "President Young, who followed President Joseph Smith, led us here. He organized these temples and carried out the purposes of his calling and office. . . . But, he did not receive all the revelations that belong to this work; neither did President Taylor, nor has Wilford Woodruff." With humility, he concluded: "There will be no end to this work until it is perfected."[13]

Modern prophets echo Joseph Smith's teachings that eternal families are created on earth through priesthood ordinances rather than being strictly procreated through physical intimacy. In 1993, Elder M. Russell Ballard stated that earthly families *help us* to qualify for eternal life within eternal families.[14] More recently, President Russell M. Nelson counseled that we create eternal families through priesthood power and by exercising faith.[15] Church leaders also advise those of us whose previous sealings have been canceled, seemingly rending our children from us in eternity, that we need not fear even though the marital bond is no longer valid. Our children are assured eternal parentage, and our eternal family relationships "will be determined by our wise and loving Father."[16]

I confess that sometimes I pause when singing the hymn "Families Can Be Together Forever," fearing this promise applies to some families, but possibly not mine. Remarriage and time have lessened the frequency of those thoughts. But still, at times, I ponder how new covenants will bridge the gap made by those done away. And where certainty gives way, faith steps in. The words of comfort voiced by Joseph Smith are a salve for my wounds. Like William Phelps, my heart sings when I think of being one with my spouse for eternity. Thoughts of Joseph Kingsbury remind me that covenants can fulfill the desires of my heart. Answers to Hyrum Smith's questions encourage me to think of celestial families outside of limiting frameworks. Joseph Smith presented a concept of eternity that accommodates all covenant families and transcends a two-dimensional ancestral diagram. Like the Saints in Nauvoo, I grab hold of the Prophet's broad teachings and revelations on eternal relationships, trusting that they include my blended family tree.

Laura Harris Hales is an independent scholar and freelance editor.

Notes

1. William W. Phelps to Sally Phelps, May 26, 1835, quoted in Bruce Van Orden, "Writing to Zion: The William W. Phelps Kirtland Letters (1835–1836)," *BYU Studies* 33, no. 3 (1993), 550; spelling and punctuation standardized.
2. "Visions, 3 April 1836 [D&C 110]," josephsmithpapers.org.
3. William Clayton, Affidavit, Feb. 16, 1874, in Affidavits about Celestial Marriage, 1869–1915, CHL.
4. "Kingsbury, Joseph Corrodon" (biographical entry), josephsmithpapers.org.
5. *Wasp* (Nauvoo, IL), Oct. 29, 1842.
6. "Blessing to Joseph Kingsbury, 23 March 1843," josephsmithpapers.org; Joseph C. Kingsbury, "Diary of Joseph C. Kingsbury," 13–14, J. Willard Marriott Digital Library, University of Utah, Salt Lake City.
7. "Smith, Hyrum" (biographical entry), josephsmithpapers.org.
8. Ronald K. Esplin, "Hyrum Smith: The Mildness of a Lamb, the Integrity of Job," *Ensign*, Feb. 2000.
9. Minutes, Apr. 6–9, 1844, p. 31, in Historian's Office, General Church Minutes, 1839–77, CHL.
10. "Blessing to Sarah Ann Whitney, 23 March 1843," josephsmithpapers.org; Lucy Walker, quoted in Lyman Omer Littlefield, *Reminiscences of Latter-day Saints: Giving an Account of Much Individual Suffering Endured for Religious Conscience* (Logan: Utah Journal Co., 1888), 46; Jeni Broberg Holzapfel and Richard Neitzel Holzapfel, eds., *A Woman's View: Helen Mar Whitney's Reminiscences of Early Church History* (Provo, UT: Religious Studies Center, Brigham Young University, 1997), 482–87.
11. Richard Lyman Bushman, *Joseph Smith: Rough Stone Rolling* (New York: Knopf, 2005), 440.
12. Wilford Woodruff and George Q. Cannon, "The Law of Adoption," *Deseret Weekly*, Apr. 21, 1894, 543.
13. Wilford Woodruff, "Discourse by President Wilford Woodruff," *Latter-day Saints' Millennial Star*, May 21, 1894, 325, spelling standardized.
14. M. Russell Ballard, "Equality through Diversity," General Conference, Oct. 1993, ChurchofJesusChrist.org.
15. Russell M. Nelson, "Spiritual Treasures," General Conference, Oct. 2019, Churchof JesusChrist.org.
16. The First Presidency issues a standard letter to parents when sealings are canceled. In addition to the letter sent to me, I have reviewed several others, which contain the same wording. (See First Presidency to Laura Dursteler, May 26, 2009, copy in possession of the author.)

"THE PRIVILEGE OF REWARDING . . . GOOD FOR EVIL": JOSEPH SMITH'S RESPONSE TO THE 1843 EXTRADITION ATTEMPT

By Nicole Christensen Fernley

In summer 1843, Missouri officials sent a sheriff to Illinois to apprehend Joseph Smith, marking Missouri's third attempt to have Joseph extradited for criminal prosecution. The details of the arrest provide a lively and fascinating narrative, and Joseph's behavior before, during, and after the extradition attempt gives us a glimpse of his personality and character.

In mid-June of that year, Joseph and Emma Hale Smith traveled some 170 miles northeast from Nauvoo to visit with the family of Emma's sister Elizabeth Hale Wasson in Palestine Grove, Illinois. The visit was likely a meaningful one for both Emma and Joseph—after nearly ten years of estrangement from Emma's family, they had reestablished ties only within the last couple of years.[1]

On June 21, William Clayton and Stephen Markham arrived in Palestine Grove after a frantic ride from Nauvoo. They warned the Prophet of an impending arrest instigated by Missouri officials. But Joseph declined to go into hiding, as he had the prior year when evading Missouri authorities. Instead, he told his friends not to be alarmed: "I have no fear. I shall not leave here. I shall find friends, and Missourians cannot hurt me. I tell you in the name of Israel's God."[2]

Two days later, while the Smith and Wasson families were eating dinner, two men came to the door, claiming to be "Mormon Elders" and asking to see "Brother Joseph."[3] These men were Joseph H. Reynolds, a sheriff from Jackson County, Missouri, and Harmon T. Wilson, a constable of Hancock County, Illinois. They had come to arrest Joseph and extradite him to Missouri on charges of treason stemming from the 1838 "Mormon War." Wilson spotted Joseph, who had left the house and was heading toward the barn. Instead of showing any writ or warrant, the officers grabbed him and thrust "two cocked pistols" against his head, repeatedly exclaiming, "God damn you! I will shoot you! I will shoot you, God damn you! I will shoot you." Joseph later reported, "I asked them what they wanted to shoot me for. 'If you make any resistance.' 'O very well,' says I, 'I have no resistance to make.' They then dragged me away."[4]

The officers shoved Joseph into a wagon, punching him in the sides with their pistols all the while, and tried to rush him away. Markham, one of Joseph's bodyguards, grabbed the horses' bridles—despite the lawmen threatening to shoot him—and held the horses long enough for Emma to bring Joseph his hat and coat. As the officers hauled Joseph to nearby Dixon, Illinois, they kept their pistols jammed into his sides for much of the journey and only desisted when Markham chided them "for their cowardice in so brutally illtreating an unarmed defenseless prisoner."[5]

After they arrived in Dixon, Joseph was held prisoner in a tavern while the lawmen arranged for fresh horses to take him to Missouri. When Joseph asked for legal counsel, Reynolds refused and threatened again to shoot him. In response, as Joseph recounted, "I turned to him, opened my bosom and told him to shoot away."[6] This unflinching attitude was on display throughout the events related here—from Joseph's casual responses to threats of shooting to his reflection afterward that he had been "cool and dispassionate" during the ordeal.[7] Joseph had years of experience in dealing with persecution, and this was not the first nor the last time his faith in God and his courage were called upon in the face of danger and violence. This was, after all, the man who went to his death a year later reportedly saying, "I am going like a lamb to the slaughter;

but I am calm as a summer's morning; I have a conscience void of offense towards God, and towards all men."[8]

Markham secured legal counsel for Joseph in Dixon, but Reynolds and Wilson refused to allow the attorneys to talk to Joseph. Several local citizens—none of whom were members of the Church—gathered outside the room where Joseph was being held and insisted that he be granted his rights. The lawmen eventually relented, and two attorneys were allowed to speak with Joseph, who told them that he had been arrested under dubious authority. He also showed them dark bruises "about 18 inches in circumference" on each side of his body caused by the lawmen punching him repeatedly with their pistols.[9] After obtaining a writ of habeas corpus, Joseph, his attorneys, his captors, and a few others eventually left Dixon via horseback and a hired stagecoach to appear before a judge authorized to hold a habeas corpus hearing. In an odd turn of events, they were also joined by Sheriff James Campbell of Lee County, Illinois, who had arrested *Reynolds and Wilson* on charges of personal injury and false imprisonment brought in a civil lawsuit filed by Joseph's attorneys.

Meanwhile, word of Joseph's arrest had reached Nauvoo.[10] On the evening of June 25, Hyrum Smith sent armed members of the city's militia, the Nauvoo Legion, to ensure that Joseph wasn't taken to Missouri without due process. Several of the troops headed north on the Mississippi River via steamboat, and others left on horseback, separating into small groups to search. As Joseph and the others traveled south together, some of the Legion members encountered their group and then turned around to travel with them. The lawmen began to feel intimidated as more and more Legion members joined the traveling party.[11] It must have been quite a sight—Joseph with his captors, and those captors with their own captor, and the whole surrounded by dozens of Legion troops on horses.

Joseph and those traveling with him promised the outnumbered lawmen that no harm would come to them. Reynolds was apparently in particular fear of a Legion member named James Flack, with whom he was already acquainted. When Joseph heard of it, he approached Flack and asked him "to bury his feelings against Reynolds" and not to harm him because Joseph had pledged to protect him.[12] An affidavit from the attorneys and stagecoach drivers traveling with Joseph stated that the Latter-day Saints did not threaten Reynolds or Wilson; instead, several Saints, including Joseph, promised that the two lawmen "should be personally safe."[13]

The party eventually made its way to Nauvoo so that Joseph could have his case heard before the Nauvoo Municipal Court.[14] When they arrived in Nauvoo on June 30, they were greeted by throngs of cheering people and a brass band playing the patriotic song "Hail Columbia." Joseph brought his fellow travelers to his home, a log house on the eastern shore of the Mississippi River, where Reynolds and Wilson were seated at the head of the table and Emma served them a midday meal.[15]

Around five o'clock in the afternoon that same day, Joseph met with a crowd of thousands of Saints gathered in a grove near the partially completed Nauvoo Temple and delivered a discourse relating all that had transpired during his arrest. Speaking of Reynolds and Wilson, he said, "I have brought them to Nauvoo and treated them kindly. I have had the privilege of rewarding them good for evil. They took me unlawfully, treated me rigorously, strove to deprive me of my rights, and would have run me to Missouri to have been murdered if providence had not interposed: but now they are in my hands. I took them to my house set them at the head of my table and set the best before them my house afforded, and they were waited upon by my wife, whom they deprived of seeing me when I was taken."[16]

He specifically asked the citizens of Nauvoo to respect the rights of Reynolds and Wilson. "However you may feel about the high hand of oppression," Joseph declared, "I wish you to restrain your hand from violence against those men who arrested me. My word is at stake—a hair of their heads shall not be harmed."[17]

Joseph's determination to protect the two men who had threatened and injured him is notable, as is his invitation for them to dine at his table. Though it is not impossible he invited the lawmen into his home as a show of power or intimidation, his actions nevertheless contrast starkly with theirs. While they treated him harshly and would have escorted him to probable death in Missouri, he guaranteed their safety and let them go on their way. His willingness to put aside hard feelings and treat these men with kindness and hospitality says much of his magnanimous personality and is consistent with his lifelong tendency to forgive those who had injured him.

In a discourse on July 9, about a week after his return to Nauvoo, Joseph proclaimed that he "had no enmity against any one." His brutal arrest was widely known in the community and likely provided a rich context that day when he taught, "Father forgive me my trespasses, as I forgive those who trespass against me. For I freely forgive all men. If we would secure and cultivate the love of others, we must love others, even our enemies—as well as friends."[18]

It would be a heartwarming story if at this point we could say that Joseph's treatment of Reynolds and Wilson resulted in a change of heart and that they regretted their earlier actions and attitudes. Unfortunately, that was not the case. The Nauvoo Municipal Court discharged Joseph "for want of substance in the warrant upon which he was arrested as well as upon the merits of said case."[19] Reynolds and Wilson did not give up their efforts to have him extradited, however, and went so far as to request that the governor of Illinois send out the state militia to retake Joseph. The governor declined, and Joseph was never extradited to face trial in Missouri.[20]

Nicole Christensen Fernley is an editor with the Joseph Smith Papers and the Church Historian's Press.

Notes

1. See Letter to David Hale, Feb. 12–19, 1841, in *JSP*, D8:36–42.
2. "History, 1838–1856, volume D-1 [1 August 1842–1 July 1843]," p. 1581. josephsmith papers.org. Quotations in this essay have been standardized for spelling and punctuation.
3. "History, 1838–1856, volume D-1 [1 August 1842–1 July 1843]," p. 1582.
4. "Discourse, 30 June 1843, as Reported by Wilford Woodruff," p. [59], josephsmithpapers .org.
5. "History, 1838–1856, volume D-1 [1 August 1842–1 July 1843]," p. 1583.
6. "Discourse, 30 June 1843, as Reported by Wilford Woodruff," p. [59].
7. "Discourse, 30 June 1843, as Reported by Willard Richards," p. [275], josephsmithpapers .org; "Discourse, 30 June 1843, as Reported by Wilford Woodruff," p. [54].
8. Doctrine and Covenants 135:4.

9. "History, 1838–1856, volume D-1 [1 August 1842–1 July 1843]," p. 1583.

10. "History, 1838–1856, volume D-1 [1 August 1842–1 July 1843]," pp. 1584–85. On the morning of June 24, William Clayton had departed from Dixon to catch a steamboat down the Mississippi River, arriving in Nauvoo around two o'clock in the afternoon of June 25.

11. "History, 1838–1856, volume D-1 [1 August 1842–1 July 1843]," p. 1587.

12. "History, 1838–1856, volume D-1 [1 August 1842–1 July 1843]," p. 1590.

13. "Letter from Edward Southwick, 29 July 1843," p. [2], josephsmithpapers.org.

14. Joseph Smith was mayor of Nauvoo at this time, and as such he was also the chief justice of the municipal court. When this case was finally heard in the municipal court, William Marks was elected to temporarily lead the court. (Docket Entry, June 30, 1843, Extradition of Joseph Smith for Treason [Nauvoo Mun. Ct. 1843], Nauvoo Municipal Court Docket Book, 55; Habeas Corpus, June 30, 1843, Extradition of Joseph Smith for Treason [Nauvoo Mun. Ct. 1843], Joseph Smith Collection, CHL.)

15. Immediately after Joseph was taken away from Dixon, Emma and the Smith children started for Nauvoo in a carriage driven by her nephew Lorenzo D. Wasson. They arrived on the evening of June 27, "having burned off one arm of the carriage coming home." ("History, 1838–1856, volume D-1 [1 August 1842–1 July 1843]," pp. 1585, 1588.)

16. "Discourse, 30 June 1843, as Reported by Wilford Woodruff," p. [56].

17. "Discourse, 30 June 1843, as Reported by Wilford Woodruff," p. [57].

18. "Discourse, 9 July 1843, as Reported by Willard Richards," p. [300].

19. Municipal Court, Minutes, July 1, 1843, Extradition of Joseph Smith for Treason (Nauvoo Mun. Ct. 1843), Joseph Smith Collection, CHL; Docket Entry, July 1, 1843, Extradition of Joseph Smith for Treason (Nauvoo Mun. Ct. 1843), Nauvoo Municipal Court Docket Book, 55–56, 60–87, 116–150.

20. For more information about the arrest, the court proceedings, and the aftermath, see "History, 1838–1856, volume D-1 [1 August 1842–1 July 1843]," pp. 1577–1604; and *The Joseph Smith Papers: Documents, Volume 12: March–July 1843* (forthcoming in April 2021).

"THE GREAT PRINCIPLE OF CHRISTIANITY IS LOVE": JOSEPH SMITH'S TEACHINGS ON CHARITY AND KINDNESS

By Gerrit J. Dirkmaat

Just 11 months before he would be brutally murdered in Carthage, Joseph Smith delivered a Sunday sermon that paraphrased the words of Jesus Christ to His Apostles: there was no greater love than "that a man lay down his life for his friends."[1] Expanding upon the idea, Joseph declared "friendship is the grand fundamental principle of Mormonism." This type of love, he asserted, would revolutionize and "civilize the world." The disciples of Jesus should therefore "pour forth love" to their fellow human beings.[2]

In the course of his life, Joseph Smith held many official titles: prophet, president, mayor, judge, general, and numerous others. But the title he seemed to relish most was that of friend. Contemporary documents reveal Joseph to be someone with a naturally humorous and kind disposition who loved other people. Certainly, he was passionate and was prone to anger when the people he loved were attacked, defamed, or betrayed. But just as certainly, Joseph was quick to forgive those that offended him at the slightest hint of contrition by the offender. Many Latter-day Saints today focus their religious efforts primarily on their immediate families, heeding the prophetic teachings that family is the basic unit of society now and in the afterlife. But Joseph also saw Latter-day

Saint theology as a broader call to love those outside of our own families, treating them as if they really were our brothers and sisters. The examples that follow are only a few that shed light on his love of all mankind.

English reformer John Finch's tour of American socialist experiments in the mid-1840s took him to various communal groups. His main purpose was to see those settlements patterned after the utopian model of his hero, socialist Robert Owen. These communes were attempting to enact the idealized sharing of land and resources among workers. But an intrigued Finch also visited the Latter-day Saint enclave in Nauvoo. Not quite an atheist, but deeply skeptical of organized religion, Finch arrived in Nauvoo expecting to find religious zealots devoted to a dour, imperial, self-righteous, and self-appointed prophet. Having heard the rumors of Latter-day Saint perfidy, he expected to be treated with suspicion and condescension, if not outright anger, for intruding into their religious haven in Nauvoo.

But as he reported his actual interactions with Joseph Smith, Finch could not help but express his surprise. He had been greeted cheerfully by Hyrum Smith and taken to stay at Joseph Smith's Mansion House, where he observed Joseph over several days and had multiple discussions with him. Joseph was not the haughty, aloof, domineering prophet Finch had envisioned but instead was "polite, obliging, and well-behaved." Finch further commented with surprise on Joseph's personality: he "was cheerful and playful in his manners" and would even wrestle with his friends in the street. Finch noted that Joseph was "merry with his customers and friends" and that Joseph's friendly disposition was reciprocated, as he was "much respected in his family and among all who came into his house."[3]

When Finch skeptically asked Joseph "how he became a prophet," Joseph responded with laughter rather than defensiveness, joking that all of his enemies claimed he was a false prophet and all of his followers believed him to be a true prophet, "so, between the both, a prophet he became." Indeed, Joseph's lack of pretension and affable personality made the agnostic Finch wonder if Smith was a religious leader at all. Finch was stunned to find Joseph "liberal and charitable in speaking of other sects." At one point Finch sardonically noted, "If he had any religion at all, which I very much doubt, he kept it entirely out of our sight except a long grace said at meals." Joseph Smith appeared very much to be a regular person.

Rather than barring the socialist from speaking to his people, Joseph invited and encouraged Finch to give several public discourses to the Latter-day Saints on Owenite ideals. Finch noted that the following week a Unitarian minister was scheduled to lecture as well. When queried why he would let outsiders with different beliefs preach to the Saints, Joseph told him that "he allowed liberty of conscience to all, and was not afraid of any party drawing his people away from him."

In a moment of soberness, Joseph expressed to Finch, as he had to the Saints in his sermon on July 23, that "he considered the great principle of Christianity was love" and that there should be "more of this love-spirit among his followers than any other sect." For his part, Finch remained unconvinced of Latter-day Saint theology but still admitted that he "experienced the greatest kindness" from Joseph Smith.[4]

Joseph believed friendship and brotherly and sisterly love should transcend religious beliefs. He taught, "[I] don't care what a character is if he's my friend." If the person was a friend, "a true friend . . . I will be a friend to him."[5] At another time he made clear that such love of others was not to be conditioned on their acceptance of the gospel: "When I have used every means in my power to exalt a man's mind, and have taught him righteous principles to no effect—he is still inclined in his darkness, yet the same principles of liberty and charity would ever be manifested by me as though he embraced it."[6]

For all of the maltreatment the Latter-day Saints received at the hands of their persecutors, Joseph was clearly touched by those few who showed Christlike love to the suffering Saints. After the nightmarish flight of so many women and children from the extermination order, assaults, and murder in Missouri, the bedraggled Saints made it across the frigid Mississippi River to Quincy, Illinois. With Joseph and many other leaders imprisoned and with almost no resources, the Saints arrived as refugees. Despite the overwhelming public view that Latter-day Saints were troublemakers at best and criminals deserving of banishment at worst, the residents of Quincy had compassion on these refugee Saints, opening their homes, their wallets, and their kitchens to feed, clothe, and provide shelter for them. After establishing the Saints in Nauvoo, Joseph and the First Presidency spoke of their gratitude to those "who in our time of deep distress, nobly came forward to our relief, and like the good Samaritan poured oil into our wounds, and contributed liberally to our necessities . . . in this labor of love."[7]

This type of compassion fueled Joseph Smith's understanding of interpersonal relationships. He wanted Nauvoo to be a similar place of refuge for those who were suffering. "We should cultivate sympathy for the afflicted among us," he urged. "If there is a place on earth where men should cultivate this spirit and pour in the oil and wine in the bosom of the afflicted it is this place and this spirit is manifest here and although he is a stranger and afflicted when he arrives, he finds a brother and a friend ready to administer to his necessities."[8]

In speaking to the women of the newly formed Relief Society in 1842, Joseph criticized the natural tendency of humanity to magnify the faults of others while minimizing their own flaws. He urged them to "not think yourselves more righteous than others; you must enlarge your souls toward others if you would do like Jesus, and carry your fellow creatures to Abram's bosom." He further implored, "You must be longsuffering and bear with the faults and errors of mankind. How precious are the souls of men [and women]!"[9] The gospel of Jesus Christ was not designed to punish sinners but to provide a means for sinners to change and repent. Joseph taught with empathy, "God does not look on sin with allowance, but when men [and women] have sinned there must be allowance made for them." Self-righteousness had to give way to love of our fellow human beings because "the nearer we get to our heavenly Father, the more are we disposed to look with compassion on perishing souls—to take them upon our shoulders and cast their sins behind our back."[10]

Placing a personal emphasis on the importance of such characteristics, Joseph explained that "nothing is so much calculated to lead people to forsake sin as to take them by the hand and watch over them with tenderness. When persons manifest the least kindness and love to me, O what power it has over my mind, while the opposite course has a tendency to harrow up all the harsh feelings and depress the human mind."[11] Near the end of his life he taught, "We must not despise a man on account of infirmity. We ought to love a man more for his infirmity."[12]

Charity and compassion for others was the essence of Joseph's life. Just weeks before he would be murdered, apparently understanding his time was short, Joseph expressed, "The only thing I am afraid of is, that I will not live long enough to enjoy the society of these my friends as long as I want to."[13] Joseph's view of heaven was one of glorious reunion, where friends and family greeted one another in the bonds of love. At one point he taught, "If I had no expectation of seeing my mother, brothers, and sisters and friends again, my heart would burst in a moment and I should go down to my grave. The expectation of seeing my friends in the morning of the resurrection cheers my soul and makes me bear up against the evils of life."[14] Relationships, like spirits, were eternal. The love of others came naturally to Joseph Smith, and his life and teachings demonstrate the extraordinary extent to which the knowledge and doctrine of Jesus Christ permeated his soul and radiated outward from his being.

Gerrit J. Dirkmaat is an associate professor of Church history and doctrine at Brigham Young University.

Notes

1. See John 15:13.
2. Journal, July 23, 1843, in *JSP*, J3:68. Quotations in this essay have been standardized for spelling and sometimes for punctuation.
3. John Finch, "Notes of Travel in the United States," *The New Moral World and Gazette of the Rational Society* (London), Oct. 5, 1844.
4. John Finch, "Notes of Travel in the United States."
5. Journal, July 23, 1843, in *JSP*, J3:66–67.
6. Council of Fifty, "Record," Apr. 11, 1844, in *JSP*, CFM:100.
7. Proclamation, Jan. 15, 1841, in *JSP*, D7:499.
8. Journal, Apr. 16, 1843, in *JSP*, J2:358.
9. Discourse, Apr. 28, 1842, in *JSP*, D9:405–6.
10. Minutes and Discourse, June 9, 1842, in *JSP*, D10:132.
11. Minutes and Discourse, June 9, 1842, in *JSP*, D10:132.
12. Council of Fifty, "Record," Apr. 11, 1844, in *JSP*, CFM:100.
13. Council of Fifty, "Record," Apr. 11, 1844, in *JSP*, CFM:100.
14. Journal, Apr. 16, 1843, in *JSP*, J2:360.

JOSEPH SMITH AND COUNCILS

By Matthew J. Grow and R. Eric Smith

Shortly before his death, Joseph Smith told a congregation of Latter-day Saints in Nauvoo, "Every man who has a calling to minister to the Inhabitants of the world, was ordained to that very purpose in the grand Council of Heaven before this world was."[1] Embedded in this statement are the profound doctrines of our premortal existence and the fore-ordination of individuals to perform tasks in mortality. But just as intriguing, the comment suggests that God governs through a council.[2]

In The Church of Jesus Christ of Latter-day Saints today, we administer the Church, both at general and local levels, through councils. Ideally, we work with our families in the same way. The principles we use in Church and family councils can be applied to our workplaces and communities. What may be surprising to Church members is how important the idea of councils was to Joseph, who came to understand the crucial role played by councils in obtaining revelation.

Early in the Church's history, Joseph learned that meetings needed to be led "as they are conducted & guided by the Holy spirit." This same revelation also implied that the guidance of the Spirit would come not just to the leader of the meeting, as it taught that spiritual gifts are distributed among different people—"to some is given one & to some is given another"—and are all used for the benefit of the whole.[3]

Joseph also pondered about how to conduct meetings according to what he called the "ancient manner."[4] In October 1831, his counselor Sidney Rigdon taught that unity was essential when Church members gathered together. He said, "God always bears testimony by his presence in counsil to his Elders when they assemble in perfect faith and humble themselves before the Lord." Following Sidney's comments, Joseph reiterated, "It is the privilege of every Elder to speak of the things of God &c, And could we all come together with one heart and one mind in perfect faith the vail might as well be rent to day as next week or any other time."[5] A week later, a conference of Church leaders sought for "the mind of the Lord" to be revealed regarding how many copies of the Book of Commandments should be printed.[6] Councils were thus not simply about administering the Church. If Church members came together in unity, sought the guidance of the Spirit, and respected the participation of all, councils would be forums in which the Lord would reveal His mind and will.[7]

In the first half of the 1830s, Joseph organized councils—including bishoprics, the First Presidency, high councils, the Quorum of the Twelve Apostles, and the Quorum of the Seventy—to administer the Church. These gave him occasion to teach the Saints more about the correct operation of councils. Joseph made clear that he had not reached his understanding of councils through reason alone. Rather, he had been shown "the order of Councils in ancient days" in a vision. By "ancient days," Joseph referred, at least in part, to the early Christian Church under the leadership of Peter.[8]

In 1834, Joseph commented that he regretted that past councils had perhaps been deprived "of some, or many blessings" because he had not taught "all the order in which a Council ought to be conducted." One principle was that members needed to come with pure hearts; explaining this, Joseph said, "we frequently, are so filled with prejudice, or have a beam in our own eye, that we are not capable of passing right descissions." In this context, purity thus meant to properly guard against bias.[9]

Furthermore, council members should take their duties seriously. "In ancient days," Joseph explained, "councils were conducted with such strict propriety, that no one was allowed to whisper, be weary, leave the room, or get uneasy in the least, until the voice of the Lord, by revelation, or by the voice of the Council by the spirit was obtained." In the Saints' councils, by contrast, Joseph had observed participants who were napping or distracted (in our day, he would undoubtedly have added looking at their phones or unsuccessfully multitasking). He encouraged Church leaders to do better.[10] Joseph also urged councils to make careful records, so that these could guide future decisions.[11]

In early 1836, Joseph met repeatedly with Church leaders to prepare them for the dedication of the Kirtland Temple. In one meeting, Joseph asked the priesthood quorums to review a set of rules that would govern the temple once it was in use. In sequence and over the course of several hours, seven separate quorums or presidencies—from the Church presidency down to the two bishoprics—discussed, debated, and approved the rules. After the final approval, Joseph expressed dissatisfaction with how some of the men had conducted themselves during the deliberations. In such settings, Joseph said, each person should "speak in his turn, and in his place" to ensure "perfect order." Moreover, before objecting to any proposal, council members should "be sure that they can throw light upon the subject rather than spread darkness, and that [their] objections be founded in righteousness which may be done by applying ourselves closely to study the, mind and will of the Lord."[12]

Understanding the creation of these councils helps solve a conundrum that Latter-day Saints can see from their study of the Doctrine and Covenants. Most of Joseph's canonized revelations came in the Church's first years, and many of them addressed questions raised by individuals. By contrast, most of Joseph's canonized revelations in the latter part of the Doctrine and Covenants do not take up individual problems but address broader doctrinal themes. Did Joseph receive fewer revelations as the years wore on? No, he charged councils throughout the Church with obtaining the will of the Lord for particular situations. Meanwhile, Joseph continued to receive revelation for the Church as a whole.[13]

The most mature expression of Joseph's understanding of councils came in his instructions to the Council of Fifty, a group composed of roughly 50 men that Joseph organized a few months before his death. The council continued to meet in Nauvoo after Joseph's death until the Saints' exodus in 1846. The Council of Fifty, Joseph taught, was a temporal or political body created to protect the Church and provide it space to flourish. He stated that it was "designed to be got up for the safety and salvation of the saints by protecting them in their religious rights and worship."[14]

Joseph spoke often to the Council of Fifty on the proper functioning of a council system. In the first meeting, Joseph stated that he "wanted all the brethren to speak their minds . . . and to say what was in their hearts whether good or bad. He did not want to be forever surrounded by a set of 'dough heads' and if they did not rise up and shake themselves and exercise themselves in discussing these important matters he should consider them nothing better than 'dough heads.'"[15] By "dough heads," Joseph seemed to have meant "yes men"—people who would tell him what they thought he hoped to hear. He understood that sometimes people would be too deferential to his authority and would thus not share freely their opinions. He had no use for that type of council. Rather, he expected active participation. Members should attend the meetings, arrive on time, speak their minds, and fulfill and then report on their assignments.

Council members should not rush to make decisions, Joseph advised, but should explore all of the options thoroughly. They should "agree to disagree long enough to select the pure gold from the dross by the process of investigation."[16] Furthermore, members should study a matter out in their own minds before agreeing to the council's decisions: "I dont want any man ever to assent to any thing in this council and then find fault with it. Dont decide in favor of any thing untill you know it."[17]

After everyone on the council had exerted his best efforts, both to seek inspiration and to study the matter out logically, Joseph taught that the council was entitled to revelation from God in its decisions. He expected council members "to exert all their wisdom in this thing" and also to receive all the wisdom they could "from the presence of God."[18] The council would then be able to arrive at unanimous decisions. Participants had a duty to help implement the decisions, since they had been made on honest, informed input.

Council members demonstrated that they had internalized these principles in their deliberations after Joseph's death. Knowing that the Latter-day Saints would have to seek refuge elsewhere, they carefully considered many possible settlement sites, including Texas, California, Oregon, and the Rocky Mountains. They studied the latest maps and reports of explorations and sent out men to gather information firsthand. As new information came in, the council eliminated possibilities that were impractical. Eventually the council focused on the valley of the Great Salt Lake. Throughout this process, council members felt that they were being guided by revelation, but not until the time for departure neared did Brigham Young feel confident of the exact destination. In January 1846, as the Saints were preparing to leave Nauvoo, Brigham declared, "The Saying of the Prophets would never be verified unless the House of the Lord should be reared in the Tops of the Mountains . . . I know where the spot is."[19]

In our own era, Church leaders have emphasized the "great spiritual power and inspired direction that come from properly conducted family, ward, and stake councils."[20] Joseph's vision of how councils can encourage vigorous and candid discussions—and thereby learn the mind and will of the Lord—remains keenly relevant.

Matthew J. Grow is a general editor of the Joseph Smith Papers Project and the managing director of the Church History Department.

R. Eric Smith is the editorial manager and a general editor of the Joseph Smith Papers Project.

Notes

1. "Discourse, 12 May 1844, as Reported by Thomas Bullock," p. [1], josephsmithpapers.org.

2. For a brief review of Joseph's teachings on the council of heaven, see *JSP*, D6:370, note 603. In addition to the sources listed there, see in particular Abraham 3:22–28; and "Discourse, 7 April 1844, as Reported by Thomas Bullock," p. 17, josephsmithpapers.org.

3. Revelation, ca. 8 March 1831–A, in *JSP*, D1:282–83 [D&C 46:2, 12].

4. Minutes, Oct. 11, 1831, in *JSP*, D2:75.

5. Minutes, Oct. 25–26, 1831, in *JSP*, D2:81.

6. Minutes, Nov. 1, 1831, in *JSP*, D2:97.

7. See Joseph F. Darowski, "Seeking After the Ancient Order: Conferences and Councils in Early Church Governance, 1830–1834," *Mormon Historical Studies* 11, no. 1 (2010): 32.

8. Minutes, Feb. 17, 1834, in *JSP*, D3:437.

9. Minutes, Feb. 12, 1834, in *JSP*, D3:429.

10. Minutes, Feb. 12, 1834, in *JSP*, D3:429. In his instructions quoted here and above from February 12 and 17, 1834, Joseph seemed particularly concerned with councils that functioned as ecclesiastical courts to hear cases of individual transgressions. But the principles he outlined apply more broadly.

11. Minutes, Feb. 27, 1835, in "Record of the Twelve, 14 February–28 August 1835," pp. 1–3, josephsmithpapers.org.

12. Journal, Jan. 14 and 15, 1836, in *JSP*, J1:151–55.

13. See Richard Lyman Bushman, *Joseph Smith: Rough Stone Rolling* (New York: Knopf, 2005), 257–58.

14. Council of Fifty, "Record," Apr. 18, 1844, in *JSP*, CFM:128.

15. Council of Fifty, "Record," Mar. 10, 1844, in *JSP*, CFM:39.

16. Council of Fifty, "Record," Apr. 4, 1844, in *JSP*, CFM:79.

17. Council of Fifty, "Record," Apr. 11, 1844, in *JSP*, CFM:93.

18. Council of Fifty, "Record," Apr. 11, 1844, in *JSP*, CFM:92.

19. John D. Lee, Journal, Jan. 13, 1846, quoted in Historical Introduction to Council of Fifty, "Record," Jan. 13, 1846, in *JSP*, CFM:522.

20. M. Russell Ballard, "Counseling with Our Councils," General Conference, Apr. 1994, ChurchofJesusChrist.org; see also, for example, "Councils in the Church" (chap. 7), in *General Handbook: Serving in The Church of Jesus Christ of Latter-day Saints* (Mar. 2020), ChurchofJesusChrist.org.

JOSEPH SMITH AND RELIGIOUS PLURALISM

By Patrick Q. Mason

"By searching the scriptures I found that mankind did not come unto the Lord but that they had apostatised from the true and liveing faith and there was no society or denomination that built upon the gospel of Jesus Christ as recorded in the new testament."[1]

So wrote Joseph Smith in 1832, as part of his first recorded attempt to describe the motivations that sent him as a young man into the grove of trees near his family farm a dozen years earlier, when he experienced his earliest vision of God. With slight variations, three of the Prophet's four firsthand accounts of the First Vision contain words to the effect that "all religious denominations were believing in incorrect doctrines and that none of them was acknowledged of God as his church and kingdom." Indeed, in his 1842 account, written to Chicago newspaper editor John Wentworth as part of a succinct summation of the Church's history to that point, Joseph recalled that God "expressly commanded" him to "go not after them," referring to the other religions of the day.[2]

"Go not after them" is not exactly a recipe for healthy interreligious dialogue and interfaith relations. Convinced that God had restored the true Christian gospel to the earth after a general apostasy of the other denominations, Joseph and the other early Saints never backed off the foundational claim that the Church they organized in 1830 was "the only true & living Church upon the face of the whole Earth" with which God was, on the whole, "well pleased."[3] Yet in the midst of a nineteenth-century American landscape characterized by religious conflict and intolerance,[4] Joseph eventually came to hold the view that at least on this side of eternity, the best approach to handling religious diversity is to embrace it. People could still hold their strong opinions about what was or wasn't true—the Saints certainly did. But by the end of his life, Joseph had repeatedly preached and modeled an ethic of religious pluralism predicated first and foremost on jealously safeguarding religious liberty, but also genuinely welcoming members of different faiths and even seeking to learn from them.

The essential foundation for religious pluralism is religious freedom. Appreciative and meaningful encounters between members of different religions cannot happen if either group is fearful for their rights or very existence. Members of the Church recognized this early on, especially after their rights were systematically trampled in the expulsion from Jackson County, Missouri, in 1833. These feelings were reinforced after state and national governments alike refused to provide the Saints with any redress for their sufferings. Thereafter, Joseph Smith advocated frequently for the protection of freedoms that had been denied the Saints. In a letter to the Church written circa February 1834, Joseph and other leading elders affirmed that all people "have the privilege of thinking for themselves upon all matters relative to conscience" and that it was fundamentally unjust to "deprive any one from exercising that free independence of mind which heaven has so graciously bestowed upon the human family as one of its choicest gifts."[5]

Missouri taught Joseph Smith and the Saints the hard lesson that Martin Luther King Jr. would write about in his famous 1963 "Letter from a Birmingham Jail," that "injustice anywhere is a threat to justice everywhere. We are caught in an inescapable network of mutuality, tied in a single garment of destiny. Whatever affects one directly, affects all indirectly."[6] In July 1834, following the failure of the Camp of Israel (now known as Zion's Camp) to restore the Saints to their lands in Jackson

County, Church leaders in Missouri responded obediently to a revelation that came to Joseph two weeks earlier instructing them to "lift up an ensign of peace, and make a proclamation for peace unto the ends of the earth."[7] In their proclamation, the Saints drew upon their experience to warn against the ability of a majority to "crush any religious sect with impunity." They recognized that if this were allowed to be the case, then "farewell to society! farewell to religion! farewell to right! farewell to property! farewell to life! The fate of our church now, might become the fate of the Methodists next week; the Catholics next month, and the overthrow of all societies next year."[8] In 1836, while serving a mission in Salem, Massachusetts, home of the infamous witch trials and not far from where a Roman Catholic convent had recently been burned to the ground, Joseph prayed, "When will man cease to war with man, and wrest from him his sacred right, of worshipping his God according as his conscience dictates? Holy Father, hasten the day."[9]

By the time the Saints were settled in Nauvoo, Joseph Smith seems to have intuited that the mere tolerance of religious difference or even a minimalistic protection of basic religious liberties is not enough. Instead, religious pluralism entails active engagement, encounter, dialogue, and understanding across religious divides. That does not mean the elimination of difference or the relativization of truth, but rather learning from the diverse perspectives and experiences inherent in variously gifted human communities.[10] On January 15, 1841, the First Presidency issued a proclamation from Nauvoo in which they extended their arms of welcome to people "of every denomination, and every sentiment of religion." "Let all those who desire to locate themselves in this place, come," the First Presidency declared, "and we will hail them as citizens and friends."[11] The Nauvoo City Council etched that sentiment into law six weeks later when they passed an ordinance declaring "that the Catholics, Presbyterians, Methodists, Baptists, Latter-Day-Saints, Quakers, Episcopalians, Universalists, Unitarians, Mohamedans, and all other religious sects, and denominations, whatever, shall have toleration, and equal priviledges in this city."[12] This statute was remarkably capacious for its day, protecting not only Protestant denominations but also chronically unpopular groups such as Catholics and Muslims. In a discourse two years later, the Prophet encouraged "Mahometans" and "Presbyteria[n]s" that even "if ye will not embrace our religion embrace our hospitalities."[13]

When in the closing months of his life Joseph Smith formed the political government of the kingdom of God, known as the Council of Fifty, he explicitly built into its structure the ideal of religious pluralism. "For the benifit of mankind and succeeding generations," he insisted, the council should include individuals who were not members of The Church of Jesus Christ of Latter-day Saints. Council members might come from other religions or no religion at all. In a society dedicated to equal rights for all, Joseph taught, every person must freely choose their god(s) and their religion. Optimistically, he surmised that the only danger connected to such freedom is that "every man will embrace the greatest light." "The principles of intollerance and bigotry never had a place in this kingdom, nor in my breast," the Prophet affirmed. "Let us from henceforth drive from us every species of intollerance."[14]

While he was a consistently strong advocate of religious freedom, Joseph Smith was not immune to the spirit of denominational rivalry. On many occasions he deployed acerbic rhetoric toward other churches, especially the Protestant denominations that prevailed in nineteenth-century America and often actively opposed the Saints. But contrary to his Puritan ancestors, who understood (and enforced) religious liberty as the right to worship God only in their way, Joseph recognized that true religious freedom guarantees people's right to be different, and even wrong. Any infringement on one religion posed a threat to all. That's why less than two weeks before his death, Joseph warned that "any man who will betray the Catholics will betray you."[15]

How could the prophet of the Restoration, who received God's direct command to refrain from joining any other church, be so open in his views toward other religions? It was because Joseph had a conviction that on this side of the veil, truth is not the exclusive property of any one person or group, but available to all of God's children. "Mormonism is truth," he instructed Church members, and "the first and fundamental principle of our holy religion is, that we believe that we have a right to embrace all, and every item of truth." In its fullest sense, truth can never be "circumscribed" by any particular creedal affirmation.[16] It was precisely because "Latter Day Saints have no creed," Joseph taught, that they "are ready to believe all true principles that exist," regardless where they come from.[17]

Joseph Smith's commitment to truth allowed his deepest convictions to exist seamlessly alongside an openness to what God, the world, and his fellow human beings still had to teach him. From hard experience, he knew that his own rights and privileges, and those of his people, went only as far as those of the least popular religious group in any given time and place. In word and deed, Joseph Smith went beyond grudging toleration of religious difference to develop the foundations of a robust Latter-day Saint ethic of religious pluralism.

Patrick Q. Mason holds the Leonard J. Arrington Chair of Mormon History and Culture at Utah State University, where he is an associate professor of religious studies and history.

Notes

1. "History, circa Summer 1832," p. 2, josephsmithpapers.org.
2. "Church History," Mar. 1, 1842, p. 707, josephsmithpapers.org; see also "History, 1838–1856, volume A-1 [23 December 1805–30 August 1834]," p. 3, josephsmithpapers.org [Joseph Smith—History 1:18–20].
3. "Revelation, 1 November 1831–B [D&C 1]," pp. 126–27, josephsmithpapers.org [D&C 1:30].
4. See John Corrigan and Lynn S. Neal, eds., *Religious Intolerance in America: A Documentary History* (Chapel Hill: University of North Carolina Press, 2010).
5. "Letter to the Church, circa February 1834," p. 135, josephsmithpapers.org.
6. Martin Luther King Jr., *Why We Can't Wait* (New York: Signet Classic, 2000 [1963]), 65.
7. "Revelation, 22 June 1834 [D&C 105]," p. 101 [201], josephsmithpapers.org [D&C 105:39].
8. "An Appeal," *The Evening and the Morning Star* 2 (Aug. 1834): 364.
9. "History, 1838–1856, volume B-1 [1 September 1834–2 November 1838]," p. 749, josephsmithpapers.org.
10. For a succinct expression of religious pluralism, see http://pluralism.org/what-is-pluralism/.
11. "Proclamation, 15 January 1841," p. 277, josephsmithpapers.org.
12. *Times and Seasons*, June 1, 1842, 3:807–8, josephsmithpapers.org; see also "Nauvoo City Council Minute Book, 3 February 1841–8 February 1845," p. 13, josephsmithpapers.org.
13. "Discourse, 29 January 1843, as Reported by Willard Richards–A," pp. [162]–[163], josephsmithpapers.org.

14. Council of Fifty, "Record," Apr. 11, 1844, in *JSP*, CFM:97, 100; see also Council of Fifty, "Record," Apr. 18, 1844, in *JSP*, CFM:128.

15. "Discourse, 16 June 1844–A, as Reported by Thomas Bullock," p. [5], josephsmithpapers .org.

16. "Letter to Isaac Galland, 22 March 1839," p. 54, josephsmithpapers.org.

17. "History, 1838–1856, volume D-1 [1 August 1842–1 July 1843]," p. 1433, josephsmith papers.org.

JOSEPH SMITH
AND EQUALITY

By Jed Woodworth

Joseph Smith is often thought to be the most democratic of American prophets. He flourished at a time when social distinctions of all kinds were being questioned, disputed, and leveled. Yet no one extended to common people the kind of privileges Joseph did. In place of a trained clergy, he gave priesthood to virtually every adult male. Against growing economic acquisitiveness, he sought to protect the poor and the marginal. "It is not given that one man should possess that which is above an other," said one early revelation.[1] Not even his role as revelator was held in reserve for himself. "The weak things of the world," another revelation said, "should come forth & break down the mighty & strong ones," so that "every man might Speak in the name of God the Lord."[2] His very life proved Jefferson's language in the Declaration of Independence that "all men are created equal." After all, if an uneducated farm boy could rise to found America's largest homegrown church, anyone could.[3]

In ways less often recognized, however, Joseph Smith's teachings were stubbornly resistant to the leveling of hierarchy. He rejected the standard Protestant insight that salvation was available to all without the mediation of priestly authority. Not only did salvation require the mediation of the Church, it ultimately ran through a single person, the "one on the earth at a time" who held the keys that governed the priesthood sealing of husband and wife, man and woman.[4] Whatever equality meant for Joseph, it did not mean the rejection of all inequalities. The Book of Abraham declared that wherever two spirits existed, one would be more intelligent than the other.[5] Social distinction seemed to be written into the basic fabric of the universe.

Joseph Smith, of course, was not alone in affirming a seemingly contradictory view of equality. From the beginning of English settlement in the New World, social distinctions persisted despite new claims to egalitarianism. "Free men" and "gentlemen" sat atop an elaborate social hierarchy, followed by lesser classes like mechanics, sailors, indentured servants, women and children, and last of all slaves.[6] The contradiction entered into the founding documents of the American republic. All people could be said to be "citizens" even while the right to vote was reserved for "free white males."[7] Jefferson could say that "all men are created equal" even while owning slaves himself.[8]

Over time, American history moved in the direction of dissolving the contradiction by collapsing one category into the other, toward the affirmation of more political and social equality, not less. The idea that "gentlemen" sat atop a social hierarchy was set aside within a generation. The provision that only free white males were entitled to vote took longer to dismantle, but within a century and a half, the vote had been extended widely, first to non–property holders, then to Blacks, and eventually to women. Beginning in the 1960s, liberation movements, both in the United States and abroad, spread like waves, arguing for still further social, economic, and racial equality. Over time, most Americans seemed content to dismiss inequality as something imposed by culture or tradition—and thus capable of revision—and not anything rooted in the nature of things. The views of Benjamin Rush, the eighteenth-century physician and American Founding Father, proved remarkably durable. "Human nature is the same in all ages and countries," he said, "and all the differences we perceive in its characters in respect to virtue and vice, knowledge and ignorance, may be accounted for from climate, country, degrees of civilization, forms of government, or accidental causes."[9]

Joseph Smith's views on equality worked in the opposite direction. Early on, his view of salvation was remarkably free of hierarchy. The Book of Mormon did not make priesthood or eternal marriage a requirement for salvation. The Lord invites all to come unto him, Nephi taught. "He denieth none that come unto him, black and white, bond and free, male and female; and he remembereth the heathen; and all are alike unto God"[10] Joseph Smith's later teachings did not reject that insight so much as they embedded it within elaborate layers of priesthood ritual. Without the ordinances of the higher priesthood, an 1832 revelation taught, "the power of Godliness is not manifest unto man in the flesh."[11] Near the end of his life, Joseph Smith introduced the temple endowment and various priesthood sealing rituals, creating further status levels in this life and in the life to come.

None of the revelations, early or late, made equality a right of birth. Joseph Smith did not affirm equality as a self-evident fact as Jefferson did. In the same passage in which Nephi preaches that all are alike unto God, he condemns those who create "envyings, and strifes, and malice."[12] In Joseph's teachings, God's highest rewards are reserved for the righteous. Privilege and status are not granted by right of birth. Even the affirmation of hierarchy did nothing to guarantee anyone's place in the life to come. Whatever status priesthood power brought, Joseph taught, could be maintained only by good behavior: "by persuasion by long suffering by gentleness and meekness and by love unfaigned."[13] Priesthood sealings alone were powerless to guarantee exaltation. "For Strait is the Gate and narrow the way, that leadeth unto the exaltation and continuation of the lives and few there be that find it."[14] Rather than expanding equality, the revelations constricted it.

Joseph Smith distilled his mature understanding of equality near the end of his life. Two months before his death, Joseph met with the Council of Fifty to deliberate on a constitution. One of the provisions in the draft document said that "God hath created all men free and equal." The provision called to mind Jefferson's language in the Declaration of Independence, but Joseph objected to the construction. Knowing that the revelations affirmed a constricted view of equality, Joseph put forward another construction.

"All men were in the designs of God created equal," he said, "and inasmuch as some had greater capacities than others, it was required of them to possess the greater philanthropy."[15]

The construction reconciled the apparent contraries in Joseph Smith's thought. In the premortal realms, spirits of lesser or greater capacity made choices. Some spirits, "on account of their exceeding faith and good works," were given particular assignments on earth for the benefit of the human family.[16] But in other ways, all were still "in the designs of God created equal." All spirits were sent to earth to be tested, to be tried. All had some calling or mission in life. "Every man who has a calling to minister to the Inhabitants of the world," Joseph would teach a few weeks later, "was ordained to that very purpose in the grand Council of Heaven before this world was."[17] Since the capacity of spirit and circumstances of birth varied, not every calling could be the same.

The acknowledgement of inequality, of greater or lesser capacity, had no bearing on whether a person had more or less social privilege. Those of greater capacity were guaranteed nothing by their choices in the premortal life or their circumstances of birth, for the same behavioral standards expected of some were expected of all. Even so, greater capacity came with social responsibility. They were required "to possess the greater philanthropy." Where much was given, much was expected.

Jed Woodworth, a historian with the Church History Department, is the managing historian of *Saints: The Story of the Church of Jesus Christ in the Latter Days*, a multivolume official history of the Church.

Notes

1. Revelation, May 7, 1831, in *JSP*, D1:302 [D&C 49:20].

2. Revelation, Nov. 1, 1831–B, in *JSP*, D2:106 [D&C 1:19].

3. For arguments on Joseph Smith's democracy, see Nathan O. Hatch, *The Democratization of American Christianity* (New Haven, CT: Yale University Press, 1989); and Robert V. Remini, *Joseph Smith* (New York: Penguin Putnam, 2002).

4. "Revelation, 12 July 1843 [D&C 132:7]," p. 1, josephsmithpapers.org.

5. "The Book of Abraham," *Times and Seasons*, Mar. 15, 1842, 3:720 [Abraham 3:19], josephsmithpapers.org.
6. Russell L. Hanson, "Equality," in *A Companion to American Thought*, ed. Richard Wightman Fox and James T. Kloppenberg (Malden, MA: Blackwell, 1995).
7. Sean Wilentz, *The Rise of American Democracy: Jefferson to Lincoln* (New York: Norton, 2005).
8. The contradiction was explored in Garry Wills, *Inventing America: Jefferson's Declaration of Independence* (Garden City, NY: Doubleday, 1978), 207–17.
9. Gordon S. Wood, *The Radicalism of the American Revolution* (New York: Vintage, 1993), 236–37.
10. 2 Nephi 26:33.
11. Revelation, Sept. 22–23, 1832, in *JSP*, D2:295 [D&C 84:21].
12. 2 Nephi 26:21.
13. Letter to Edward Partridge and the Church, ca. Mar. 22, 1839, in *JSP*, D6:394 [D&C 121:41].
14. "Revelation, 12 July 1843 [D&C 132:22]," p. [3], josephsmithpapers.org.
15. Council of Fifty, "Record," Apr. 18, 1844, in *JSP*, CFM:118.
16. Alma 13:3.
17. "Discourse, 12 May 1844, as Reported by Thomas Bullock," p. [1], josephsmithpapers.org.

A "MOST REMARKABLE AND WONDERFUL MAN": EMMELINE B. WELLS REMEMBERS JOSEPH SMITH

By Cherry Bushman Silver

By happenstance—or by divine guidance—16-year-old Emmeline B. Woodward arrived in Nauvoo, Illinois, in mid-May 1844. Upon landing, she and her party were greeted by the prophet of the Restoration. She never forgot her first impression of Joseph Smith, and she increasingly drew on his charisma and character to provide a standard for her own work in uplifting women.

She reflected 40 years later on the crises of 1844: "Many events of interest to me transpired in that year. I went to Nauvoo Jos. Smith & Hyram were martyred, my little Eugene, my only son, was born and died his father left me alone in a strange city and wandered away and never returned, I never saw him again, broken-hearted young and desolate without home, money or any friends I was left to my fate, and although I felt no special guidance yet the hand of Providence was over me and must have guided me to the safe haven I found."[1]

Emmeline lived a long life—and a productive one. After her young husband, James Harris, left her to go to sea, she married two more times, first to Newel K. Whitney and after his death to Daniel H. Wells, both Church leaders. She lived in obscurity, she said, during the years she reared her five daughters[2] but became a public figure when she began to edit the semimonthly newspaper the *Woman's Exponent*. She directed the grain-storage cause. She supported the woman suffrage movement. She assumed more and more leadership in the Relief Society, serving as fifth general president between 1910 and 1921. She had a remarkable memory for people and facts and was known as a witty conversationalist and capable defender of her faith. She memorialized the Prophet Joseph Smith in her talks and essays, citing his championing of women. She included him in a novel and reflected on his life in her private diaries.

Personal Encounter with Joseph Smith

Emmeline's party arrived in Nauvoo from Massachusetts in a company of converts and returning missionaries. Never having seen the Prophet, she "had not formed any idea of him except of his wonderful power." Then she saw his figure and felt his influence: "At last the boat reached the upper landing, and a crowd of people were coming toward the bank of the river. As we stepped ashore the crowd advanced, and I could see one person who towered away and above all the others around him; in fact I did not see distinctly any others. His majestic bearing, so entirely different from any one I had ever seen (and I had seen many superior men) was more than a surprise. It was as if I beheld a vison; I seemed to be lifted off my feet, to be as it were walking in the air, and paying no heed whatever to those around me. I made my way through the crowd, then I saw this man whom I had noticed, because of his lofty appearance, shaking hands with all the people, men, women and children. Before I was aware of it he came to me, and when he took my hand, I was simply electrified,—thrilled through and through to the tips of my fingers. . . . The one thought that filled my soul was, I have seen the Prophet of God, he has taken me by the hand, and this testimony has never left me in all the 'perils by the way.' It is as vivid today as ever it was. For many years, I felt it too sacred an experience even to mention."[3]

Nauvoo Memories

That description of Emmeline's first encounter appeared in the December 1905 issue of the *Young Woman's Journal* 100 years after

Joseph's birth. It is the story she told to the end of her life when invited to speak to youth groups and ward meetings.

Other details from June 1844 in Nauvoo came to her mind when she wrote an autobiographical novel called *Hepzibah*, which she serialized in the *Woman's Exponent* in 1890–91. "Their first Sunday in Nauvoo, Joseph the Prophet preached, and Hepsie knew the moment he stepped upon the platform, and she saw his magnificent presence, and the influence he brought with him upon the whole congregation, that he was in very deed a Prophet of God."[4]

After the excommunication of William Law and the printing of the *Nauvoo Expositor*, she felt deep concern for the Prophet's life. Her husband, James, joined the guard to protect Joseph Smith by day and slept in his barn at night.[5] Then came the time of darkness: "Joseph's going to Carthage to deliver himself up with the others who were accused spread dismay and consternation through the City of Nauvoo, the people were almost wild, hundreds, yes, thousands would gladly have gone in his stead; they mourned even then and when the dreadful news of the massacre came it was as if a thunderbolt had fallen in the midst of the City, and a dark cloud hung like a sable pall over all, that none seemed able to pierce."[6]

Diary entries on June 27 in 1891 and 1894 reinforced those impressions: "How well I remember that day and time. How dark the clouds seemed to hang over the city of Nauvoo, it was as though the sun could not shine."[7] Again, "All of us who remember the tragedy will recall the dreadful feeling that pervaded the City of Nauvoo and rested with such a heavey [heavy] weight upon the heads and hearts of the Saints and all who dwelt in the vicinity."[8]

Joseph Smith and the Rights of Women

Emmeline arrived in Nauvoo too late to join the Female Relief Society, yet she made her own copy of the minutes of the meetings and inscribed her own notes on them.[9] She became one of the guardians and interpreters of Joseph Smith's founding sermons to the women of the Church. As the sisters prepared to celebrate Relief Society's 50-year jubilee in the Salt Lake Tabernacle in March 1892, Emmeline went with Zina D. H. Young and other women to the local florist to prepare a suitable symbol: "While at Reedings, we ordered an immense key of green & white three feet long to be made for the Jubilee to represent the tree of knowledge Joseph Smith turned for the women of this generation since which time women have been developing powers and attributes which had previously lain dormant and also claiming independence and freedom in civil political and religious matters unheard of before."[10]

In that sentence, Emmeline credited Joseph Smith and his turning of the key for the whole women's movement. He invited women to accept new knowledge, to develop "powers and attributes," and to acquire "independence and freedom" in both secular and religious matters.

To honor the centenary of his birth in 1905, Emmeline reprinted major portions of the Female Relief Society of Nauvoo minutes in the *Exponent*.[11] Perhaps someone challenged her interpretation or general president Bathsheba Smith's, for a few days later she and Bathsheba spent two or three hours reading from the record of the first Relief Society.[12] In the next issue, Bathsheba as president and Emmeline as secretary retracted an introductory sentence: "'President [Joseph] Smith stated that the meeting was called for the purpose of making more complete the organization of the Church by organizing the women in the order of the Priesthood.' We find by comparing it with the original record no such statement was made."[13] In their minds, however, Joseph Smith had invited possibilities for spiritual authority, which they welcomed.

In defining how Joseph strengthened the Relief Society, Emmeline suggested focus and methods. In her editorial "A Hundred Years of Progress," she noted that "he was the first man to organize the women of the Church into a philanthropic society, taking the initiative himself, retiring from the meeting while they elected their own officers, advising them to observe parliamentary usage in their meetings. This was March 17, 1842, long before women's organizations had become a part and parcel of the world's activities."[14]

Finally, she defended his character. She recognized that people of the world demeaned Joseph Smith. Some at national women's meetings had turned their scorn on her because of his teachings. In defense, Wells proclaimed that he offered "advanced ideas of womanhood" and himself exemplified an elevated manhood: "The women of the world who deride the name and who defame the character of Joseph Smith should take a little time to look up on his advanced ideas of womanhood. His gentle, chivalrous and reverential manner towards all women was a distinguishing trait in the character of this most remarkable and wonderful man. One could not meet him even casually without feeling the potent influence of the atmosphere that enveloped him, as entirely different from other men of the same period."[15]

When she alluded to Joseph Smith, she connected him not only with manhood but with spiritual power. For instance, while in England in the summer of 1899 with the International Council of Women, she attended a Latter-day Saint church service. "A great outpouring of the Holy Spirit and a power that was a refreshing from on high rested upon Prest [DePlatte] Lyman," she wrote in her diary. "I realized something of the spirit of Joseph Smith and could have prophesied then and there but held my peace except to respond in a few words when called upon."[16]

Emmeline B. Wells, the last general Relief Society leader to testify of meeting Joseph Smith personally, valued his mentoring of women in leadership, philanthropy, and spiritual gifts. Although she encountered him only briefly at age 16, she never lost her admiration for him. If anything, her sense of his superior thinking increased over the remaining 75 years of her life.

Cherry Bushman Silver is researcher, annotator, and coeditor of the Diaries of Emmeline B. Wells.

Notes

1. Emmeline B. Wells, Diary, Jan. 18, 1888, L. Tom Perry Special Collections, Harold B. Lee Library, Brigham Young University, Provo, UT (hereafter Perry Special Collections). Images of Wells's diaries are available online at Lee Library Digital Collections. Annotated transcripts of the Wells diaries are being published electronically by the Church Historian's Press.
2. Wells, Diary, Mar. 1, 1881, and Aug. 3, 1901.

3. Emmeline B. Wells, "Joseph Smith, the Prophet," *Young Woman's Journal*, Dec. 1905, 22:554–56.
4. [Emmeline B. Wells], "Hepzibah," Chapter XX, *Woman's Exponent*, May 1, 1890, 18:180.
5. [Emmeline B. Wells], "Hepzibah," Chapter XXI, *Woman's Exponent*, May 15, 1890, 18:187.
6. [Emmeline B. Wells], "Hepzibah," Chapter XXI, *Woman's Exponent*, May 15, 1890, 18:188.
7. Wells, Diary, June 27, 1891.
8. Wells, Diary, June 27, 1894.
9. Copy in Emmeline B. Wells Collection, Perry Special Collections.
10. Wells, Diary, Mar. 14, 1892.
11. "The Relief Society," *Woman's Exponent*, Nov. 1905, 34:36.
12. Wells, Diary, Dec. 30, 1905.
13. "Correction," *Woman's Exponent*, Jan. 1906, 34:44; see "Nauvoo Relief Society Minute Book," in *The First Fifty Years of Relief Society: Key Documents in Latter-day Saint Women's History*, ed. Jill Mulvay Derr et al. (Salt Lake City: Church Historian's Press, 2016), 23–131.
14. Emmeline B. Wells, "A Hundred Years of Progress," *Woman's Exponent*, Jan. 1906, 34:45.
15. Emmeline B. Wells, "A Hundred Years of Progress," *Woman's Exponent*, Jan. 1906, 34:45.
16. Wells, Diary, July 30, 1899.

PROTECTING NAUVOO:
THE LAST DAYS OF
JOSEPH SMITH

By Adam H. Petty

One can only imagine the scene that Joseph looked out upon as he climbed the wooden scaffolding across the street from his home, the Nauvoo Mansion. A host of men were gathered, and not by accident. These were members of the city's militia, the Nauvoo Legion, and they had been ordered out to defend Nauvoo from what seemed like an imminent mob attack.[1] It was the afternoon of June 18, 1844, and the past eight days had been full of fear and trembling as Joseph tried to work out the temporal salvation of his people.

The crisis had started on Mulholland Street. There, in a nondescript office, stood the press of the *Nauvoo Expositor*. This newspaper, published by Joseph's enemies in Nauvoo, furiously attacked the Prophet's actions, teachings, and moral character. The *Expositor*'s first and only issue went out to the public on June 7.[2] Joseph, as mayor of Nauvoo, met with the city council on June 8 and 10 to discuss how the city's government would respond. While the council's deliberations ranged far and wide, the specter of another Missouri loomed over the proceedings as Joseph and others argued that the paper's content would incite mob violence against the Latter-day Saints.[3] On the evening of June 10, the city council passed a resolution declaring the *Expositor* a nuisance and instructing Joseph to remove the press in a manner of his own choosing. That night a posse of men under the command of the city marshal destroyed the *Expositor*'s press on Joseph's orders.[4]

It was only the beginning of sorrows. Despite Joseph's attempt to avoid mob violence by destroying the press, the mob came all the same, using the press's destruction as justification for its actions.[5] Threats against Joseph and against Nauvoo came thick and fast. The *Expositor*'s proprietors threatened vengeance on Joseph, and Thomas Sharp's *Warsaw Signal* threatened the Latter-day Saints with extermination.[6] Word came of mobs gathering. The nearby towns Warsaw and Carthage became armed camps.[7]

Things appeared black. On June 12, Joseph was arrested on a charge of riot in relation to the *Expositor*'s destruction. Joseph, however, refused to go to Carthage to stand trial, fearing for his safety if he left Nauvoo. Instead, he applied for a writ of habeas corpus that was granted, resulting in a hearing and his ultimate release.[8] This legal maneuver only inflamed the tensions in Hancock County.[9] The situation was spinning out of control. By June 16, Joseph had determined that "the only way to prevent sheddi[n]g of blood was to get the Gove[r]nor in person. to come down" to Hancock County. That same day he wrote Governor Thomas Ford, requesting that he do just that.[10] Joseph also issued a proclamation trying to explain why the city council had acted as it did in the case of the *Expositor*.[11] Joseph's messengers, however, never found Ford, and the proclamation only provided sport for the *Warsaw Signal*.[12] On June 17, Joseph and the others charged with riot were tried by Hancock County justice of the peace Daniel H. Wells, who was not a member of the Church, and they were acquitted.[13]

That evening Joseph issued orders to mobilize the Nauvoo Legion, and on June 18 the Legion mustered near the Masonic Hall and then marched down Main Street to the Nauvoo Mansion, where Joseph addressed them. On a makeshift stand, Joseph urged the members of the Legion to defend their families against the threat of extermination. He also declared martial law in the city, meaning that no one could enter or leave without a pass.[14] In the days that followed, Joseph issued orders to gather arms and powder, set patrols to protect the city, and pledged his farm as collateral to obtain supplies for the people. Joseph and others also went out along the likely routes that the mob would use to attack Nauvoo and scouted out positions. On the evening of June 22, he ordered the Legion to dig entrenchments to the east of the city to face any potential attack from that direction.[15]

That order was never carried out because late that night Joseph received a long and scathing letter from Thomas Ford accusing him of gross outrages against the law and ordering him to surrender himself in Carthage for trial on the charge of riot.[16] Apparently alarmed by this letter and unwilling to deliver himself into the hands of an angry mob, Joseph and a few associates crossed the Mississippi River into Iowa Territory on June 23. Later that day, a group from Nauvoo came over and persuaded Joseph to surrender himself. Joseph then returned to Nauvoo and sent word to Ford that he and the others charged with riot would surrender themselves.[17] By June 25, Joseph and his companions were in Carthage facing the charge of riot, for which they posted bail, meaning they would have been free to go. While in Carthage, however, Joseph and Hyrum were also charged with treason, a nonbailable offense, for declaring martial law and calling out the Nauvoo Legion.[18] Trapped in the jail at Carthage, they were murdered by a mob two days later.[19]

Through all these events Joseph was charged with protecting the Saints and the city from mob violence. Destroying the *Expositor's* press was insufficient. Proclamations and official explanations fell short. Even mobilizing the Legion and putting the city under martial law were not enough. No, in the end Joseph saved Nauvoo by choosing to face certain death in Carthage. Some of the Saints in Nauvoo clearly perceived this. Vilate Kimball observed on June 24 that Joseph and Hyrum "giveing themselves up, is all that will save our city from destruction."[20] Similarly, William Clayton noted on June 24 that Joseph expected "nothing but to be massacred" if he went to Carthage. Joseph, however, saw "no alternative," according to Clayton. "He must either give himself up or the City be massacred by a lawless mob under the sanction of the Governor."[21]

It is during these mad days in June that something of Joseph's character becomes visible. Here was a man who spent the last weeks of his life desperately trying to defend his people. Here was a man who ultimately put his life on the altar and like a lamb went to the slaughter, reminding all of us that "greater love hath no man than this, that a man lay down his life for his friends."[22]

This essay has presented only the barest sketch of Joseph's last days, and it only hints at the myriad events, pressures, dangers, and decisions that bombarded Joseph in June 1844. Yet this man who was willing to sacrifice his all to defend the Saints is the Joseph that I have come to know during my time working on the Joseph Smith Papers. I have paid the price to gain this knowledge. It has required time, effort, and diligence to pore over the surviving records and piece together an understanding of things. It has come bit by bit as I have studied and pondered things in my mind.

It is all too easy for people to jump to superficial conclusions about Joseph. In his April 7, 1844, sermon, the Prophet warned those listening to not be hasty in judging him. "You never knew my heart," he told them. "No man knows my history; I cannot tell it. I shall never undertake it; if I had not experienced what I have, I should not have known it myself. . . . When I am called at the trump of the ark-angel, and weighed in the balance you will all know me then."[23] Later, in a sermon on May 12, he touched on a similar theme. "I never told you I was perfect," Joseph said, "but there is no error in the revelations which I have taught— must I then be thrown away as a thing of nought?"[24] In 1844, the Latter-day Saints faced a dilemma. Would they stand by Joseph or would they listen to his detractors?

Joseph still has his critics today, just like he did in 1844, and modern Latter-day Saints face the same choice. Will we stand by Joseph? Joseph's pleas to the Saints still ring true: I am a true prophet. I will show you. Remember, you don't really know me and you won't until the day of judgment. I am not perfect, but the revelations are. Will you stand by me?

Adam H. Petty is a historian and documentary editor for the Joseph Smith Papers Project and the author of *The Battle of the Wilderness in Myth and Memory* (Baton Rouge: Louisiana State University Press, 2019).

Notes

1. Journal, June 18, 1844, in *JSP*, J3:290; William Clayton, Daily Account of Joseph Smith's Activities, June 18, 1844, in *JSP*, J3:336.
2. *Nauvoo Expositor*, June 7, 1844.
3. Nauvoo City Council, Minutes, June 8 and 10, 1844, in "Nauvoo City Council Rough Minute Book, February 1844–January 1845," pp. 11–31, josephsmithpapers.org.
4. "Mayor's Order to Nauvoo City Marshal, 10 June 1844," josephsmithpapers.org; Journal, June 10, 1844, in *JSP*, J3:277.
5. "Unparralleled Outrage at Nauvoo," *Warsaw Signal*, June 12, 1844, [2].
6. Journal, June 11, 1844, in *JSP*, J3:279; "Preamble and Resolutions," *Warsaw Signal*, June 14, 1844, [1].
7. Journal, June 11, 13, and 15–16, 1844, in *JSP*, J3:279, 281, 283–84, 286; Thomas G. Wilson, Affidavit, June 16, 1844, Joseph Smith Office Papers, CHL; Thomas Ford, *A History of Illinois from Its Commencement as a State in 1818 to 1847* (Chicago: S. C. Griggs, 1854), 339; Vilate Kimball to Heber C. Kimball, June 9, 1844, Kimball Family Correspondence, CHL.
8. Journal, June 12, 1844, in *JSP*, J3:279–80; Events of June 1844, in *JSP*, CFM:194–95; William Clayton, Journal, June 12, 1844, in *An Intimate Chronicle: The Journals of William Clayton*, ed. George D. Smith (Salt Lake City: Signature Books, 1991), 132–33; "Letter to Thomas Ford, 22 June 1844–B," josephsmithpapers.org.
9. Events of June 1844, in *JSP*, CFM:195; "Letter from Thomas Ford, 22 June 1844," josephsmithpapers.org.
10. Journal, June 16, 1844, in *JSP*, J3:286; "Letter to Thomas Ford, 16 June 1844," josephsmithpapers.org.
11. "Proclamation, 16 June 1844," josephsmithpapers.org.
12. Journal, June 17, 1844, in *JSP*, J3:289; Samuel James to Willard Richards, June 30, 1844, Willard Richards Journals and Papers, CHL; "Joe's Proclamation," *Warsaw Signal*, June 19, 1844, [2].
13. Journal, June 17, 1844, in *JSP*, J3:288.
14. History of the Nauvoo Legion, Draft 1, Nauvoo Legion (Ill.) Records, 1841–45, CHL; Journal, June 17–18, 1844, in *JSP*, J3:289–91; William Clayton, Daily Account of Joseph Smith's Activities, June 18, 1844, in *JSP*, J3:336; "Military Order to Jonathan Dunham, 17 June 1844–A," josephsmithpapers.org; "Mayor's Order to Nauvoo City Marshal, 18 June 1844."
15. History of the Nauvoo Legion, Draft 3, Nauvoo Legion (Ill.) Records, 1841–45, CHL; Journal, June 20 and 22, 1844, in *JSP*, J3:293, 300; Albert P. Rockwood, Statement, Sept. 7, 1856, Joseph Smith History Documents, CHL; History of the Nauvoo Legion, Draft 1; "Military Order to Jonathan Dunham, 22 June 1844," josephsmithpapers.org.
16. "Letter from Thomas Ford, 22 June 1844."
17. Willard Richards, Journal Excerpt, June 23, 1844, in *JSP*, J3:305; Theodore Turley to Hosea Stout, Oct. 28, 1855, Joseph Smith History Documents, CHL; Stephen Markham to Wilford Woodruff, June 20, 1856, Historian's Office, Joseph Smith History Documents, CHL; "Letter to Thomas Ford, 23 June 1844," josephsmithpapers.org; Vilate Kimball to Heber C. Kimball, June 9, 1844.
18. Willard Richards, Journal Excerpt, June 25, 1844, in *JSP*, J3:307, 312; Ford, *History of Illinois*, 337.
19. "Two Minutes in Jail," *Nauvoo Neighbor*, July 24, 1844, [3].

20. Vilate Kimball to Heber C. Kimball, June 9, 1844.
21. William Clayton, Journal, June 24, 1844, as quoted in *JSP*, J3:306, note 8.
22. John 15:13.
23. "Discourse, 7 April 1844, as Reported by *Times and Seasons*," josephsmithpapers.org.
24. "Discourse, 12 May 1844, as Reported by Thomas Bullock," josephsmithpapers.org.

NOTE ON CITATIONS

The essays in this collection often draw on manuscripts housed in the Church History Library, The Church of Jesus Christ of Latter-day Saints, Salt Lake City. That repository is abbreviated as CHL.

The essays also frequently cite the Joseph Smith Papers website and print volumes. For brevity, citations to the website give the title of the cited document, a page number if relevant, and the overall site URL, josephsmithpapers.org. When the print volumes are cited, a short citation form is used. The short citation gives the initials *JSP*, an abbreviation for the volume number, and the page number. The short forms for the volumes cited in this collection are listed below with their corresponding full citations.

JSP, CFM / Grow, Matthew J., Ronald K. Esplin, Mark Ashurst-McGee, Gerrit J. Dirkmaat, and Jeffrey D. Mahas, eds. *Council of Fifty, Minutes, March 1844–January 1846.* Administrative Records series of *The Joseph Smith Papers,* edited by Ronald K. Esplin, Matthew J. Grow, and Matthew C. Godfrey. Salt Lake City: Church Historian's Press, 2016.

JSP, D1 / MacKay, Michael Hubbard, Gerrit J. Dirkmaat, Grant Underwood, Robert J. Woodford, and William G. Hartley, eds. *Documents, Volume 1: July 1828–June 1831.* Vol. 1 of the Documents series of *The Joseph Smith Papers,* edited by Dean C. Jessee, Ronald K.

Esplin, Richard Lyman Bushman, and Matthew J. Grow. Salt Lake City: Church Historian's Press, 2013.

JSP, D2 / Godfrey, Matthew C., Mark Ashurst-McGee, Grant Underwood, Robert J. Woodford, and William G. Hartley, eds. *Documents, Volume 2: July 1831–January 1833.* Vol. 2 of the Documents series of *The Joseph Smith Papers,* edited by Dean C. Jessee, Ronald K. Esplin, Richard Lyman Bushman, and Matthew J. Grow. Salt Lake City: Church Historian's Press, 2013.

JSP, D3 / Dirkmaat, Gerrit J., Brent M. Rogers, Grant Underwood, Robert J. Woodford, and William G. Hartley, eds. *Documents, Volume 3: February 1833–March 1834.* Vol. 3 of the Documents series of *The Joseph Smith Papers,* edited by Ronald K. Esplin and Matthew J. Grow. Salt Lake City: Church Historian's Press, 2014.

JSP, D4 / Godfrey, Matthew C., Brenden W. Rensink, Alex D. Smith, Max H Parkin, and Alexander L. Baugh, eds. *Documents, Volume 4: April 1834–September 1835.* Vol. 4 of the Documents series of *The Joseph Smith Papers,* edited by Ronald K. Esplin, Matthew J. Grow, and Matthew C. Godfrey. Salt Lake City: Church Historian's Press, 2016.

JSP, D5 / Rogers, Brent M., Elizabeth A. Kuehn, Christian K. Heimburger, Max H Parkin, Alexander L. Baugh, and Steven C. Harper, eds. *Documents, Volume 5: October 1835–January 1838.* Vol. 5 of the Documents series of *The Joseph Smith Papers,* edited by Ronald K. Esplin, Matthew J. Grow, and Matthew C. Godfrey. Salt Lake City: Church Historian's Press, 2017.

JSP, D6 / Ashurst-McGee, Mark, David W. Grua, Elizabeth A. Kuehn, Brenden W. Rensink, and Alexander L. Baugh, eds. *Documents, Volume 6: February 1838–August 1839.* Vol. 6 of the Documents series of *The Joseph Smith Papers,* edited by Ronald K. Esplin, Matthew J. Grow, and Matthew C. Godfrey. Salt Lake City: Church Historian's Press, 2017.

JSP, D7 / Godfrey, Matthew C., Spencer W. McBride, Alex D. Smith, and Christopher James Blythe, eds. *Documents, Volume 7: September 1839–January 1841.* Vol. 7 of the Documents series of *The Joseph*

Smith Papers, edited by Ronald K. Esplin, Matthew J. Grow, and Matthew C. Godfrey. Salt Lake City: Church Historian's Press, 2018.

JSP, D8 / Rogers, Brent M., Mason K. Allred, Gerrit J. Dirkmaat, and Brett D. Dowdle, eds. *Documents, Volume 8: February–November 1841.* Vol. 8 of the Documents series of *The Joseph Smith Papers,* edited by Ronald K. Esplin, Matthew J. Grow, Matthew C. Godfrey, and R. Eric Smith. Salt Lake City: Church Historian's Press, 2019.

JSP, D9 / Smith, Alex D., Christian K. Heimburger, and Christopher James Blythe, eds. *Documents, Volume 9: December 1841–April 1842.* Vol. 9 of the Documents series of *The Joseph Smith Papers,* edited by Matthew C. Godfrey, R. Eric Smith, Matthew J. Grow, and Ronald K. Esplin. Salt Lake City: Church Historian's Press, 2019.

JSP, D10 / Kuehn, Elizabeth A., Jordan T. Watkins, Matthew C. Godfrey, and Mason K. Allred, eds. *Documents, Volume 10: May–August 1842.* Vol. 10 of the Documents series of *The Joseph Smith Papers,* edited by Matthew C. Godfrey, R. Eric Smith, Matthew J. Grow, and Ronald K. Esplin. Salt Lake City: Church Historian's Press, 2020.

JSP, D11 / McBride, Spencer W., Jeffrey D. Mahas, Brett D. Dowdle, and Tyson Reeder, eds. *Documents, Volume 11: September 1842–February 1843.* Vol. 11 of the Documents series of *The Joseph Smith Papers,* edited by Matthew C. Godfrey, R. Eric Smith, Matthew J. Grow, and Ronald K. Esplin. Salt Lake City: Church Historian's Press, 2020.

JSP, H1 / Davidson, Karen Lynn, David J. Whittaker, Richard L. Jensen, and Mark Ashurst-McGee, eds. *Histories, Volume 1: Joseph Smith Histories, 1832–1844.* Vol. 1 of the Histories series of *The Joseph Smith Papers,* edited by Dean C. Jessee, Ronald K. Esplin, and Richard Lyman Bushman. Salt Lake City: Church Historian's Press, 2012.

JSP, H2 / Davidson, Karen Lynn, Richard L. Jensen, and David J. Whittaker, eds. *Histories, Volume 2: Assigned Historical Writings, 1831–1847.* Vol. 2 of the Histories series of *The Joseph Smith Papers,* edited by Dean C. Jessee, Ronald K. Esplin, and Richard Lyman Bushman. Salt Lake City: Church Historian's Press, 2012.

JSP, J1 / Jessee, Dean C., Mark Ashurst-McGee, and Richard L. Jensen, eds. *Journals, Volume 1: 1832–1839.* Vol. 1 of the Journals series of

The Joseph Smith Papers, edited by Dean C. Jessee, Ronald K. Esplin, and Richard Lyman Bushman. Salt Lake City: Church Historian's Press, 2008.

JSP, J2 / Hedges, Andrew H., Alex D. Smith, and Richard Lloyd Anderson, eds. *Journals, Volume 2: December 1841–April 1843.* Vol. 2 of the Journals series of *The Joseph Smith Papers,* edited by Dean C. Jessee, Ronald K. Esplin, and Richard Lyman Bushman. Salt Lake City: Church Historian's Press, 2011.

JSP, J3 / Hedges, Andrew H., Alex D. Smith, and Brent M. Rogers, eds. *Journals, Volume 3: May 1843–June 1844.* Vol. 3 of the Journals series of *The Joseph Smith Papers,* edited by Ronald K. Esplin and Matthew J. Grow. Salt Lake City: Church Historian's Press, 2015.

JSP, MRB / Jensen, Robin Scott, Robert J. Woodford, and Steven C. Harper, eds. *Manuscript Revelation Books.* Facsimile edition. First volume of the Revelations and Translations series of *The Joseph Smith Papers,* edited by Dean C. Jessee, Ronald K. Esplin, and Richard Lyman Bushman. Salt Lake City: Church Historian's Press, 2009.

INDEX